Beyond Bullet Points, 3rd Edition

Using Microsoft° PowerPoint° to
Create Presentations That Inform,
Motivate, and Inspire

CLIFF ATKINSON

PUBLISHED BY
Microsoft Press
A Division of Microsoft Corporation
One Microsoft Way
Redmond, Washington 98052-6399

Library of Congress Control Number: 2011923735
ISBN: 978-0-7356-2735-2

Seventh Printing: March 2015

Printed and bound in the United States of America.

Microsoft Press books are available through booksellers and distributors worldwide. For further information about international editions, contact your local Microsoft Corporation office or contact Microsoft Press International directly at fax (425) 936-7329. Visit our Web site at www.microsoft.com/mspress. Send comments to mspinput@ microsoft.com.

Acquisitions Editor: Kim Spilker
Developmental Editor: Valerie Woolley
Project Editor: Valerie Woolley
Editorial Production: Waypoint Press
Copy Editor: Roger LeBlanc
Cover: Twist

The images used in the following figures are copyright © iStockphoto.com and the artist. For more information about an image, enter the file number in the Search box at the iStockphoto.com website.

1-8: Building, #2201015; 1-9: Gavel and flag, #804982; 1-10: Money, #2557065; 1-12: Prescription, #2996720 X-Ray, #1231514; 2-14: PDA, #12816202; 6-14: Magnifying glass, #307057; 8-4: Clipboards, #576498, #3793238, #3831334; 8-5: Clipboard, #1825380; 8-6: Toolbox, #1459715 Charts, #2168557; 8-9: Brain, #2565668; 8-16: Light bulb, #8315449 Stopwatch, #13901118 Money, #5509580; 8-19: Closed sign, #10507982; 10-8: Racers, #2158582 Stopwatch, #2208715 Hurdle, #3272327 Racetrack, #2548145; 10-12: Calendar, #3513709 Monitor, #496871 Checklist, #223288; 10-13: Paper, #773703 Org Chart, #815535 Buildings, #976238 Yoga pose, #1850531; 10-19: Oil well, #3418353 Adding machine ribbon, #877076 Spreadsheet, #926275 No Sale, #3627711 Money tray, #1886778; 10-21: People, #141425 Cars, #3146730 Taxis, #506002 Airplane, #829923; 10-22: People, #340892 Map, #2497505; 10-25: Watch, #590167 Gears, #2748397; 10-29: DNA, #129259; 10-33: Dartboard, #2669473 Darts, #3483998 Credit card, #2140018 Calculator, #3328335 Percentages, #3211485; E-4: People, #450125

Contents

What do you think of this book? We want to hear from you!

Microsoft is interested in hearing your feedback so we can continually improve our books and learning resources for you. To participate in a brief online survey, please visit:

microsoft.com/learning/booksurvey

What do you think of this book? We want to hear from you!

Microsoft is interested in hearing your feedback so we can continually improve our
books and learning resources for you. To participate in a brief online survey, please visit:

microsoft.com/learning/booksurvey

Acknowledgments

MY THANKS to Kim Spilker and the teams at Microsoft Press and O'Reilly, who graciously provided me with the opportunity to update this book in a third edition. Thanks to my editing team of Valerie Woolley, Steve Sagman, and Roger LeBlanc, and to Brenda Bazylewski and the iStockphoto community for the stock photography used in many of the presentation examples.

Thanks to those who inspired the foundation of the BBP approach most profoundly: Richard E. Mayer's important work on multimedia learning, Barbara Minto's revolutionary critical-thinking methodology, Jonathan Pryce's insights on structuring and outlining information, the engineers who developed the STOP proposal-writing method at Hughes Aircraft, and the media producers who practice their craft here in Los Angeles.

A special thanks to the many BBP readers and workshop participants—your courage in applying BBP often against great odds gives me hope that BBP will continue to make a difference in the world.

Dedication

To my partner, Andrew.

—Cliff Atkinson

About the Author

Cliff Atkinson is an acclaimed writer, popular keynote speaker, and an independent consultant to leading attorneys and Fortune 500 companies. He designed the presentations that helped persuade a jury to award a $253 million verdict to the plaintiff in the nation's first Vioxx trial in 2005, which Fortune magazine called "frighteningly powerful."

Cliff's bestselling book *Beyond Bullet Points* was named a Best Book of 2007 by the editors of Amazon.com, and has been published in three editions and translated into a dozen languages including Chinese, Korean, and Russian. The book expands on a communications approach he has taught internationally at top law firms, government agencies, business schools and corporations, including Sony, Toyota, Del Monte, Nestlé, Nokia, Deloitte, BBDO, The NPD Group, Ipsos, Facebook, Bristol-Myers Squibb, Intel, GE, the American Bar Association, and the United Nations International Criminal Tribunal.

Cliff's work has been featured in the Los Angeles Times, The New York Times and the The Wall Street Journal.

Cliff received his B.A. in English and journalism from Baylor University in Texas and his M.B.A. from Richmond, The American International University in London. After serving as a captain in the U.S. Air Force, he held marketing and consulting positions for start-up companies in San Francisco during the dot-com boom. Cliff currently resides in Washington D.C.

Introduction

I ORIGINALLY WROTE *Beyond Bullet Points* in 2005 to offer a new way for people to create Microsoft PowerPoint presentations more effectively. I never imagined that shortly after the book's publication, the impact of the Beyond Bullet Points (BBP) approach would make headlines in the *New York Times*, the *Wall Street Journal*, and the *Los Angeles Times*. Since then, interest in BBP has elevated the first edition of this book to bestseller status, at one point reaching the #4 sales rank out of all books at Amazon.com. It turns out that BBP is striking a chord with people who have a simple desire—to move beyond the bullet points that keep both presenters and audiences trapped, frustrated, and alienated from one another.

People are finding that BBP really works for them and that once they try this approach, they can't go back to the old way of using PowerPoint. Since the first edition of this book was published, BBP has been even more thoroughly road-tested and resoundingly audience-approved. Individuals report a process that is practical, orderly, focused, and disciplined, and organizations are finding a methodology that is attainable, effective, efficient, and scalable.

BBP is working today across an incredible range of professions and purposes. It will help you frame and facilitate a conversation with your audience, and it will guide you on how and where and why to use PowerPoint. Lately, questions about BBP have shifted from "How do I do this?" to "How does my organization do this?" which indicates that the approach is taking hold at a deeper level and setting the stage for a broader movement of people who support and use BBP every day.

The underlying system of BBP in this book is the same as in the first two editions, offering a way to turn general theories about communication into the practical things you do when you open a new PowerPoint presentation tomorrow morning.

How this Book Is Organized

As in the previous edition of this book, I take you step by step, chapter by chapter, through the BBP process. Chapters 1 through 3 provide an overview of the reasons why you should try BBP and how the process looks, and

Chapters 4 through 10 explain specifically the detailed steps of how to use BBP. A bonus Chapter 11, available at the companion content Web page for the book and at *www.beyondbulletpoints.com*, introduces a fun exercise called BBP Visual Improv. This book is designed to be a practical guide that you keep close at hand while you work on PowerPoint presentations, as well as a source of ongoing inspiration.

For many people, BBP turns the conventional thinking about PowerPoint presentations upside-down and unlocks the potential that has always been available in the software tool, as well as in the people who use it. The heart of this book is really about people communicating with people. By using a commonly available software tool to help you to do that, you can find focus, clarity, and engagement. I hope you'll find that and much more in this book, as you make and tell your own presentation stories *beyond bullet points*.

Where to Get the Companion Content

The companion content Web page for this book includes copies of key tools described in the book; a bonus chapter, Chapter 11, which introduces a fun exercise called BBP Visual Improv; and PDF versions of the BBP Ground Rules and BBP Checklists that you can use as a desktop reference. These files, as well as other information, can be downloaded from *www.beyondbulletpoints.com* or the following page:

http://go.microsoft.com/fwlink/?Linkid=213936

Your Companion eBook

The eBook edition of this book allows you to:

- Search the full text
- Print
- Copy and paste

To download your eBook, please see the instruction page at the back of this book.

How to Get Support & Provide Feedback

The following sections provide information on errata, book support, feedback, and contact information.

Errata & Book Support

We've made every effort to ensure the accuracy of this book and its companion content. If you do find an error, please report it on our Microsoft Press site:

1. Go to *www.microsoftpressstore.com*.

2. In the Search box, enter the book's ISBN or title.

3. Select your book from the search results.

4. On the book's catalog page, find the Errata & Update tab.

5. Click View/Submit Errata.

You'll find additional information and services for your book on its catalog page. If you need additional support, email Microsoft Press Book Support at *mspinput@microsoft.com*. Please note that product support for Microsoft software is not offered through the addresses above.

We Want to Hear from You

At Microsoft Press, your satisfaction is our top priority and your feedback our most valuable asset. Please tell us what you think of this book at

> *http://www.microsoft.com/learning/booksurvey*

The survey is short, and we read every one of your comments and ideas. Thanks in advance for your input!

Stay in Touch

Let's keep the conversation going! We're on Twitter:

> *http://twitter.com/MicrosoftPress*

CHAPTER 1

The Perfect PowerPoint Storm

EVERY SUMMER, the residents of Angleton, Texas brace themselves for the possibility that a fearsome hurricane might bear down on their Gulf Coast town near Houston. But nothing could prepare them for the hot and humid July day in 2005 when a different kind of storm hit their quiet town of 18,000 people. The doors of the old gray county courthouse in the town square opened to a flood of television crews who crowded the hallways looking for a place to film. A group of newspaper reporters surged into the main courtroom, squeezing into uncomfortable wooden benches and tapping updates on their laptops to the newsrooms of the *New York Times*, the *Wall Street Journal*, the Associated Press, *Fortune*, and Reuters.

The journalists were in Angleton to cover the news event of the day: the opening statements of a major legal trial that would begin with a Microsoft PowerPoint presentation. Everyone in the courtroom stood when the jurors filed into the room and settled into their seats. The room was silent, here at the eye of the storm, when a man stood up to face the jurors. Little did anyone know that this lawyer was about to unleash a storm of his own from his laptop computer. After all, this was no ordinary PowerPoint presentation he was about to give—it was a Beyond Bullet Points presentation. Like many of the hurricanes that have passed through Texas, this presentation would make headlines for its devastating force.

The lawyer who was about to speak was no stranger to PowerPoint, or to the courtroom. Born and raised in Texas, Mark Lanier specializes in representing plaintiffs in personal injury trials and has a long string of winning verdicts for his clients. Early on, he worked as a lawyer in large law firms, but later he started his own firm and eventually moved it to the outskirts of Houston. Mark would soon demonstrate that these days anyone with a laptop computer and PowerPoint software—and an effective strategy for using them—can make as great an impact as a person with unlimited resources.

Mark turned to his client, the plaintiff in this case, who was sitting in the first row with her family. "Your Honor," Mark said, "if I may begin by introducing to the jury and to the Court my client." As Carol Ernst stood, Mark introduced her and her daughter. Carol's husband, Bob, had died of a heart attack, and she suspected that a painkiller her husband had taken, Vioxx, was a cause of the heart attack. So she filed a lawsuit against the defendant, the drug's manufacturer, Merck & Co., Inc. Mark would represent Carol throughout the trial.

As Carol sat down, Mark walked toward the jury box past the row of lawyers sitting at the defense table. These lawyers were from two internationally recognized law firms hired by the defendant. With billions of dollars in their war chest, the company could afford the best. Facing such a formidable opponent with deep pockets, Mark knew he would need to be at the top of his game and use the tools and techniques he had to the best of his ability to make the greatest impact.

Mark paused at the jury box and made eye contact with each of the 12 jurors. Before the jurors arrived, Mark had wheeled the lawyers' podium to the side of the courtroom because he didn't want a piece of furniture, or anything else, to stand between him and his audience. Mark had a folksy style when he talked to jurors in the courtroom, speaking with a Texas drawl, in colorful language, and in a conversational manner. But by now, Mark's legal opponents knew that to interpret his simple style as unsophisticated would be a big and expensive mistake, because of his strong track record of successful verdicts in jury trials.

The judge had instructed the jurors earlier that when they took their oath, they had become court officials like himself and the lawyers. The jurors were charged with administering justice in this case, by listening to all the evidence in open court and then making a decision based on the facts and the judge's instructions and reading of the law. Like any audience, they sat ready to hear what the presenter would say.

KNOW YOUR AUDIENCE

You need to know your audience well before you start planning your presentations. Mark knew some things about his audience in the jury box—the legal teams from both sides had prepared a written questionnaire for the jurors, in which they found that the jurors were in their 20s and 40s, high-school educated, and from a range of professions, including an electrician, a college student, a construction worker, a product technician, a homemaker, a secretary, and a government employee. The lawyers also had an opportunity to ask jurors questions in person during a Q&A session called *voir dire*. In your own presentations, the better you know your audience, the better you'll be able to customize your material to them.

As you might be able to relate to, most experienced speakers say they get nervous before a big presentation. Likewise, Mark must have felt some nervousness, but not just because the jurors were watching him closely. Plaintiffs' attorneys like Mark can spend upward of $1 million to bring a case to trial on behalf of their clients, and if they lose, they literally have lost everything they put into the case. The defendant had a great deal to lose as well, because this was the first case to go to trial against the pharmaceutical company. Beyond any negative media coverage the case might bring to the company, a verdict against the company could have a big impact on its bottom line—it could lose millions of dollars in an unfavorable verdict, and possibly lose billions of dollars in market value if its stock price dropped on the news.

Author's note — Mark Lanier discovered the first edition of *Beyond Bullet Points* at an online bookseller as he was preparing for this trial, and he invited me to fly to Texas to help him use the BBP approach to create his opening statement. We followed the approach in this book step by step as we structured his presentation, and I selected the graphics and designed slides similar to the ones that appear in this chapter. By following the detailed descriptions of the BBP approach through the examples in the rest of this book, you'll be able to apply the same effective approach to your own presentations.

Based on what the plaintiff and defendant had at stake in this trial, the courtroom presentation was about as high-stakes as a PowerPoint presentation can get.

Stepping onto the Media Stage

Mark glanced down at his laptop computer, which sat facing him on a small table below the jury box, out of sight of the jurors. What he saw on his laptop screen was a feature in PowerPoint called Presenter view, similar to the screen shown in Figure 1-1, which gave Mark a special view of the presentation that only he could see. Like the teleprompter that broadcasters use to present their speaking notes, this sometimes-overlooked PowerPoint feature gives you the ability to see additional information that does not appear on the screen the audience sees. For example, at the upper left of his screen, Mark could see the blank blue slide that the jurors were currently looking at. And he also could see his speaker notes at the upper right, reminding him of the points he planned to make while each slide was displayed on screen, as well as a row of small previews of his upcoming slides at the bottom of the screen, helping him to make a smooth transition from one slide to the next.

See Also	To learn how to use Presenter view for your BBP presentations, see Appendix B, "Presenting BBP with Two Views."

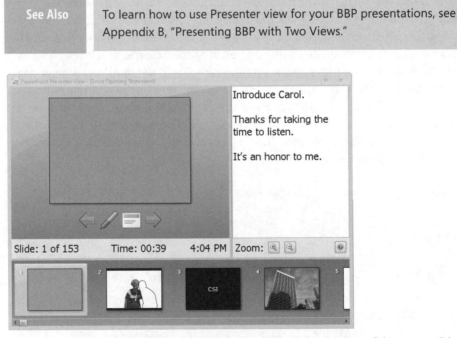

FIGURE 1-1 A feature in PowerPoint called Presenter view gave Mark a view of the current slide the jurors saw on screen, along with his own speaker notes and thumbnail views of upcoming slides.

As he began speaking, Mark's thumb pressed the button on a remote control device like the one shown in Figure 1-2, which he cupped in his hand at his side where the audience would not notice it. This remote would be his constant companion for the next couple of hours, as he used it to advance the PowerPoint slides while he spoke, giving him flexibility to slow down or speed up to match his narration and ensure that the experience appeared seamless to the jurors.

FIGURE 1-2 Remote control devices offer presenters the ability to advance the slides of a PowerPoint presentation without using the keyboard.

"It's extremely important to me that you hear what this case is about," Mark said. "So I've put together...different exhibits to try and help it stick in your brain and help you focus on what we think are critical points." When Mark clicked the remote control button, it signaled his laptop computer to advance to the first image in the PowerPoint presentation. Although the jurors could not see the laptop below the jury box, they did see an image of Carol and Bob appear on the 10-foot screen directly behind Mark, as illustrated in Figure 1-3. From where the jurors sat, it appeared that Mark was in a giant television set, as the images on the screen would soon start dissolving and changing behind him in a seamlessly choreographed media experience.

FIGURE 1-3 The images from Mark's PowerPoint presentation filled the 10-foot screen behind him.

The projected colors, images, and words were so thoroughly integrated into the presentation experience that turning off the projector would have been like eliminating the set of a theater production or the screen in a movie theater. Never breaking eye contact with the jurors or looking back at the screen, Mark now began to tell a gripping story that would lay out the evidence of the plaintiff's case through the next two and a half hours of the presentation.

A Singular Story

What was notable about Mark's PowerPoint slide, shown on its own in Figure 1-4, was not so much what was on it, but rather what was not on it. You would probably expect the slides of a PowerPoint presentation to be filled with bullet points, but here the jurors saw only the visual power of a single, simple photograph. Such full-screen images are rare in PowerPoint presentations, but this image fit in perfectly with what Mark would do next.

FIGURE 1-4 A family photo of Bob and Carol showed the happy couple after they were married.

With a photograph of the couple on the screen as his backdrop, Mark began telling an anecdote to introduce Bob and Carol to the jurors. "But let me tell you a little bit about Bob," Mark said. "Bob was a great fellow who always took [Carol] to wonderful, interesting places. They went to the kite festival in Washington State. They went to the balloon launch in Albuquerque. They had a lot of fun. He got her into tandem bike racing. They weren't the winning kind of athletes. They just did it to be together, and it was a good, fun way for them to live together."

Mark knew that telling the details of an anecdote like this one about Carol and Bob is an effective way to introduce a new and complicated topic to an audience. With a simple story of a bike race, the jurors could quickly imagine what Carol and Bob's relationship and lives were like. And seeing the family photograph would make it easier for jurors to relate to the plaintiff, perhaps reminding the jurors of similar photos they have taken or seen in their own families. The photo and specific details of the couple's life together would work powerfully to quickly introduce Carol and Bob to the jury and make an emotional connection with them. This slide worked much more effectively than a list of bullet points ever could, because we don't live our lives in bullet points—we live in images and stories.

"They did get married after being together for a number of years," Mark explained. "Interestingly enough, they were introduced over exercise. And you'll hear Carol talk about her...daughter...being the matchmaker between Carol and Bob." Here Mark added a detail informing the jurors that they would hear from Carol herself on the stand, establishing a sense of anticipation that they would get to hear from her firsthand. Mark knew that hinting at events to come is an effective way to grab any audience's interest. And by using the specific details about Carol and Bob while the photograph was displayed on screen, he connected the audience's emotions to the image.

Mark clicked the remote control again and displayed the same photograph, except now the background behind the photograph had disappeared, as shown in Figure 1-5. As the new photograph appeared, Mark said, "They had a wonderful time together. But ultimately...the picture starts to fade and things start to go different. And let me tell you why." People are not used to seeing family photographs where the background suddenly disappears, so this visually set the stage that something unexpected was about to happen to Carol and Bob. The emotions of the audience that Mark had associated with the photograph suddenly were stripped away.

FIGURE 1-5 The next slide shows the same photograph with the background stripped away to indicate that something unexpected had happened.

Clicking again, Mark displayed a new version of the photograph, except in this one, Bob was missing from the photograph. In his place was a thick black line like the chalk outline from a crime scene, as shown in Figure 1-6. "You see, Bob Ernst is dead today," Mark said. "One of my witnesses that I want to bring in the case I cannot bring you. Bob Ernst cannot come in here today. He is no longer here. He didn't know he was going to need to be here. He didn't leave us anything in video. He didn't leave us anything in writing that would talk about the issues that we need to talk about."

This striking photograph visually communicated to the jurors that the worst had happened—that Bob and Carol's happiness ended abruptly and unexpectedly when Bob died of a heart attack. The black outline around where Bob had been in the photo visually brought home the point that Bob's death suddenly had left a hole in Carol's life, and in her heart.

FIGURE 1-6 This slide shows Bob missing from the photograph, with only a thick black line to indicate where he once was.

Mark knew that his audience came from a part of Texas that was growing increasingly conservative and that the jurors might not be predisposed to award a big verdict to a plaintiff in a product liability case like this. But with the thick black outline that indicated where Bob had been, Mark also introduced a powerful new outline for his presentation. If the jurors were not going to be friendly toward a product liability case, Mark was now visually reframing his opening statement to a new story line that the conservative jurors would find more engaging—a murder mystery. In this third photograph, the black outline subtly communicated a familiar story setting that the jurors immediately would understand—a crime scene from a television show. This unexpected use of a familiar convention from TV would surprise the jurors and make the idea stick in their minds. This slide would then thematically transition to the next, pivotal, slide in the presentation.

Mark clicked the remote again, and this time a black slide appeared with the phrase *CSI: Angleton* on it, similar to the slide shown in Figure 1-7, as he said, "If we were going to put it into a TV show, this would be 'CSI: Angleton.' ...What you're going to do is... follow the evidence, like any good detective would."

FIGURE 1-7 Next the words "CSI: Angleton" appeared on the screen as Mark told jurors that they would be like crime scene investigators, sorting through the evidence to figure out what caused Bob's death.

In an entertaining fictional story, the main character is someone an audience observes from a distance. But in a nonfiction presentation, making the audience the center of the action can dramatically increase their sense of involvement. You'll learn how to always make your audience the main character of your presentation story when you plan your first five slides in Chapter 4, "Planning Your First Five Slides."

In keeping with classical storytelling form, Mark's next step would be to present the main characters with a problem they would have to face.

The Heart of the Problem

Mark clicked the remote control to advance to the next slide, showing an image of a headquarters building, similar to Figure 1-8, as he said, "The evidence is going to lead you to one place"—the front steps of one of the largest pharmaceutical companies in the world. Mark explained that he would show a great deal of evidence from many sources that all proved the company's drug was a cause of Bob's heart attack. But then he added, "There are lots of different ways it can be painted," and jurors would have to eventually weigh the evidence against everything else they would hear.

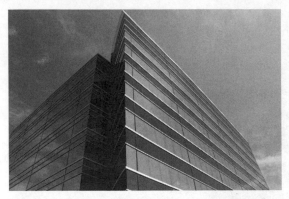

FIGURE 1-8 Next Mark showed a photo of the headquarters building of the pharmaceutical company, similar to this, and told jurors that the evidence in the case would lead to the company's doorstep.

Mark clicked the remote button to show the next slide, a photograph of a gavel and flag, similar to Figure 1-9, as he said, "You're going to hear all of this evidence because... your job to do is to get us to justice...Nobody else has this power. A judge can't do it... Politicians can't do it. Nobody else can do it. This is where you can make a difference in the world."

The image of the gavel along with Mark's narration reinforced the problem the jurors faced: they will see the evidence against the company, and they will have to sort through it and bring the situation to justice. You'll learn how to create similar dramatic tension in your presentations in Chapter 3, "Building a Foundation with the BBP Story Template," when you plan the two specific slides that present your audience with an unresolved problem that your presentation will help them to solve.

FIGURE 1-9 With a gavel and flag displayed on screen, Mark explained that the jurors could bring the situation to justice.

Next, as Mark began to click to a slide similar to the one shown in Figure 1-10, he said, "How are you going to do it? My suggestion to you is, again, you've got to follow the evidence. First of all, I'm going to show you a motive." The word *motive* appeared on the screen (left) along with a picture of a stack of money. "I'm going to show you the means," he said, as the word *means* and an image of pills similar to this one appeared on the screen (middle). "I'm going to show you the death," he said, as the word *death* and the familiar outline of Bob appeared next to Carol on the screen (right).

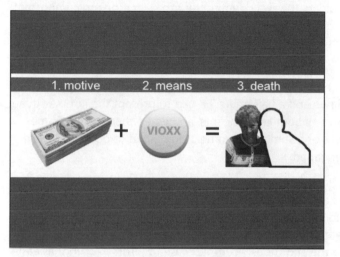

FIGURE 1-10 This summary slide visually distills the entire case into a single image. The horizontal bars above and below the icons are red to indicate that this slide stands out as the most important in the presentation.

With these slides, Mark asked the jurors to follow the simple formula that underlies every murder-mystery story: *motive + means = death*. Even jurors who don't watch TV would know this familiar structure from books, board games, or stories in the news. Earlier, Mark hinted at a murder-mystery motif with the black outline and again with the CSI reference, and now at the most important part of the presentation, he fully established the murder-mystery motif as the structure for the entire presentation to come. You'll learn more about how you find your story thread and integrate verbal and visual motifs into your own presentation starting in Chapter 4.

This single slide distills the essence of the entire story into a single image—you'll create a similar slide in Chapter 7, "Sketching Your Storyboard," and Chapter 8, "Adding Graphics to Your Slides." Although the slide appears simple, it is extremely sophisticated in its effect because it reduces a complex case into something easy to understand and follow.

Distilling the Essence

As he was in the planning stage of his presentation, Mark faced a vast amount of information that he could potentially present to his audience, as you certainly do in your own presentations. For Mark, it would be tough to explain the complex science behind how the drug worked, how it was developed, and how it was reviewed and studied. It would be confusing to recount the details of every event, every person involved, and the sequence in which the case unfolded. It was a daunting task to select the most important evidence to explain the case from more than 3 million documents and countless hours of videotaped depositions from witnesses.

On top of the vast amount of information to choose from, Mark faced the constraints of a limited amount of time to communicate to his audience, just as you do in your presentations. In no more than two and a half hours, he had to present the jurors with an overview of the case, educate them about key concepts, and equip them with a framework to understand the six weeks of testimony to come. And he had to do all this while keeping jurors interested and engaged.

Just as you'll do in Chapter 5, "Planning the Rest of Your Slides," Mark solved the problem of potentially overwhelming his audience by distilling his presentation into three roughly equal parts that he would spend equal amounts of time explaining. With his three key points identified, and using the murder-mystery motif as a familiar structure, Mark verbally and visually introduced the enormously complex case to jurors as being "as easy as 1-2-3" to understand, using this summary slide as he spoke.

Next Mark clicked the remote to show the slides containing his key points, similar to the images shown in Figure 1-11, as he introduced each of the three sections of the presentation. Instead of overwhelming jurors with 3 million documents, Mark now guided them along what appeared to be a very simple story as he introduced the three most important parts of the case, which he then explained in more detail as his presentation moved forward. Now the jurors could relax as they listened and watched the story unfold.

In any presentation, the audience can't possibly remember all the information they see and hear, but it helps if you give them graphical cues to the presentation's organization and the slides' relative importance. The look of these three slides was based on the style of the earlier summary slide, carrying forward the story visually to complement Mark's verbal explanation. The simple split-screen layout of the slides, the use of the striking red color, and the consistent graphical style ensured that when these slides appeared, they would stand out as the most important among all of the slides. You'll learn more about how to apply these techniques when you sketch your own storyboard in Chapter 7.

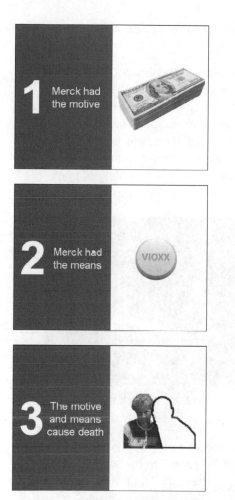

FIGURE 1-11 As he introduced each of the three sections of the opening statement, Mark displayed slides that carried forward the theme from the earlier summary slide, including the red backgrounds on the left half of each slide.

Mixing Mediums

With this simple yet clear and engaging introduction to his opening statement, Mark had succeeded in presenting a framework that would be easy for jurors to follow. He continued to integrate the story seamlessly through the remaining slides over the next couple of hours. Although your own presentations will likely not last as long, the same

BBP approach will give you the ability to quickly scale down any presentation from 45 minutes to 15 to 5.

As Mark continued through the presentation, many slides in the presentation looked similar to the ones shown in Figure 1-12. The slides were designed so that the jurors' attention would first go to the most important information at the top of the screen—a headline that summarized the main point at hand, like a newspaper headline. Next the jurors would see a simple graphic that illustrated the specific headline. Last the jurors' attention would shift from the screen to Mark, who explained the point of the slide in more detail. The range of visuals used on the slides included a wide variety of photographs, medical illustrations, documents, screen captures, timelines, and more.

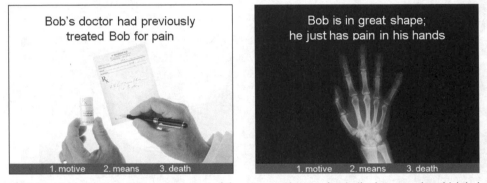

FIGURE 1-12 The slides within each section of the presentation used a similar layout style, which helped the jurors quickly understand the information.

Mark clicked through the 153 slides of this presentation at a pace of less than one minute per slide, which allowed his audience to digest the information on the screen before moving forward to the next slide and the next part of the story. This pace kept the jurors visually interested.

Conventional PowerPoint slides can overwhelm audiences with too much information on the screen, but Mark's presentation contained only one idea per slide, giving jurors time to digest each point as they listened to Mark's verbal explanation. Instead of reading bullet points from the screen, Mark used his slides as visual cues to prompt him on the next point he would make, allowing him to speak with a natural and spontaneous style that came from the depth of his knowledge and authority on his topic. And instead of looking at the screen to see what was on it, Mark kept his attention focused on the jurors, making eye contact with each person throughout the presentation.

Beyond the PowerPoint slides, Mark also used a range of other media and physical props to engage with the audience over the course of the presentation. At times, he switched the screen to a document projector, where he displayed physical paper documents and highlighted passages on the pages with a yellow marker as he explained the significance of the evidence. Later he used a large paper flip chart that he calls a "double-wide," where he wrote out key terms and concepts with large markers. Sometimes he switched from the slides to a brief video that illustrated a point. Other times, he used physical props such as a plastic model of a heart held up in his hand to teach jurors the science behind heart attacks.

Mark used different types of media to keep things varied and interesting throughout the presentation and to keep the experience from feeling too slick and produced. But after using each type of media, Mark always returned to the PowerPoint presentation on the 10-foot screen because it was a visually unifying tool he could use to move the story forward. The shifting and dissolving images holding the audience's interest on the large screen seamlessly came together with Mark's physical presence, and his voice filled in key details while remaining consistent with the visual presentation. In the Angleton courtroom, PowerPoint had taken on a new role—it was now a tremendously persuasive backdrop that would have a major impact on the jurors in the eye of the PowerPoint storm in this Angleton courtroom.

Fade to Gray

After Mark finished his presentation, the judge allowed a break, and the jurors left the courtroom. Now it was the defense team's turn to present its opening statement. They got their PowerPoint presentation ready on their own laptop computer, and they rolled back the podium to where it had been before Mark moved it, in front of the jury box. When the jurors returned, the defense lawyer walked up to the podium, looked down at his printed notes, and began to read his opening statement to the jurors.

In the crucial first few minutes of the presentation, when it is essential to make an audience feel like the presentation is all about them, the lawyer recited the details about the admirable history of the company. Instead of making the presentation human by telling an anecdote about a real person, he cited dry data about the millions of people the company aims to reach with its various drugs. As he read the prepared script in formal and impersonal language, someone else on his team advanced the PowerPoint slides forward on the computer, sometimes missing a cue and leaving a disconnect between what the lawyer said and what the jurors saw on the screen. The lawyer occasionally turned back to look at the screen behind him to point at a complicated chart or a long passage of text.

Rather than display a dynamic and engaging visual experience, the lawyer next showed a slide with a formal photograph of the company's former CEO in a coat and tie as he talked about the CEO and his family, his biography, his public service, and his civic involvement. Missing the chance to connect with the everyday people in the jury with color and character, the defense lawyer continued on with slides that showed formal photographs of other corporate executives, and he talked about their Ivy League educations, detailed biographies, and long lists of accomplishments. Missing the point that less is more, later the lawyer displayed the familiar bullet points, charts, and long passages of text that the jurors strained to read.

The defense lawyer's relationship with the jurors never warmed up with the chilly and formal tone of the prepared talk. The podium that was now in front of the jurors had erected a wall between the presenter and his audience, the prepared script took away the lawyer's natural voice and spontaneity, and the PowerPoint slides on the screen became a 10-foot distraction from the lawyer who was speaking.

At the end of the defense's presentation, everyone stood as the jurors left the courtroom, and then the court adjourned for the day. If what lawyers believe is true, the two presentations the jurors had just experienced would play a significant role in the verdict they would reach at the end of the trial. Whatever the jurors thought that day, the journalists in the room wasted no time in pronouncing their verdict about how they thought the two PowerPoint presentations had gone.

Stark Choices

The news media cover opening statements of legal trials every day, but it's unusual when the topic of the coverage is the presentation style itself. According to the coverage of this opening statement the next day, something exceptional had happened in the Angleton courtroom. According to *Fortune*'s account, Mark "gave a frighteningly powerful and skillful opening statement," speaking "without notes and in gloriously plain English" and taking on the defendant "with merciless, spellbinding savagery" (Roger Parloff, "Stark Choices at the First Vioxx Trial," *Fortune*, July 15, 2005). The reporter had not noticed that Mark did have a form of notes—his PowerPoint presentation in Presenter view on his laptop below the jury box. The *New York Times* reported that in comparison with Mark's opening, the defense lawyer's presentation was "staid" and that "he read portions of his statement and illustrated his talk mostly using blue-and-yellow PowerPoint pie charts and long excerpts of letters from the Food and Drug Administration" (Alex Berenson, "Contrary Tales of Vioxx Role in Texan's Death," *New York Times*, July 15, 2005).

According to *Fortune:* "The trial offers jurors a stark choice between accepting Lanier's invitation to believe simple, alluring and emotionally cathartic stories" and the defense's "appeals to colorless, heavy-going soporific Reason. Lanier is inviting the jurors to join him on a bracing mission to catch a wrongdoer and bring him to justice." In contrast, the *Fortune* article continued, the defense "is asking the jurors to do something difficult and unpleasant like—well—taking medicine."

Six weeks later, the trial ended, and the jurors entered the jury room to deliberate. After a day and a half of discussion, the jurors made a decision, and the journalists and lawyers filled the courtroom again to hear what they would say. The jurors awarded the plaintiff a stunning $253 million verdict. Amid the storm of international headline news, the pharmaceutical company's market capitalization fell $5 billion (Alex Berenson, "Jury Calls Merck Liable in Death of Man on Vioxx," *New York Times*, August 20, 2005).

After the verdict was announced, the *Wall Street Journal* reported one juror as saying "'Whenever [the defense] was up there, it was like wah, wah, wah,' . . . imitating the sounds Charlie Brown's teacher makes in the television cartoon. 'We didn't know what the heck they were talking about'" (Heather Won Tesoriero, "Merck Loss Jolts Drug Giant, Industry," *Wall Street Journal*, August 22, 2005).

The impact of the PowerPoint presentation in Mark's opening statement proved to last long after the trial. Six months later, Mark met with the Angleton jurors during a focus group session to see what they remembered about the trial, and the jurors vividly recalled the specific story and images that Mark presented in his opening statement.

Winds of Change

Although using PowerPoint helped win the day in Angleton for the plaintiff, that particular story did not end there, as many more Vioxx cases went to trial in other courtrooms around the U.S. Later the pharmaceutical company's market capitalization recovered, and Merck agreed to settle all Vioxx claims in 2007 with a $4.85 billion settlement fund. But what was unlocked in Angleton that July day was an example of the dramatic results an effective PowerPoint approach can have on a single presentation in a single room with a single audience.

The BBP approach had never been used in a courtroom before the Angleton trial, but since that day, its impact is still reverberating through the legal profession. Today, if a legal team faces a courtroom opponent who is using BBP, they know that they have to somehow respond and raise the bar of their own presentations. Legal teams that have faced opponents using BBP in the courtroom have started to adopt the story themes and graphics that the other side uses. For example, in trials against the pharmaceutical company that followed the Angleton verdict, the defense lawyers began using the "CSI" theme in their presentations. When Mark faced them again, he used techniques to counter what the defense lawyers did, raising the bar even higher.

The same sorts of impacts are being felt in other professions as well, as BBP begins to transform the status quo for presenters everywhere. As you consider applying BBP to your own presentations in this book, it might seem hard to imagine how to apply these types of techniques to your specific profession. But beyond lawyers and law firms, many people in many other professions and organizations are accomplishing significant results with this approach, including presenters in major corporations, governmental agencies, universities, research firms, and nonprofit organizations. Within these groups, people use BBP in a wide range of functions such as marketing, sales, training, and education. In this book, you'll find examples of presentations from different fields and for different purposes so that you see how to apply BBP to your own situation.

Everything Mark and many others have accomplished using the BBP approach is explained in detail in this book. In Chapter 2, "Realigning Our PowerPoint Approach with the Research," you'll learn the underpinnings of BBP along with the key research findings you need to know, and in Chapter 3, you'll see an overview of the three steps of the BBP approach. Then you'll get right to work on planning your first five slides in Chapter 4 and the rest of your slides in Chapter 5. In Chapter 6, "Setting Up Your Storyboard and Narration," you'll set up your storyboard and narration; in Chapter 7, you'll sketch the storyboard; and in Chapter 8, you'll add graphics. You'll get advice on delivering BBP presentations in Chapter 9, "Delivering Your BBP Presentation," and you'll see how BBP plays out through a wide range of presentation contexts and purposes in Chapter 10, "Reviewing a Range of BBP Examples," and. The companion Web site to this book, at *www.beyondbulletpoints.com*, offers advanced resources to the fast-growing community of people using BBP. By the end of this book, you should be well equipped with the knowledge and tools you need to start applying BBP to your own presentations.

The Power of BBP in Your Hands

Mark's presentation in Angleton is only a sample of how to use BBP to unlock the engaging, compelling stories inside of you. When Mark entered the Angleton courtroom that hot July day to present his opening statement, he had the same PowerPoint software you have. He just used it in an innovative way that produced dramatic results and made headline news. The book in your hands right now gives you the power to do the same.

CHAPTER 2

Realigning Our PowerPoint Approach with the Research

BEYOND BULLET POINTS (BBP) gets dramatically better results than the conventional bullet point approach because beneath the simple, clear, and compelling visual stories is a sophisticated foundation that determines everything you say, show, and do during a presentation. This chapter will explain why BBP works so well and why the conventional approach so often falls short of expectations.

Three Bedrock Tools of PowerPoint

Throughout its 20 years of existence, PowerPoint software has always offered the ability to work on your presentation in three key views: Normal view, Notes Page view, and Slide Sorter view. Although the rest of the PowerPoint features added since then are nice to have, these three views continue to be the bedrock tools you need to create your presentations.

> **See Also** This chapter focuses on the three views you use when you prepare your slides in advance of a PowerPoint presentation. For more information about the two views you can use when you present slides to an audience—Slide Show view and Presenter view—see Appendix B.

Normally when you create a text slide in PowerPoint with the standard bullet point approach, you first start in Normal view, as shown on the left in Figure 2-1, where you click to add a title to the title area and then click to add text in the content area below. If you have more to say verbally about the slide but can't fit the extra words in the content area, you might be one of a few people to visit Notes Page view, shown in the middle in Figure 2-1, where you see the slide area at the top and an adjacent text box in the notes area at the bottom that does not appear on screen during a presentation. And after you've created your slides, you might visit Slide Sorter view, shown on the right, to take a look at all of your slides together as small thumbnails.

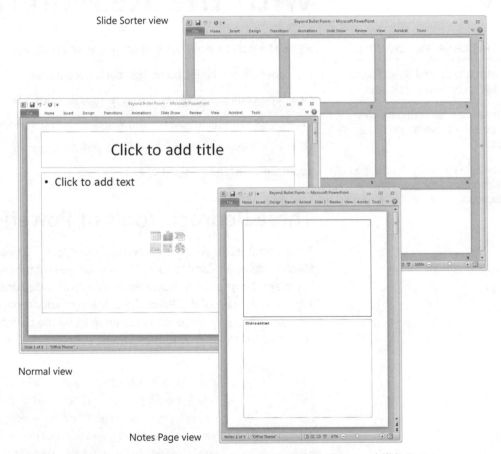

FIGURE 2-1 The three working views in PowerPoint: Normal, Notes Page, and Slide Sorter.

This ordered sequence of using PowerPoint in Normal, Notes Page, and then Slide Sorter views is the norm today. The secret to unlocking the power of BBP is to flip this sequence and always work in PowerPoint in Slide Sorter view first, then in Notes Page view, and finally in Normal view. As this chapter explains, when you discover this new order for using the same features that have been around for two decades, you will teach an old PowerPoint dog new tricks. And when you apply the new sequence to your own presentations, you'll see how BBP taps into the powerful potential of PowerPoint that has been waiting for you all along.

Realignment 1: Use Slide Sorter View to Manage the Volume of Information in Your Presentation

Open a new, blank PowerPoint presentation, and on the View tab, in the Presentation Views group, click Slide Sorter, as shown in Figure 2-2. Although you might be used to looking at Slide Sorter view only occasionally, if ever, the first trick of BBP is to always begin working in PowerPoint in this view. You'll do that starting in Chapter 6 after you finish writing the outline for your presentation. If you're wondering why it's so important to elevate the status of this little-used view from the least important to the most important way to look at your presentations, you need to step out of the PowerPoint mindset altogether for a bit and ask some uncommon questions first.

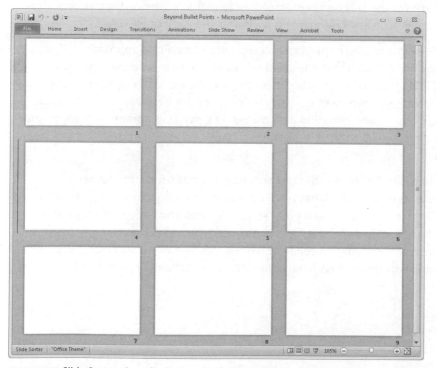

FIGURE 2-2 Slide Sorter view, displaying all of your slides as small thumbnails.

In Search of "Research Reality"

In most conversations about PowerPoint, the discussion usually focuses on which size font to use, how to insert a video clip, and whether the background of a PowerPoint template should be blue, black or another color. One thing you never hear is a conversation about any research related to PowerPoint presentations. Despite the widespread use and influence of PowerPoint software in many professions, you would be hard pressed to find research that demonstrates that the underlying theory, impact, or effectiveness of the conventional bullet point approach is better than any other approach.

For example, you won't find research indicating that presenting with bullet points on a PowerPoint slide is more effective than presenting without them, or studies showing that using a PowerPoint design template to make every slide background the same produces better learning than not using a design template, or a quantitative justification and rationale for commonly accepted PowerPoint design guidelines such as the 6-by-6 rule, which states that every slide should have six lines of text with six words per line.

This lack of comparative studies on PowerPoint approaches has created a void in terms of research-based guidelines on how best to use the software, and this void has been quickly filled with popular myths and cultural habits. In other words, the main reason we approach PowerPoint the way we do is simply because that's the way that we've always done it, and not because any research says it's better than any other way.

Although there is little research specifically comparing PowerPoint approaches, there is a significant body of research that has direct relevance to those who use spoken words and projected images to communicate. Researchers in the fields of cognitive science and educational psychology have been studying for decades the best ways to help people learn new information using narration and images. Their work is a treasure trove of information that is directly relevant and applicable to you when you use PowerPoint to create presentations.

The only problem is that currently the research dots are not connected to our PowerPoint bullet points. That is what you'll do now as you apply three key parts of this research to the three views of PowerPoint. As you do that, you'll see how these three "research realities" quickly dispel the myths and break the habits that stand in the way of effective presentations. These three research realities also will show clearly why BBP works so well and why the conventional approach to PowerPoint does not deliver results as effectively.

RESEARCH ON MULTIMEDIA LEARNING

This chapter is inspired by the work of Richard E. Mayer, Ph.D., a professor of psychology at the University of California, Santa Barbara. Ranked as the most productive researcher in the field of educational psychology in the world, Mayer is the author of 23 books and more than 350 other publications and has been researching multimedia learning and problem solving for almost 20 years. In his books and related articles and papers, Mayer proposes a way to understand the use of multimedia that promotes meaningful learning and lays out a set of principles for designing any multimedia experience based on his own research and that of others. For more information about the research on multimedia learning and its implications for PowerPoint presentations, see:

- Richard E. Mayer, Ed., The Cambridge Handbook of Multimedia Learning (Cambridge University Press, 2005).

- Cliff Atkinson, "The Cognitive Load of PowerPoint: Q&A with Richard E. Mayer," www.beyondbulletpoints.com (March 2004).

Research Reality 1: You Have to Respect the Limits of Working Memory

Whether or not you think about it consciously, you probably accept fundamental assumptions about communication that literally shape your thinking in ways large and small. If you commonly talk about communication in terms of a "sender" who transmits a "message" to a "receiver," you might assume that you "send" information through an unobstructed channel, like a pipeline, and the audience will "get it," fully intact, at the other end of the pipeline, as shown in Figure 2-3.

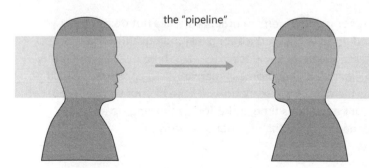
the "pipeline"

FIGURE 2-3 The pipeline concept assumes that there is an unobstructed channel between you and your audience.

With the pipeline in mind, you assume that you can produce a PowerPoint presentation in whatever way you like, as shown on the left in Figure 2-4. After you send this PowerPoint presentation through the pipeline, you assume that its receivers will "get it" on the other side, as shown on the right. Under this assumption, your work is then done. The only criterion for success is that you "delivered" the PowerPoint presentation through the pipeline. If for some reason the audience didn't get what you delivered, of course, it's not your fault as a presenter—after all, you delivered the PowerPoint presentation, and what they did with it is their problem, not yours.

The pipeline assumption is at work when people make statements like, "We showed them the facts, but they just didn't get it," or, "The presentation went right over their heads." When a verdict in a legal trial goes against one party, it is common for people to say the jury just didn't "get" the evidence, or when a sales presentation does not succeed, the presenter might say the audience just didn't "get" the benefits of the product or service. It is hard to separate the pipeline metaphor from our thinking because it is woven into the words and expressions we use commonly every day.

What you present to your audience   What you assume the audience learns

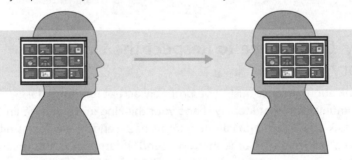

FIGURE 2-4 With the pipeline in mind, you assume that your audience will "get" whatever you "deliver" to them.

Although the pipeline metaphor is convenient, in practice it does not deliver what you might assume it does. According to leading educational psychologist Richard E. Mayer, if you give a multimedia presentation to an audience, there are three possible outcomes, as shown in Figure 2-5. The first possible outcome is that your audience experienced *no learning* (upper right). This is the worst-case scenario—in spite of your work in preparing your presentation and your audience's time and effort in showing up and paying attention, no learning happened to make the experience worthwhile.

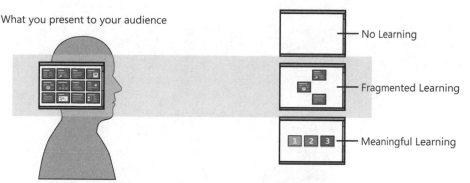

FIGURE 2-5 In reality, audiences do not automatically get what you send through the pipeline.

A second possible outcome is that your audience remembered perhaps the bullet points on slides 12 and 33 and the diagram on slide 26—but that's all they remembered. In this scenario, they remember only bits and pieces of the presentation because they experienced *fragmented learning* (middle right). In fragmented learning, the audience members remember at least some things; but from a presenter's perspective, you have no control over what they learned because the fragments could be *any* pieces of information among many, and you don't know which ones.

The third possible outcome is that the audience remembered exactly what the presenter intended—they experienced *meaningful learning* (lower right). Meaningful learning is what any group wants to achieve in their time together—the people in the audience understand what the presenter intended, and they are able to apply the information after the meeting.

Audiences routinely report that PowerPoint presentations today are "Forgettable!" and "What's the point?" It's rare to hear an audience and a presenter agree that meaningful learning has occurred. In order to turn the situation around, you literally need to change the shape of the metaphor that guides the way you think about human communication.

During a PowerPoint presentation, the memory of an audience member is the critical human element that determines how well new information is received, processed, and stored in the human mind. Researchers who study the mind generally accept that there are three types of human memory, as shown in Figure 2-6.

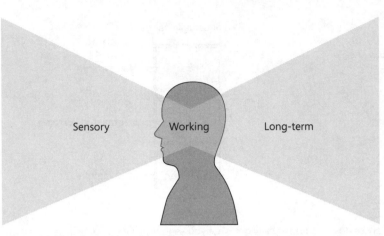

FIGURE 2-6 The three types of human memory: sensory memory, long-term memory, and working memory.

The first type is *sensory memory.* Sensory memory is the part of the mind where your audience members briefly store the initial impressions of sights and sounds as they look at and listen to the environment around them. Sensory memory is potentially unlimited in capacity, although sights and sounds might persist in sensory memory for less than a second.

The second type is *long-term memory*—the part of the mind where your audience members store information over an extended period of time, from as little as 30 seconds to as long as a lifetime. In a presentation context, this is where you would like your audience to store the new information you intend to communicate to them. Beyond just remembering the new information, you also would like them to be able to access and apply the information from long-term memory when needed. Like sensory memory, long-term memory is also potentially unlimited in its capacity.

The third type is *working memory* (sometimes called *short-term memory*)—the part of the mind where your audience members hold their attention. The theories underlying working memory are complex, but essentially, working memory is a temporary holding area for information. As sensory memory briefly holds sights or sounds, working memory then pays attention to some of them and holds them for a matter of seconds while it works to integrate them into long-term memory.

While sensory memory and long-term memory each have unlimited capacity, working memory is severely limited in its capacity to process new information. In an influential paper published in 1956, George A. Miller observed that people could hold a small number of "chunks" that they mentally form in what we now understand as working memory. Although the capacity of chunks was thought to be around seven for most people, depending on the type of information, working memory expert Nelson Cowan recently revisited Miller's classic work and now estimates the capacity of working memory for new information at three or four chunks.

> **See Also** For more information about the capacity of working memory, see:
>
> ■ George A. Miller, "The Magical Number Seven, Plus or Minus Two: Some Limits on Our Capacity for Processing Information," *Psychological Review* **63**, 81–97 (1956).
>
> ■ Cliff Atkinson, "The Science of Making Your PowerPoint Memorable: Q&A with Nelson Cowan," *www.beyondbulletpoints.com* (June 2004).

Although the limits of working memory have been acknowledged for 50 years, the concept has never been fully absorbed or integrated into our day-to-day practice and understanding of human communication. The pipeline metaphor has such a strong grip on our collective consciousness that we have effectively resisted the adoption of the research that contradicts it. Yet as much as you might want to believe that there is an unobstructed pipeline between sender and receiver, the reality is that the limits of working memory put a major crimp in that metaphor.

In order to align your own assumptions about communication with what researchers accept about the way human memory works, you'll need to drop the old pipeline metaphor and pick up a new metaphor—the *eye of the needle*, as shown in Figure 2-7.

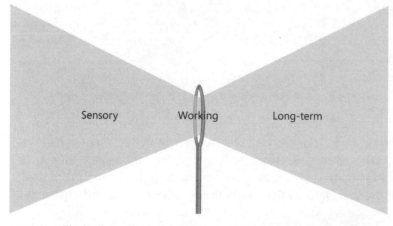

Sensory   Working   Long-term

FIGURE 2-7 The limited capacity of working memory to process new information creates a narrow passage—much like the eye of a needle—that stands between the information you present sensory memory and the information that is integrated into long-term memory.

Keeping this new metaphor in mind when you create presentations, you know that you have a potentially unlimited amount of new information that you could show someone's sensory memory (left). You want the new information to be retained in long-term memory (right). But working memory is so constrained in its capacity to process new information that it creates a narrow passage, much like the eye of a needle (center). This extremely small space of the "eye" of working memory constitutes the most formidable challenge you face as a presenter.

This new metaphor visually explains why audiences report either no learning or fragmented learning. If you present working memory with more new information than it can handle, as shown on the left in Figure 2-8, the eye of the needle is easily overloaded and will process and integrate into long-term memory what it can—only bits and pieces out of the entire presentation, as shown on the right. As much as you might want your audience to learn the new information you present, they will never be able to learn it unless you help that information properly pass through the eye of the needle.

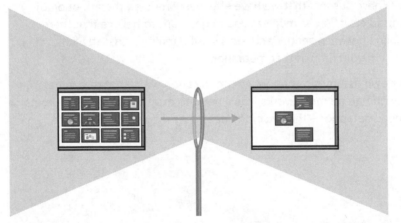

FIGURE 2-8 When you show more information than working memory can handle, audience members remember only bits and pieces.

The impact of reducing excess load on working memory has been documented by researchers including Mayer, who conducted a study using two multimedia presentations. The first presentation featured interesting but irrelevant graphics, and the second presentation provided the same information, but without the interesting but irrelevant graphics.

Mayer measured the impact of the two approaches on audiences in terms of two criteria: *retention*, the ability of the audience to simply recall the information, and *transfer*, the ability to creatively apply the new information. Audiences who experienced the second presentation retained 69 percent more information and were able to apply 105 percent more creative solutions using the information than those who experienced the first presentation. This study offers research-based evidence to support the saying "Less is more"—the less you overload working memory with extraneous information, the more learning improves.

BBP Respects the Limits of Working Memory

With the eye of the needle metaphor in mind, take a look at how a BBP presentation appears in Slide Sorter view, as shown in Figure 2-9. Studies have found that people learn better when information is broken up into digestible pieces, and here in Slide Sorter view, you see each specific digestible piece—in the form of a single slide that contains only one main idea that is clearly summarized by a headline. This eases your audience through your story and explanation frame by frame, one piece at a time.

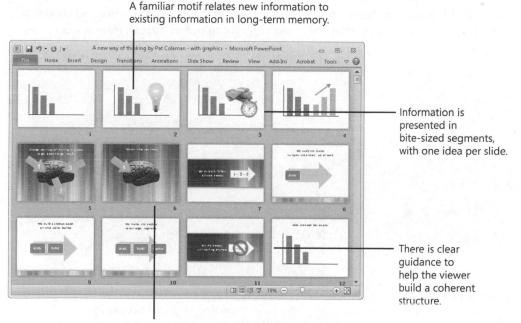

A familiar motif relates new information to existing information in long-term memory.

Information is presented in bite-sized segments, with one idea per slide.

There is clear guidance to help the viewer build a coherent structure.

Slide layouts and backgrounds call attention to the most important slides first.

FIGURE 2-9 Slide Sorter view shows a presentation that is broken up into digestible chunks for easier handling by working memory.

In the Slide Sorter view of a BBP presentation, your eye immediately goes to the most important slides because you use layouts and backgrounds to cue your audience to where they are. This approach draws from the hard work you do when you distill your complex ideas to the essence and identify your key points, as you'll see in Chapter 5. These visual cues also indicate the slides in the presentation that explain your key points, and provide backup detail.

In Chapters 6, 7, and 8, you'll use consistent layouts and backgrounds on related slides in a presentation to create visual and verbal continuity among them, but when you reach a different type of slide, the layouts and backgrounds will change. This orients both presenter and audience to where they are in the story, and the changing slide layouts and backgrounds offer your audience visual variety to keep their interest.

You also see from Slide Sorter view that BBP uses a visual motif through a presentation. Researchers have found that you improve the ability of working memory to process new information by applying familiar organizing structures. This works because an important quality of working memory is that it is a two-way street. Although working memory has only limited capacity to handle *new* information as that information arrives, as shown on the left in Figure 2-10, it also has unlimited capacity to pull in *existing* information from long-term memory, as shown on the right.

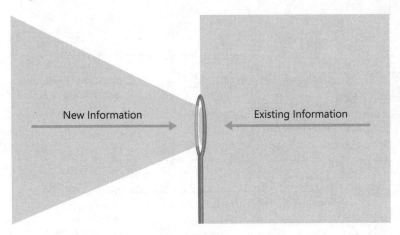

FIGURE 2-10 Working memory is limited in its capacity to process new information (left), but it is unlimited in its capacity to process existing information from long-term memory (right).

This plays out in the classic test of working memory, when a researcher presents someone with new information in the form of a series of unrelated numbers, such as *1 2 1 5 1 5 2 3 5 4*. The number of these individual chunks of information that someone can recall is considered the capacity of that person's working memory.

However, people can remember more of the same set of numbers when working memory pulls from long-term memory a structure they already know. This organizes the new information into meaningful chunks that hold the same information in a more memorable way, such as 212-555-1234—the familiar structure of a U.S. telephone number.

Thus a "chunk" is defined by the *audience* as they apply a meaningful structure from their long-term memory to new information. You help your audience accelerate understanding of new information with BBP by introducing a familiar "chunking" structure to new information you present. For example, in Chapters 4 and 5, you choose a familiar motif that resonates with your audience, and then later in Chapters 7 and 8, you extend the motif visually across the slides.

See Also	For more information about using familiar structures to overcome the limited capacity of working memory to process new information, see John Sweller, "Implications of Cognitive Load for Multimedia Learning," in *The Cambridge Handbook of Multimedia Learning*, Richard E. Mayer, Ed., pp. 19–30 (Cambridge University Press, 2005).

The Old Way Ignores the Limits of Working Memory

For comparison, take a look at a conventional PowerPoint presentation in Slide Sorter view, as shown in Figure 2-11. Audiences might not know about the limited capacity of working memory, but they do know what they're talking about when they say presentations like this are a "Data dump!" and "Overwhelming!" They've been down the road to overload before, and Slide Sorter view shows exactly how the conventional approach takes them there. The new information is clearly not presented in bite-size pieces; instead, it fills every slide, slide after slide, with overwhelming detail.

Information is not presented in bite-sized segments.

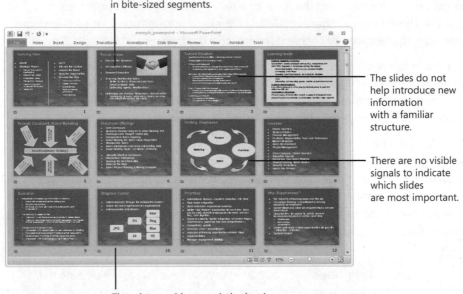

The slides do not help introduce new information with a familiar structure.

There are no visible signals to indicate which slides are most important.

There is no guidance to help the viewer build a coherent structure.

FIGURE 2-11 Slide Sorter view of a conventional PowerPoint presentation reveals no digestible pieces and no cues about the presentation's structure or organization.

What you see here is visual overwhelm rather than visual organization. Using the same predesigned background for all of the slides gives them a uniform look, but it also prevents you from using a range of design techniques to visually highlight the most important information on single slides or across slides. It also makes the overall presentation appear visually repetitive, which causes boredom that quickly shuts down attention.

> **MYTH VS. TRUTH**
>
> **Myth:** There's no need for me to use graphical cues to point out the organization of the presentation.
>
> **Truth:** Research shows that people learn better when you use visual cues to highlight a presentation's organization.

See Also   For more information about the research described in the Myth vs. Truth sidebars in this chapter, see Richard E. Mayer, Ed., *The Cambridge Handbook of Multimedia Learning* (Cambridge University Press, 2005).

Looking at this big-picture view of the presentation, you can't see immediately the location of the most important slides. Instead, every idea has equal visual weight, and there are no cues given by the slide backgrounds about relative importance of ideas. Working memory, with its limited capacity to process new information, has to sort things out on its own and is presented here with the impossible task of holding all this new information while it figures out what's most important to know.

MYTH VS. TRUTH

Myth: People will learn more if I show more.

Truth: Research shows that people learn better when information is presented in bite-size pieces.

You also see that there is no structure that ties each of the individual slides together into a coherent whole—this presentation is just a series of bulleted lists and diagrams, slide after slide. There is no familiar framework that the audience already has in long-term memory that can guide working memory to make sense of the new information.

Realignment 2: Use Notes Page View to Synchronize What You Show and What You Say

Now that you've realigned the way you use Slide Sorter view with the research, it's time to move on to another seldom-seen view in PowerPoint. Click the View tab, and in the Presentation Views group, click Notes Page, to switch to Notes Page view, shown in Figure 2-12. As described earlier, Notes Page view lets you see the on-screen slide above, along with an off-screen notes area that the audience does not see. The second trick of BBP is to always work in Notes Page view after Slide Sorter view, which you'll do starting in Chapter 6. There are research-based reasons to do that, as you'll see next.

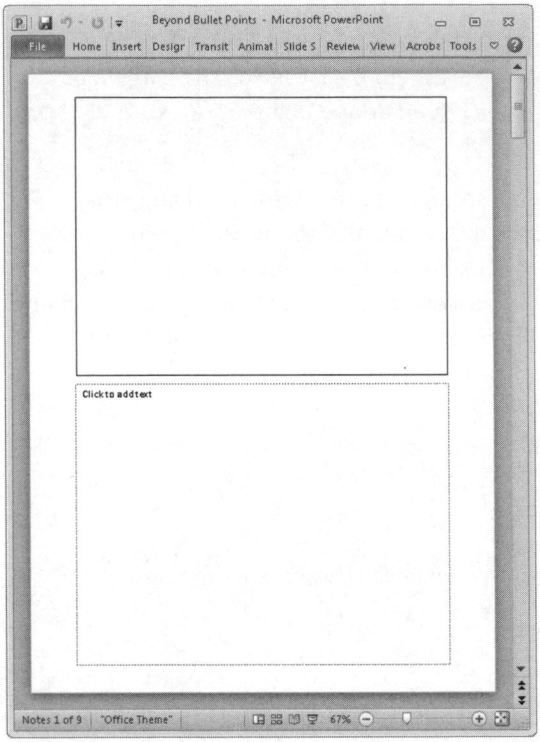

FIGURE 2-12 Notes Page view includes the on-screen slide area above and an off-screen notes area below.

Research Reality 2: You Have to Address the Two Channels

The next research reality, the concept of *dual channels*, states that people receive and process new visual and verbal information in not one, but two separate but related channels. Allan Paivio described his theory of *dual coding* in the 1970s, and during the same decade, Alan Baddeley and Graham Hitch described a similar two-channel structure in working memory.

Today, the concept has become a widely accepted standard among researchers. In the dual-channels model, the images someone sees are processed through a *visual channel*, the domain of images including photographs, illustrations, charts, and graphs, as illustrated conceptually in Figure 2-13 (top). What a speaker narrates is processed through the *verbal channel* (bottom), which is the domain of language.

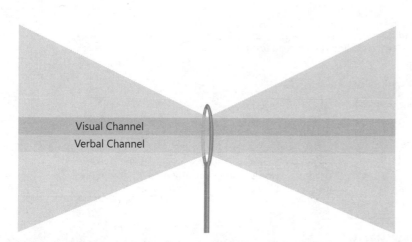

Visual Channel

Verbal Channel

FIGURE 2-13 The second research reality is that working memory receives information through two channels—a visual channel and a verbal channel.

Although text on a screen is a visual element, working memory quickly verbalizes the words and sends them through the verbal channel. Research over the years has found that the way information is presented to these two channels has a big impact on the effectiveness of working memory.

See Also For more information about the dual-channels concept, see:

- Alan D. Baddeley and Graham Hitch, "Working Memory," in *The Psychology of Learning and Motivation. Advances in Research and Theory*, G. H. Bower, Ed., Vol. 8, pp. 47–89 (Academic Press, 1974).

- Allan Paivio, *Mind and Its Evolution* (Lawrence Erlbaum Associates, 2007).

BBP Addresses the Two Channels

You see how BBP addresses the reality of dual channels by looking at a typical slide in Notes Page view, as shown in Figure 2-14. A clear headline at the top of the page always summarizes the point—you'll write out these headlines in Chapters 4 and 5. The off-screen text box in the bottom half of the page contains what you will say aloud while the slide is on screen—you'll write out your narration for each slide in Chapter 6. And last you'll add a simple graphic to the slide area that you see in the top half of the page to complement the headline and the verbal narration in Chapter 8.

BBP plans for visuals in the slide area and
spoken words in the off-screen text box below.

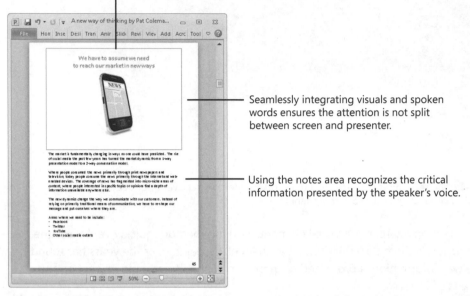

Seamlessly integrating visuals and spoken
words ensures the attention is not split
between screen and presenter.

Using the notes area recognizes the critical
information presented by the speaker's voice.

FIGURE 2-14 With BBP, you use Notes Page view to manage the visual channel in the on-screen slide area above and the verbal channel in the off-screen text box below.

Writing out the spoken information in the off-screen text box before you add a graphic significantly reduces the amount of information you otherwise would place in the slide area and instead keeps the slide area simple and clear. This helps working memory focus attention on the single point that you explain verbally during this slide. Instead of reading the headline verbatim, you let the audience quickly read and digest it on their own.

BBP uses Notes Page view in this way to tightly integrate screen and narration in order to make the most efficient use of the two channels of working memory. Looking at the visual and verbal areas together in Notes Page view is like looking at a single frame in a filmstrip, which is made up of a sequence of connected visual frames, each with a corresponding chunk of audio.

When you design for multimedia such as film, you apply a different set of conventions than the ones used for print because a film model has two coordinated informational tracks—a visual track that contains pictures and an audio track that contains the spoken words.

AN EFFECTIVE SCREEN AND HANDOUT

By viewing your slides in Notes Page view like the frames in a filmstrip, you align your approach with the dual channels—the information that is presented to the visual channel is in the on-screen slide area, and the information presented to the verbal channel is in the off-screen text box. This approach also creates a well-balanced handout that you print in Notes Page format, as shown in Figure 2-14. By using PowerPoint this way, you ensure that you produce both an effective live presentation and an effective printed document.

It is no accident that the structure of a filmstrip is conspicuously similar to the dual-channels concept. When you watch a film with sound, your mind coordinates the different information from the soundtrack and the visual frames on screen.

For almost a century, filmmakers have managed to communicate complex ideas to audiences around the world with synchronized images and sound, with little if any text on the screen. Likewise, working memory can easily coordinate visual and verbal channels if they are properly coordinated and presented.

With the screen behind the speaker, the audience sees and quickly digests the slide and then pays attention to the speaker and his or her verbal explanation. The entire experience appears seamless to the audience.

Using the off-screen notes area in Notes Page view also takes into account the fact that the speaker has a voice during a presentation, which offers a critical source of information that has to be planned and integrated into the experience.

BBP fundamentally changes the media model for PowerPoint from paper to a filmstrip. But the difference between a filmstrip and the BBP approach is *pacing*. In film and television, you commonly view 24 to 60 frames per second. A BBP presentation runs at the speed of conversation—about one frame per 30-60 seconds—allowing time for the audience to digest the new information and then focus next on the presenter. This even and appropriate pacing ensures that your audience experiences only the right things at the right times.

The Old Way Addresses Only One Channel

If you choose not to address both the visual and verbal channels, you see from the Notes Page view of a conventional slide shown in Figure 2-15 that you load up the slide area at the top with all of the information you want to communicate both visually and verbally. Because half of the available real estate available for information in Notes Page view is not used—the off-screen text box below is empty—the slide area becomes the single place to hold both spoken words and projected images.

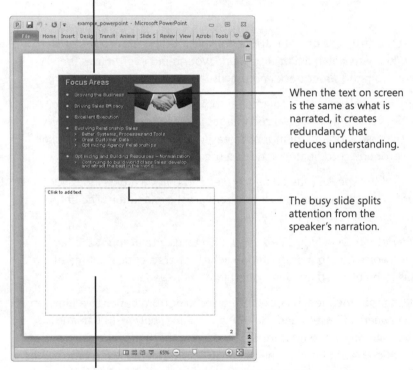

Placing all information on the slide area results in an overwhelming amount of information on the slide.

When the text on screen is the same as what is narrated, it creates redundancy that reduces understanding.

The busy slide splits attention from the speaker's narration.

Not using the notes area ignores a critical source of information, the speaker's voice.

FIGURE 2-15 The conventional PowerPoint approach does not incorporate the dual-channels concept and instead places both visual and verbal information in the slide area.

When you do not align your PowerPoint approach with the dual-channels concept, you impair learning in a number of ways. For example, ignoring the off-screen text box creates a scarcity of resources in the slide area, which predictably produces overloaded slides. Words will usually take priority over visuals, so you will tend to see slides filled with text.

Visuals added to these already crowded slides are usually reduced to the size of postage stamps so they can be squeezed between the boxes of text. These dynamics produce slides that are overly complex and difficult to understand.

When this type of slide is displayed during a presentation, the audience tries to make sense of the overloaded slide instead of paying attention to the speaker. When they do shift attention to the speaker, they soon look back at the slide and work hard to try to synchronize the two sources of information. Researchers call this the *split-attention effect*, which creates excess cognitive load and reduces the effectiveness of learning. You can observe similar dynamics when you're watching a film or TV show and the sound is slightly out of sync—it's very noticeable because your working memory has to do the extra work of continually trying to synchronize the mismatched images and narration.

> **MYTH VS. TRUTH**
>
> **Myth:** I don't need to worry if what I say doesn't match up with my slide.
>
> **Truth:** Research shows that people understand a multimedia presentation better when they do not have to split their attention between, and mentally integrate, multiple sources of information.

Another problem with ignoring the off-screen text box in Notes Page view is that you do not recognize and plan for a primary source of information during PowerPoint presentations—your own voice. The result is that the relationship between your spoken words and projected visuals is not fully addressed. You might assume that the information on your slide can stand alone, without verbal explanation, but a PowerPoint slide does not exist in a vacuum—you are standing there speaking to your audience while you project the slide.

You must effectively plan how your spoken words and projected images relate to each other. And if you write nothing in the off-screen notes area, you will be unable to take advantage of Presenter view, as shown in Figure 2-16 and described in Appendix B, to manage your presentation because nothing will appear in the speaker notes pane on the right to guide you while you cover all the points you want to make.

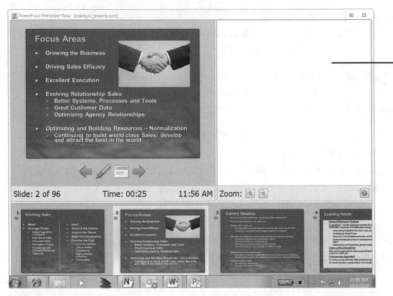

If you do not use the off-screen notes when you set up your slides, no speaker notes will appear here to guide you during your talk.

FIGURE 2-16 If you don't write out what you will say in the notes area in Notes Page view, there's little point in using Presenter view, because nothing will appear in the speaker notes pane and the text on the slides is too small to read on the slide thumbnails.

Audiences might not know about dual-channels theory, but they do know how they feel when presenters don't integrate the concept into their PowerPoint approach. When presenters read bulleted text from the screen, audiences complain that the presenter should "E-mail it to me!" or "Just give me the handout!" This frustration has a research basis—writing out the text of your presentation on your slides and then reading it to your audience contradicts the widely accepted theory of dual channels.

You might assume that presenting the same information in multiple ways will reinforce your point. But if you present the same information to the two channels, you reduce the capacity of working memory and in turn reduce learning by creating what researchers call the *redundancy effect*.

When someone speaks, you process the verbal information at one speed. When the speaker also displays the text of the speech, you process the same information at a different speed—your mind first takes in the text visually and then verbalizes it for processing in the verbal channel.

Because the same information is arriving through the same channel at different speeds, working memory has to split attention between the two sources of information as it works hard to reconcile them. This redundancy quickly overloads working memory and impairs learning.

AN INEFFECTIVE SCREEN AND HANDOUT

By addressing only one channel in your presentation, as shown earlier in Figure 2-15, you create both split attention and redundancy in a live presentation. And by not capturing what is said verbally in the off-screen notes area, you also miss the chance to use PowerPoint to create an effective handout by printing the slides in notes page format.

Redundancy also happens when the same information is presented both visually and in text because the same information is entering through two channels and the mind has to exert more effort to reconcile them. This reduces the efficiency of working memory and can lead to the cognitive overload that so frustrates audiences.

MYTH VS. TRUTH

Myth: It's OK to read my bullet points from the screen.

Truth: Research shows that people understand a multimedia presentation better when the words are presented as verbal narration alone, instead of both verbally and as on-screen text.

To explore the redundancy effect, Mayer conducted experiments using two multimedia presentations. The first presentation included the same material both narrated and displayed with text on the screen, and the second presentation included the narration with the text on the screen removed. Audiences who experienced the second presentation retained 28 percent more information and were able to apply 79 percent more creative solutions using the information than those who experienced the first presentation.

Thus, the dual-channels concept turns one of our core assumptions about PowerPoint upside-down. Contrary to conventional wisdom and common practice, reading bullet points from a screen actually hurts learning rather than helps it. Research shows that when you subtract the redundant text from the screen that you are narrating, you improve learning.

If you choose not to align your PowerPoint approach with dual channels, you diminish the potential effectiveness of your presentations. When you place both verbal and visual material in the slide area, the busy slide splits the audience's attention between screen and presenter, which creates additional load on working memory. And when you present the same information in both visual and verbal form, you create redundancy that overloads working memory. You resolve the situation in BBP by effectively coordinating visual and verbal information in Notes Page view.

Realignment 3: Use Normal View to Guide Attention on the Screen

Now that you've realigned Notes Page view with the research, it's time to get back to normal in terms of the way you're used to working in PowerPoint. Click the View tab, and in the Presentation Views group, click Normal to display Normal view, as shown in Figure 2-17. The third trick of BBP is to always work in Normal view last, which you'll do in Chapters 7 and 8. The third research reality will guide you through the reasons why.

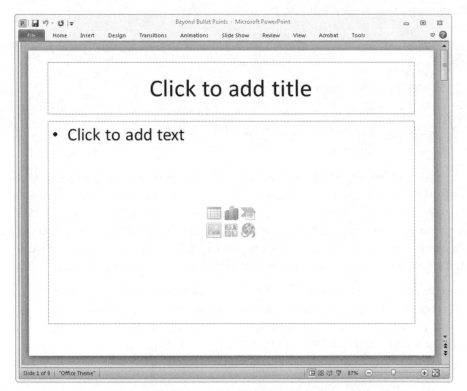

FIGURE 2-17 The most common way to work in PowerPoint is in Normal view.

Research Reality 3: You Have to Guide Attention

The third research reality confronts the PowerPoint assumption that you create your slides however you want and your audience will understand them. In the pipeline metaphor, a presentation exists by itself, independent of the people who receive it—a presenter simply pours information into the passive minds of the audience.

Yet researchers have long known that the mind is not a passive vessel, but rather it is an active participant in the process of learning. It is the minds of your audience that have to create understanding out of the new information they process in working memory.

You play an important role in helping your audience create understanding by designing slides in specific ways that guide the attention of working memory to the most important visual and verbal information, as illustrated in Figure 2-18.

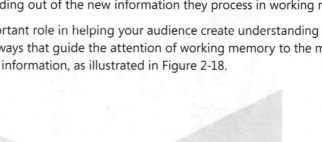

FIGURE 2-18 The third research reality is that you must guide the attention of working memory.

BBP Guides Attention

As described earlier, with the BBP approach, each slide has a headline when you start working in PowerPoint. You then write out what you will say verbally in the off-screen text box in Notes Page view and then add a simple graphic in Normal view to produce a slide, as shown in Figure 2-19.

The graphic clearly and simply illustrates the main point of the slide.

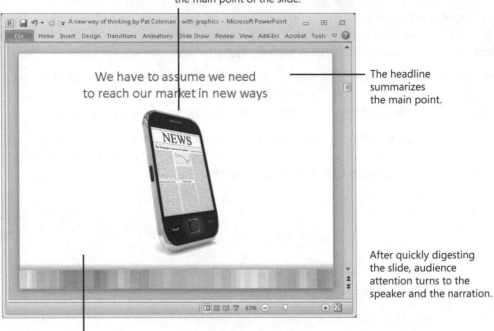

We have to assume we need to reach our market in new ways

The headline summarizes the main point.

After quickly digesting the slide, audience attention turns to the speaker and the narration.

There is no extraneous information to distract attention.

FIGURE 2-19 A BBP slide, shown here in Normal view, guides the attention of working memory from the headline to the graphic to the person speaking.

The simplicity of this slide belies the sophisticated impact it has as it effectively guides the attention of working memory. It is crystal clear where working memory should focus first—on the headline at the top of the slide. People are used to reading newspaper headlines that summarize the main point of a story in a single sentence, and here the complete sentence headline serves the same function.

The audience doesn't have to work hard to figure out the point you want to make—instead, you have cleared the way for them to focus on the idea at hand rather than be distracted by unnecessary cognitive work.

HEADLINE RESEARCH

Michael Alley, author of *The Craft of Scientific Presentations: Critical Steps to Succeed and Critical Errors to Avoid* (Springer, 2005), conducted a study using two PowerPoint presentations, each with a different headline format. One presentation included only sentence fragments at the top of each slide, and the second presentation included a complete sentence at the top that summarized the most important point of the slide. In tests to measure the knowledge and comprehension of the information in the presentations, the audiences who experienced the slides with the complete sentence headlines saw an average improvement in test scores of 11 percentage points over the audiences who saw the slides with the sentence fragments. When you use the title area of the slide to summarize your point for your audience members, you properly guide their attention, and in the process you ease the burden on their working memory to figure out your point.

Research has found that visuals can improve learning, but only if they illustrate the point you are making. In Chapter 7, you will sketch the appropriate graphics for each slide by focusing on the slide headlines, and then in Chapter 8, you will add the specific graphics. Because you choose only graphics that relate to the specific point at hand, the graphics tell a major part of the story as they communicate information through the visual channel in sync with your verbal explanation. This makes effective use of working memory by using both the visual and verbal channels, rather than just the verbal channel alone. It also ensures that working memory is not distracted by graphics that don't relate specifically to the information at hand. Likewise, the slide background contains no extraneous information that would add more cognitive load.

The simple elements of a BBP slide work together to guide the complete presentation experience. First the audience members quickly digest the headline, then they view the simple graphic that illustrates the headline, and then they turn their attention to the verbal explanation of the speaker. The result is an engaging multimedia experience that balances visual and verbal elements and contributes to meaningful understanding.

The Old Way Does Not Guide Attention

In the conventional PowerPoint slide shown in Figure 2-20, it's not easy to see where the presenter intends to guide attention. Such a busy slide assumes that viewers have the working memory capacity to read through all the material as they might with a written document—all while they are listening to you speak. As described earlier in the discussion of the dual-channels theory, it is easy for too much material on this slide to split the attention of the audience between screen and presenter or to impair learning by using both on-screen text and narration to explain the same information.

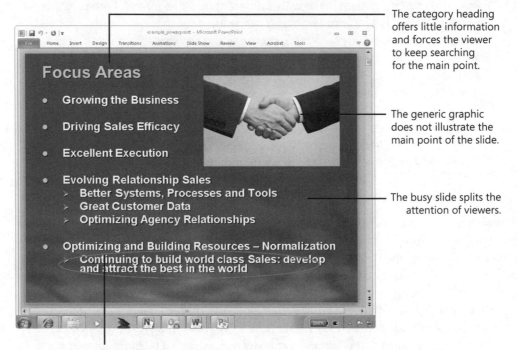

The category heading offers little information and forces the viewer to keep searching for the main point.

The generic graphic does not illustrate the main point of the slide.

The busy slide splits the attention of viewers.

The generic list approach offers no structure that ties the list items together.

FIGURE 2-20 The conventional PowerPoint approach does not help working memory to select the most important information.

If you grew up writing essays and reports on paper or as Microsoft Office Word documents, it's a natural transition to think of a PowerPoint slide as a piece of paper where you start writing out your thoughts. But one of the fundamental assumptions about a piece of paper is that it can stand alone—a presenter normally does not need to be there to explain it. The only problem is that this example PowerPoint slide is accompanied by the narration of a live presenter—yet the slide does not take that fact into account.

Another problem with thinking of the slide area as a piece of paper is that you are much more likely to fill it with text instead of a graphic. Although text on a screen is initially processed through the visual channel, as described earlier it is quickly verbalized and sent through the verbal channel—thus text-filled slides essentially ignore the capacity of the visual channel to efficiently process information in sync with the verbal channel.

> **MYTH VS. TRUTH**
>
> **Myth:** Graphics are nice to have, but they're not essential.
>
> **Truth:** Research shows that people learn better from words and pictures than from words alone. This applies when the pictures illustrate what the words say, not when pictures are added for decorative effect.

One of the reasons the example slide does not guide attention is that it uses a *category heading*—like those you see in almost all PowerPoint presentations. A category heading like "Focus Areas" can help you quickly brainstorm a list of information, but as you see here, it does nothing to guide you to a quick understanding of what is the most important information on the slide. Simply categorizing and listing information does not entail the critical thinking it takes to determine the point of the lists in the first place.

Category headings don't say anything specific, and to uncover the mystery of what you are trying to communicate when you use them, your audience members need to invest extra capacity of working memory they don't have to connect all the dots of the bullet points below the headings. And these headings put an extra burden on you and your audience as you both struggle to see the focus of your ideas through the sequence of slides in your presentation. As your audience views these headings and their corresponding stacks of bulleted lists, slide after slide, it's no wonder that they find the presentation unfocused, hard to understand, and overwhelmed with unnecessary details.

Although the slide includes a photograph of a handshake, it does not illustrate the specific point of the slide and was likely added for visual decoration to "spice it up". This runs counter to the research that shows that the less you overload working memory with extraneous information, the more people learn.

> **MYTH VS. TRUTH**
>
> **Myth:** People learn more when I wow them with special effects and spice up my presentations with razzle-dazzle.
>
> **Truth:** Research shows that people learn better when extraneous information is removed from a presentation.

Audiences might not know about the research that indicates that you need to guide their attention, but they do know what they are talking about when they frequently say conventional presentations are "incoherent lists" with "no direction" and "a jumble." Instead of guiding working memory through the experience, this example slide creates unnecessary work by not quickly getting to the clear point, by not tapping into the visual channel, and by creating split attention and redundancy with the narration of a live presenter.

THE MISALIGNED TEMPLATE

Many organizations create a corporate PowerPoint template in an effort to ensure that every presentation created in the organization has a similar graphical style. Although these templates can ensure a similar look across presentations, if they ignore the three research realities described in this chapter, they also diminish the effectiveness of presentations of all the presenters who use them.

A Well-Trained Tool

These three research realities reveal a stark contrast between BBP and the conventional approach to PowerPoint and explain why BBP gets dramatically better results. Now you can personally connect the dots between this research by adopting a new metaphor, the eye of the needle, and by using the BBP approach to guide you through the challenges of creating powerful and effective presentations.

Forget the old ways of using PowerPoint, because as you saw in this chapter, when you ignore the research realities, you use an approach that is broken, ineffective, and frustrating for audiences. Instead, when you choose an approach that fixes the problems, you produce experiences that audiences find engaging and meaningful.

That's because you have now reoriented the three fundamental views of PowerPoint to align with the research, and with these new ideas in mind, you are ready to unlock the power of BBP in your own presentations as you turn now to Chapter 3.

Building a Foundation with the BBP Story Template

PREPARING A PRESENTATION is complex and difficult from a couple of perspectives. From a presenter's point of view, you have many things you want to say and show during a presentation, and you would like your audience to integrate the new information into clear understanding in long-term memory, as shown in Figure 3-1.

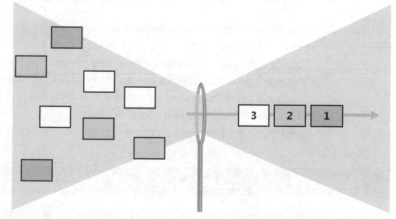

FIGURE 3-1 The formidable challenge every presenter faces—the limited capacity of working memory.

But as you saw in Chapter 2, you also know what is happening from the audience's point of view in terms of memory. *Sensory memory* can see and hear a potentially unlimited amount of verbal and visual information, but only for a fleeting second. *Long-term memory* can hold a potentially unlimited amount of information from 30 seconds to up to a lifetime. Yet the capacity of *working memory* to handle new information, the eye of the needle, is relatively limited for the few seconds it pays attention to what you are showing and saying.

That means that effectively communicating a message is not as easy as creating a Microsoft PowerPoint presentation and assuming that you deliver it through an unobstructed pipeline to the passive minds of your audience. Instead, you have to set PowerPoint myths aside and engage the three research realities you learned about in Chapter 2—finding the right amount of new information to engage the limited capacity of working memory without overloading it, engaging both the visual and verbal channels, and guiding the working memory of your audience to help them integrate new information into their long-term memory.

Some of the techniques you will use to accomplish this are new, some you already know, and some are old methods used in new ways. If you're completely new to using PowerPoint, you won't have to unlearn old habits; instead, you'll find here a better way to use PowerPoint from the start.

What Does the Road Ahead Look Like?

This book shows you step by step how BBP is applied in depth to one specific example presentation on a topic most people can relate to—introducing a new idea—and shows how BBP handles a situation where you need to both inform and persuade an audience. The example is intended to be delivered as a 45-minute presentation, so you get a sense of what it takes to produce a presentation that long. You adapt the same BBP process to a wide range of presentation timeframes, topics, contexts, and purposes—Chapter 9 gives you a tour of more examples to review for inspiration.

WHAT TOOLS DO I NEED FOR BBP?

This book includes most of what you need to get started with BBP. Of course, you'll also need a computer with both Microsoft Office Word and PowerPoint installed. As you begin or continue to work with BBP, the companion Web site to this book at *www.beyondbulletpoints.com* offers additional resources, courses, and a community to help you create BBP presentations smarter, faster, and easier from start to finish.

If you work for yourself or by yourself, you have no choice but to apply BBP on your own, and you'll do just fine. But you'll get the most out of the process if you unlock the benefits it produces for teams. BBP offers organizations a process where they might not have had one before and often aligns PowerPoint with the group's communications strategy for the first time.

You should get as many people involved in the BBP process as possible, especially team leaders, marketers, graphic designers, and even some of your potential audience members. When BBP brings together these separate groups, the efficient process of producing presentations increases the speed of decision making, reduces revisions, and improves the quality and impact of PowerPoint communications for both presenters and audiences.

BBP will also reveal that people on your team have unexpected talents that will surprise you—perhaps computer engineers will turn out to be good at graphic design, graphic designers will be good at wordsmithing a logical argument, and statisticians will be good at facilitating the social process.

Sewing Up Understanding with BBP

When you face the limited capacity of the working memory of your audience to process new information, a core challenge is not creating the visuals and narration, but rather determining the underlying structure that will shape those elements in the first place. A structure focuses your ideas and helps you figure out what you want to say and how you want to say it. That's where an incredibly powerful structural tool you will use comes into play—the BBP Story Template.

The Heart and Brain of BBP: The Story Template

With the lessons of the dual-channels theory from Chapter 2 in mind, you see that film-making is an appropriate model for designing multimedia presentations because it plans and manages both visual and verbal information simultaneously.

Filmmakers know that the best way to start planning a film is with the written word, in the form of a script. A script is much shorter and less detailed than a novel because it assumes that the visuals and dialog will play a major role in telling the story. The best scripts distill stories to their bare essence and strip away anything that does not contribute to a story's singular focus.

When a writer completes a script, the document then becomes a powerful organizing tool that literally puts everyone on the same page. The script is the starting point for planning and producing visuals and dialog, and it serves as a way for everyone involved in the project to be clear on what everyone else is saying and doing. If you were a filmmaker and you started filming before you had a script—similar to working on a PowerPoint presentation without a written structure—you would probably waste time and resources while you changed your focus and figured out the story along the way.

Although putting your thoughts in writing adds a new step to your usual PowerPoint process, doing so will save you time and effort later. When you begin writing your PowerPoint script in Chapter 4, you won't have to start with an empty page, because you'll use the story template shown in Figure 3-2 to guide you every step of the way.

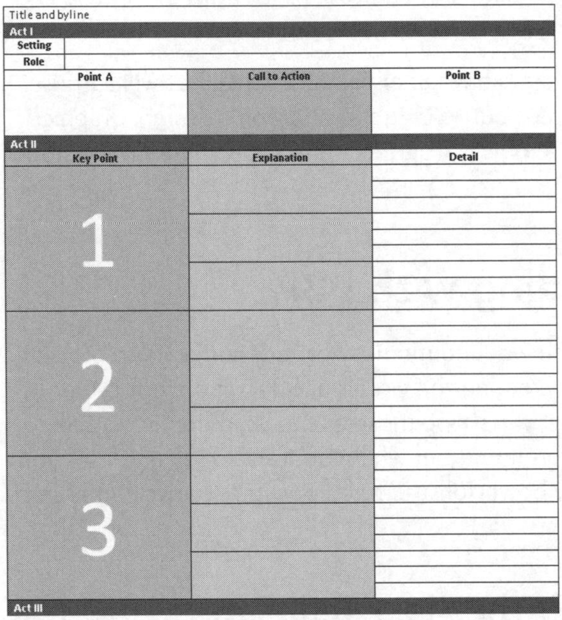

FIGURE 3-2 The BBP Story Template, which you will complete in Word.

The story template serves as a central organizing tool for the entire presentation. It is a visual interface for the structure of your presentation, helping you see the big picture on a single page or two before you commit to adding a visual and verbal track to individual slides.

The Built-in Story Structure

To understand the story template, you have to go back in time a few years. The Greek philosopher Aristotle recorded the classical elements of storytelling 2400 years ago, including the concept that a story has a beginning, a middle, and an end. When you adapt this timeless idea to your PowerPoint presentations, you'll ground your communications in a powerful technique that works.

The story template includes three sections, or *acts*, that form a classical story structure and correspond to the beginning, middle, and end of your presentation. Each act in the template is delineated by a horizontal black bar extending across the page, as shown in Figure 3-3.

Act I begins your story by setting up all of the essential elements that comprise every story, including the setting, the main character, an unresolved state of affairs, and the desired outcome. Act II drives the story forward by picking up on the unresolved state of affairs in Act I and developing it through the actions and reactions of the main character in response to changing conditions. Act III ends the story by framing a climax and a decision that the main character must face to resolve the situation, revealing something about his or her character. This time-tested structure keeps your audience interested in your presentation and eager to find out what happens next.

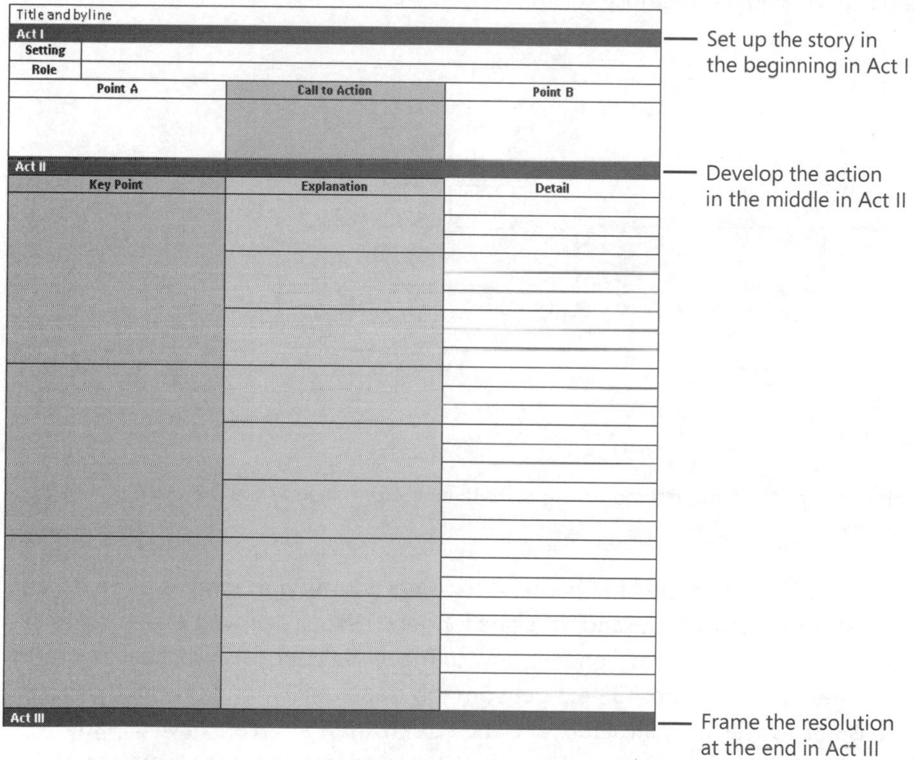

Set up the story in the beginning in Act I

Develop the action in the middle in Act II

Frame the resolution at the end in Act III

FIGURE 3-3 The BBP Story Template incorporates a classical story structure.

This three-part story structure follows natural patterns that underlie the way we think and understand. No one needs special training or technology to understand a classical story structure because it's the way humans have been communicating with one another throughout history. A story structure frames the context for communication and focuses attention by making information specific and relevant to an audience. Story literally ties together scattered pieces of information. By incorporating these fundamental ideas in your current PowerPoint story, you'll be building on a solid foundation that ensures your presentation is focused, clear, and engaging.

As mentioned in Chapter 2, the long-term memory of your audience already contains existing structures that can help working memory organize and integrate new information. One of the most well-known configurations is this three-act structure that forms the foundation for countless stories, novels, theatrical productions, films, and television shows. When you tap into this familiar structure that already exists in your audience's long-term memory and apply it to the structure of the new information you present, as shown in Figure 3-4, you are well on your way to creating a clear pathway through the limited capacity of working memory.

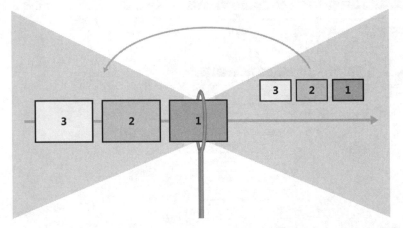

FIGURE 3-4 Introducing the familiar three-act structure to new information as you present it to working memory.

The research principles described in Chapter 2 have been around as long as 50 years, and the idea of a story structure thousands of years longer. These are proven ideas and techniques that work—the present challenge is how to make the concepts practical as you work on your next presentation. To help get your job done quickly and efficiently, these fundamentals of classical story structure and the screenwriting process have already been adapted to your PowerPoint needs and incorporated into the story template.

In addition to a classical story structure, your story template also incorporates persuasive techniques that are useful for many types of presentations in different contexts. These include using Aristotle's concept that to persuade, you must appeal to emotion, reason, and personal credibility. Even if your intent is to simply *inform* an audience about something, you still have to *persuade* them to pay attention. Why should they listen? What's in it for them? Act I of your story template will make sure that you persuade your audience to focus on your message, and Act II will make sure that you provide the logical reasoning they need to make a decision. You will infuse the entire presentation with personal credibility in terms of verbal clarity and conciseness and add visual credibility by matching your graphics and aesthetics with your audience.

Theory Becomes Practical

The innovation of the BBP Story Template is that it brings together theory and a process into a practical tool you open up and use to structure and start every presentation. Everything you do here in the story template shapes the visuals and narration to come and sets up your ideas in a way that preconfigures and aligns information to best prepare it for its passage through the working memory of your audience. The story template ensures that every presentation accomplishes what you intend—by understanding your audience members, tailoring your material to them, getting to the point, and establishing a priority and sequence for your ideas.

You don't have to be an expert storyteller or an expert in cognitive theory; the template makes structuring your story as easy as filling in the blanks. In the cells of the story template, you'll write out a complete sentence that describes what is happening at each point in your story, similar to writing a newspaper headline. As you fill in the blanks, you'll be writing the actual story that you'll present. When you've finished, you'll have a completed one-page or two-page script. This process ensures that you stay focused on your ideas and include all the elements that make up a good story.

ALTERNATIVE STORY TEMPLATE TOOLS

This book shows you how to use a Word document as your BBP Story Template, but it's not the only tool you use. BBP readers have found innovative alternatives by re-creating the story template structure with Microsoft Excel, Post-It Notes, a flipchart, and a whiteboard. Figure 3-5 shows a BBP Story Template created using mind-mapping software called MindJet MindManager—an especially flexible and scalable tool for creating presentations that extend beyond 45 minutes into multiple-hour, daylong, and multiday timeframes. For more resources related to these alternative tools, visit *www.beyondbulletpoints.com*.

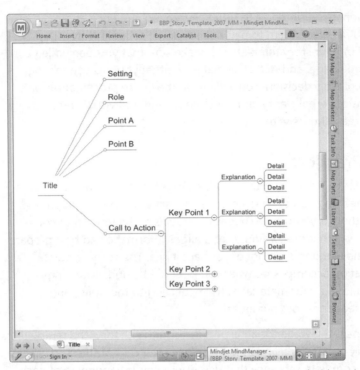

FIGURE 3-5 An alternative version of the story template created with a mind-mapping tool gives you the ability to create presentations that extend across multiple hours and days.

When you write your script using the story template, you focus on your ideas first rather than your graphics. After you complete the template in Word, you'll import the headlines into PowerPoint, where each complete sentence you wrote will become the headline of a slide, as shown in Figure 3-6. This ensures that before you start working in PowerPoint, you already know the main point you intend to make on each slide.

This pivotal technique of turning your story template into a set of PowerPoint slides will help you to transform your written words into the foundation of a visual story. This will make your job of finding visuals easier by establishing exactly what you need to illustrate on every slide, and it will help your audience to understand your new information much faster by indicating clearly in the title area the meaning of every slide.

You'll begin applying BBP step by step in Chapter 4; the following is a preview of how the three steps of BBP will unfold as you apply BBP to the specific presentation example in this book. Here you see how each slide finds its context in the bigger presentation picture by following the three steps of BBP that help you, and your audience, sew up effective understanding.

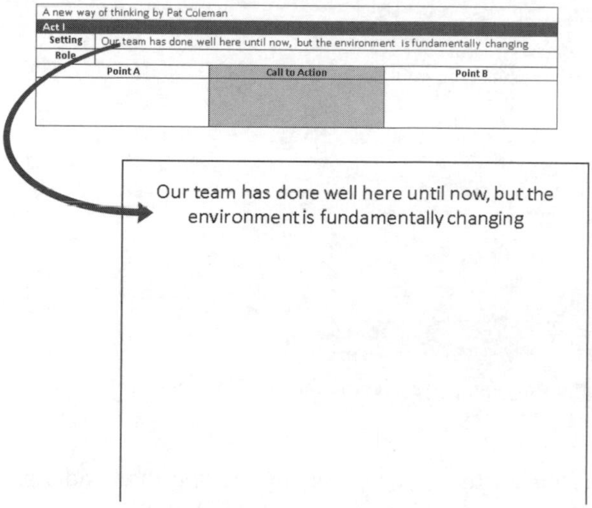

FIGURE 3-6 Each headline you write in the story template becomes a headline on a slide.

Step 1: Choose a Story Thread and a Pattern to Follow

You need to quickly make an emotional connection with an audience to motivate them, and you see the specific words that do that in Act I, where you write out the classical elements of a strong story beginning. The first five headlines you write in Act I of the story template will connect emotionally with an audience, define a problem they face, and explain how they can solve it. This forms the story thread that will carry attention through the entire presentation. You will reinforce the strength of the thread to carry new information through the working memory of your audience by applying a familiar pattern in the form of a verbal and visual *motif*, or recurring theme.

After you complete Act I and the rest of the story template, you'll import these five headlines into PowerPoint, where each statement becomes the headline of a PowerPoint slide, as shown in Figure 3-7.

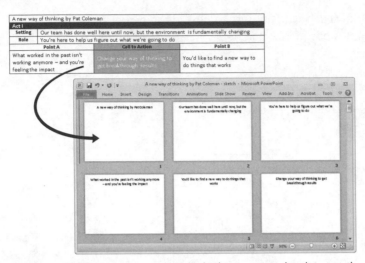

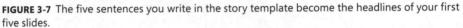

FIGURE 3-7 The five sentences you write in the story template become the headlines of your first five slides.

When you view the first five slides in Slide Sorter view, you see by reading the headlines of the slides the story thread that will carry your specific sequence of ideas through the eye of the needle of working memory of your audience, as shown in Figure 3-8; this sequence will also provide the framework for your visuals and narration.

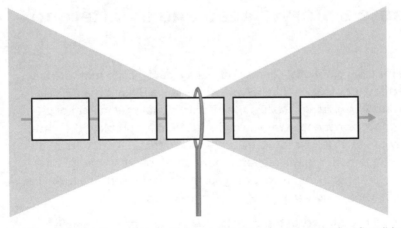

FIGURE 3-8 Act I defines what you'll show to working memory in the first five slides.

Step 2: Pull Through What's Most Important First

You set in motion a number of powerful processes in Act I of the story template that continue to play out as you create the rest of the slides in your presentation. Just as in Act I, you'll break up your ideas in Act II into digestible pieces by writing out complete-sentence headlines in the story template. Later, each sentence will become the headline of a slide, as shown in Figure 3-9.

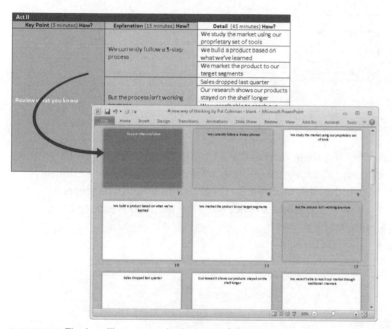

FIGURE 3-9 The headlines you write in Act II of the story template become the headlines of the rest of your Act II slides.

The challenge of any presentation is not to show *all* the information you have but, instead, to select the *appropriate* information to present. The story template guides you through the important process of selecting only the ideas your audience needs to know and breaking them into digestible chunks that are easier for your audience to understand.

A logic-tree structure is built into Act II of the story template, as shown in Figure 3-10; this structure helps you put the most important information at the top level of attention, to increase memorability and application. A presentation should have three or four key points, and you literally can see them in Act II, where you clarify and identify these top-level points, create a logical and clear structure, and perhaps most important, leave out nonessential information.

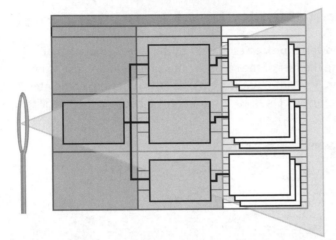

FIGURE 3-10 A built-in logic-tree structure prioritizes your ideas from most important to least.

Completing Act II of the story template can be the hardest thing you do in BBP if you're new to this way of thinking. But the investment in learning will sharpen your critical-thinking skills and ensure that the new information in your presentation appears in the order and sequence needed to prevent overloading the working memory of your audience, as shown in Figure 3-11.

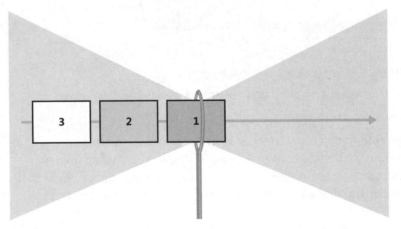

FIGURE 3-11 Act II makes sure that you present the correct priority and sequence of slides to working memory.

Step 3: Guide the Visual and Verbal Strands with Your Storyboard

With the click of a mouse, you'll transform your Word story template into a PowerPoint storyboard. You'll work with your storyboard in Slide Sorter view to review your story structure and sequence, check your pacing and flow, and use visuals to tie together the various parts of your story. This planning ensures that you continually build on and improve your strong story foundation with a single unified set of visuals and words.

Next you will quickly apply layouts with slide backgrounds that indicate the three hierarchical levels of Act II slides, as shown in Figure 3-12, to set up preliminary visual cues that designate which slides are more important than others and how those slides fit into a sequence. After you do this, you'll be able to easily see the three most important slides in your presentation—the dark gray ones. You'll also be able to see your second-most important slides—the light gray ones—and your third-most important slides—the white ones—to easily locate and hide them if you need to quickly scale down the presentation to a shorter amount of time. These slides are the foundation for the fully designed layouts and backgrounds you use to cue working memory when you add graphics in Chapter 8.

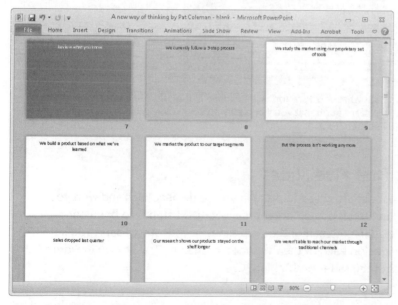

FIGURE 3-12 Next you'll cue working memory by applying layouts with preliminary slide backgrounds to the three hierarchical levels of Act II slides.

Next you'll plan the narrated soundtrack of the presentation by writing out the verbal explanation for each headline in the off-screen text box in Notes Page view, as shown in Figure 3-13. If you don't have time to write out your full narration, just take a few notes here. In line with the dual-channels theory described in Chapter 2, this helps you seamlessly integrate each visual with its verbal explanation. After capturing in the notes area a record of the rich verbal explanation that will accompany the slide, you then will choose the simplest possible visual to illustrate the headline of each slide.

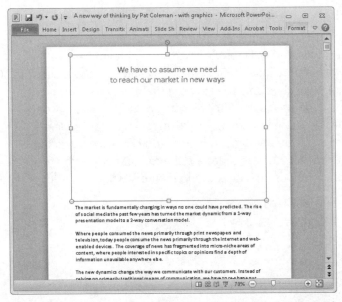

FIGURE 3-13 First you write out what you'll say for each headline in the off-screen notes area (bottom). After you have recorded the information that you'll convey with your voice, you next add a simple graphic to the on-screen slide area (top).

Sketching the First Five Slides

With your clear and concise story line in place in your slide headlines and with your narration written out in the off-screen notes area, your next step is to brainstorm an illustration for each headline of each of the Act I slides of your storyboard. You'll do that by sketching a visual idea on each of the five slides in Chapter 7, as shown in Figure 3-14, either using printouts of the slides or a Tablet PC.

When you do this, your focus is on making full use of the powerful visual channel of your audience members by sketching out a crisp and compelling visual story that complements your clear and concise headlines. Just as your headlines tell a story with only words, your sketches now should complement, enhance, and intensify that story on individual slides, as well as across slides. Here you'll also plan for both on-screen and off-screen media such as physical props, demonstrations, video, dialog, or other types of media or interactive techniques.

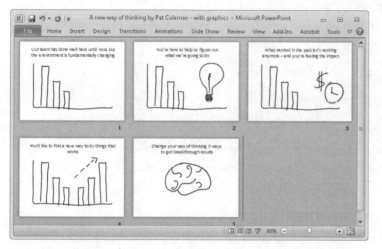

FIGURE 3-14 Once you have a storyboard, sketch a graphic on each of the five slides.

Sketching the Rest of the Slides

As with Act I, completing the story template for Act II creates a solid foundation that will help you choose exactly what you'll show and say as you present the working memory of your audience with new information. With this infrastructure in place, you'll have endless creative options to make the crisp and clear underlying story even more powerful. Here on the Act II slides, as shown in Figure 3-15, you'll visually carry through the motif you establish in Act I to help working memory better select and organize the large amount of new information.

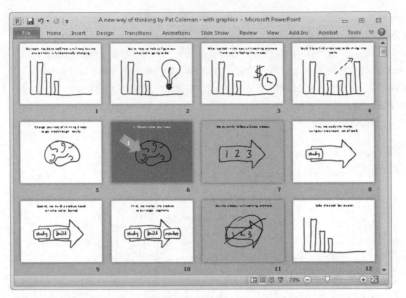

FIGURE 3-15 You'll continue sketching graphics on each of the remaining slides.

Applying Custom Layouts

After your team has agreed to and signed off on the sketches, the last step is to find and add a specific photograph, chart, or other graphic to each of the slides. But before you do that, you'll apply custom layouts to each of the different sections of your storyboard, according to the way you sketched the layout of each slide. As shown in Figure 3-16, this creates a visual foundation for the slides based on the hierarchy from the story template.

By applying layouts and backgrounds, you use graphical indicators that cue working memory to the relative importance of each slide, as shown in Figure 3-17. In this example, the striking solid background indicates the most important slides; the slides with the horizontal graphic are the second-most important, and the slides with the footer graphic are the third-most important.

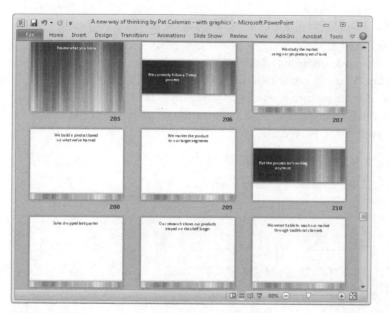

FIGURE 3-16 Storyboard with custom layouts applied.

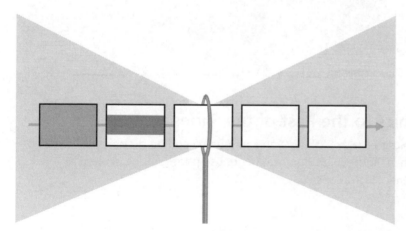

FIGURE 3-17 The slide layouts and backgrounds cue working memory to each slide's relative importance within the big picture.

Adding Graphics to the First Five Slides

The last step is to find and add graphics to each of the slides using your sketches as a guide. Here is where you savor the fruits of the labor of writing Act I in the story template, because you know you've got the specific PowerPoint slides that will ensure that you start strong in your presentation, as shown in Figure 3-18. The visual and verbal clarity you achieve is possible through using the story template, which has established the foundation for everything you have done.

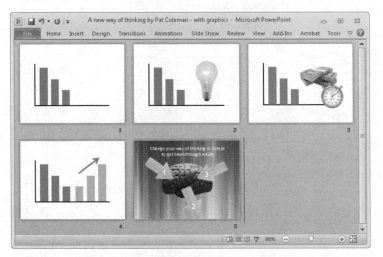

FIGURE 3-18 Adding graphics to the first five slides of Act I.

Adding Graphics to the Rest of the Slides

After you add graphics to the Act I slides, you continue by adding graphics to the rest of your slides, as shown in Figure 3-19. Here you might use photographs, screen captures, logos, charts, and other illustrations.

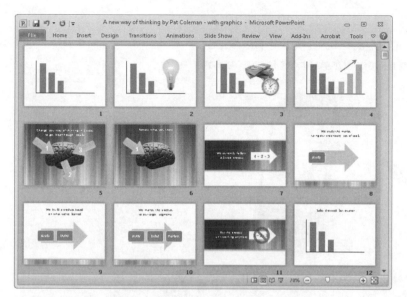

FIGURE 3-19 Adding graphics to the remaining slides.

Stepping into the Screen

Using the approach described in this book, you'll be well-equipped to produce a media experience that will get you the results you want anytime you give a presentation. Focusing and distilling your ideas using a story template and clarifying them using a storyboard blends your message with your media and significantly expands your ability to enhance your presentation with sophisticated media tools and techniques.

Now the large screen directly behind you, as shown in Figure 3-20, completely integrates your voice and body into a media experience greater than the sum of its parts. This approach brings together a range of media techniques—including those from stage, screen, theater, and television—and blends them together with your body and your clear message into a seamless presentation experience.

FIGURE 3-20 BBP immerses the audience in the experience and ensures that the attention of the audience is not split between screen and speaker.

When you project your slides on a large screen, they work as visual triggers that increase your confidence as a speaker. You're no longer tied to the uncomfortable task of reading text off the screen and unintentionally ignoring your audience. Instead, the clear headline and graphic quickly prompt you to use your natural voice and authority as you explain them.

Presenting in Multiple Views

Making use of Notes Page view to write out your narration in advance increases your ability to present confidently during a live PowerPoint presentation. While your audience sees the simple slide on the screen shown on the upper left in Figure 3-21, your Presenter view in PowerPoint on your own computer displays a speaker notes pane on the right that shows what you wrote in the off-screen text box in Notes Page view. Zoom in on the notes to enlarge the size of the font so that the text is easy to see.

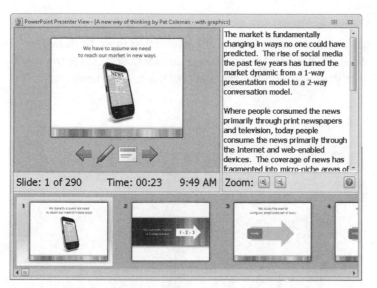

FIGURE 3-21 Presenter view allows you to see the clear and focused on-screen slide that the audience sees, alongside the text you wrote in the off-screen notes area in Notes Page view.

Presenting with a Tablet PC

With BBP, you make maximum use of a Tablet PC by writing directly on the screen to increase engagement and dialog, as shown in Figure 3-22. Chapters 7, 8, and 9 will show you a range of ways to sketch and use graphics to prompt interaction using a Tablet PC.

FIGURE 3-22 Presenting a BBP slide using a Tablet PC.

Presenting Online

Your visually engaging BBP slides are a great fit with online meeting tools, as shown in Figure 3-23. Because the slides are designed to be visually simple, they increase the need for people to pay attention to your voice on the other end of the telephone or computer speakers.

FIGURE 3-23 Presenting online using an online meeting tool.

Documenting the Experience

As described in Chapter 2, aligning your approach with the dual-channels theory allows you to use PowerPoint in a way that produces both an effective presentation and an effective printed handout, as shown in Figure 3-24. Looking at Notes Page view on the left, the on-screen slide area contains a headline and a simple graphic, while the off-screen notes area captures what is spoken aloud by the presenter. Keeping the narration off the screen creates effective slides (upper right), along with effective handouts (lower right).

When you distribute the PowerPoint file to people who were not present for the live presentation of visuals and narration, you send the notes pages, not the slides. Print out the notes pages to create a physical copy, or create a PDF version that you distribute electronically.

Using Notes Page view taps into the unique value PowerPoint offers you as a communications tool, because no other tool can produce a single file that works effectively like this on a screen, on a piece of paper, and even online.

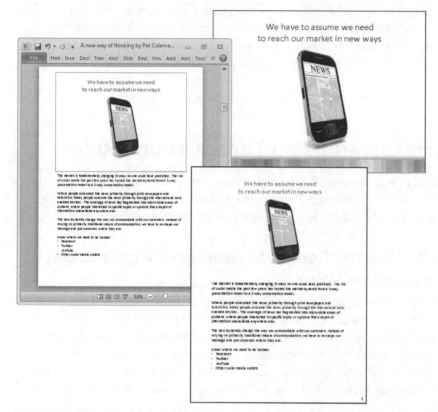

FIGURE 3-24 Notes Page view, showing a well-designed slide and a well-designed handout with the complete verbal explanation of the slide.

Getting Started with the BBP Story Template

To get started, download a copy of the BBP Story Template from *www.beyondbulletpoints.com*, and save it on your local computer.

THE BBP GROUND RULES AND CHECKLISTS

As you follow the steps in upcoming chapters, you'll find sets of BBP Ground Rules for writing your story template, sketching your storyboard, adding graphics, and producing the presentation experience. You'll also find at the end of key chapters a checklist of items to make sure that you've covered them. Refer to Appendix A for a complete list of the ground rules and checklists to print and keep handy as you work with BBP.

Writing Headlines Using Three Ground Rules

Everything you do in your presentation from this point forward will build on the headlines you write in your story template. To make your headlines as effective as possible, review the three important ground rules that apply to every statement you write.

Rule 1: Write Concise, Complete Sentences with a Subject and a Verb in Active Voice

To effectively communicate your message consistently and clearly through your entire story, your headlines must be complete sentences with a subject and a verb. Write the sentences in active voice—for example, "Our top competitors launched five new products last quarter" rather than in the passive voice, "Five new products were launched by our top competitors last quarter." Keep your language dynamic and direct; the same principles, techniques, and rules that define good writing also define good headlines in your template.

| See Also | For an excellent reference guide to writing the headlines of your story template clearly and concisely, see William Strunk Jr. and E. B. White's, The Elements of Style (Longman, 2000). |

Writing headlines in the form of complete sentences imposes a discipline on your ideas by forcing you to turn them into coherent thoughts and remove any ambiguity. Later, when you import your headlines into the title area of your PowerPoint slides, your audience will have no doubt about what you want to communicate because they can read it for themselves at the top of each slide. Write your headlines using sentence case, with the initial word capitalized and the rest in lowercase.

When you write your headlines for Act I, constrain them to only one line that fills the width of the cell without extending to a second line. The columns in your template for Act II are narrower, so you are able to extend those headlines to a maximum of about two and a half lines. Constraining your headlines to these limits keeps you from being wordy and ensures that your headlines will fill a maximum of two lines when you send them to the title area of your PowerPoint slides.

> **Tip** ✓
>
> If you're looking for practical examples of how to write concisely, look no further than the headlines of a newspaper. When writing a headline, an editor has limited space to communicate an idea clearly, so the language needs to be clear, direct, and engaging.

It might be a challenge to keep your headlines brief, but that's part of the process of boiling down your complicated ideas to their essence. This distillation will help you to get right to the point in your presentations.

Rule 2: Be Clear, Direct, Specific, and Conversational

Each statement in your story template will speak directly to your audience when it fills the title area of a slide, so use a conversational tone that is simple, clear, and direct. Say what you mean in plain language. When you make your point, include the details that give it specificity, color, and impact. Tailor your words to the level of understanding of everyone in the audience and place nothing in the headline that is not in the audience's vocabulary.

The point of the headline is to help your audience understand your point as efficiently as possible—if you use words unfamiliar to them, you create obstacles to understanding, and they will wonder what the individual words mean instead of attending to the overall message. The exception to using simple words is if everyone in the audience has prior understanding of the technical language you are using.

When you write your headlines, imagine that you are addressing a few members of your audience sitting in chairs next to your desk. Because you're simply having a conversation, your voice should be relaxed and casual—not tense and formal. This conversational tone will help you keep your headlines from getting wordy. Later, when your audience reads your headlines in the title area of your slides, the conversational tone will help them to feel more relaxed and open to your ideas. Although presenters might assume formal language gives them more authority, research shows people learn better when information is presented in a conversational style rather than a formal style.

THREE GROUND RULES FOR WRITING HEADLINES

Your story template depends on a special writing style that boils down your story to its essence. Follow these three ground rules to keep your writing on point:

- **Rule 1:** Write concise, complete sentences with a subject and a verb in active voice.
- **Rule 2:** Be clear, direct, specific, and conversational.
- **Rule 3:** Link your ideas across cells.

Rule 3: Link Your Ideas Across Cells

As you'll see in Chapters 4 and 5, you'll be breaking up your ideas into smaller pieces as you write your thoughts in the cells of the story template. As you do that, you want to make sure that you link your ideas so that they flow to one another as you read them across the cells. You make sure you do this by choosing a consistent tense across all headlines—you'll generally create a more dynamic, in-the-moment feeling to your story if you use the present tense. You should also link your ideas by using a parallel sentence structure across cells, which keeps everything sounding clear and coherent. Linking your cells verbally in the story template becomes important when you sketch and add graphics to your storyboard visually, as you'll see in Chapters 6, 7, 8, and 9.

THE WRITING ON THE WALL

Although writing is usually considered a solitary experience, don't write your PowerPoint script alone. Invite the members of your team to join you in a conference room. To get started, attach a projector to your laptop computer and display your story template as a Word document on the screen. When the story template is projected onto a wall, it becomes a tool for a group of people to see, create, discuss, debate, and agree on the structure of any presentation. Organizations have found the story template tool to be a breakthrough innovation because it guides a collaborative process, gives people ownership, taps into collective brainpower, and literally gets everyone on the same sheet of paper.

Now that you've prepared your story template and reviewed the ground rules, it's time to get specific and start with the beginning—the first five slides of your presentation.

CHAPTER 4

Planning Your First Five Slides

WHEN YOU STAND UP to make a presentation, your audience has many other things on their minds that compete with their attention to you and your information. You have to break through the clutter quickly, or you lose your chance to focus their working memory on the new information you'll present. In addition to the limited capacity of working memory, you also have only a limited amount of time to make a first impression. In the first moments of a presentation, an audience forms an opinion about you and determines your credibility to talk about the topic in the first place. This puts you in a critical situation where you really need to get it right the first time.

A presentation—like a story—is a sequence of ideas over a finite period of time. People naturally follow this linear structure when they tell one another stories, whether in person or in novels and films. The beginning of a story defines your specific opportunity to lay down the sequence of ideas that will make the most efficient use of your audiences' limited capacity for new information and your limited time to make a first impression. If this sequence is put together well, it can quickly and efficiently engage your audience.

What Will You Show, Say, and Do in the First Five Slides?

There are many theories about what it takes to focus your audience and make an impact in the first few minutes of a presentation. But whatever you believe, now you have to make specific decisions that will turn your abstract ideas into practical form. Next week, or whenever you present, you'll be the specific person standing at the front of a specific room, with a specific presentation on your computer. With Beyond Bullet Points (BBP), you have a place to begin—the document that holds your story template is the specific place where you start the practical work you need to do to get ready for that day.

With your story template document open, locate the Zoom toolbar on the lower right of the screen, and click and drag the Zoom toolbar so that Act I fills the screen, as shown in Figure 4-1. Here you see the five cells where you'll write the five headlines of Act I following the three ground rules described in the "Writing Headlines Using Three Ground Rules" section in Chapter 3.

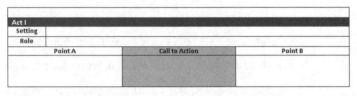

FIGURE 4-1 The five cells where you'll write the five headlines in Act I of the story template.

Although you'll be working in a Microsoft Office Word document for now, it's helpful to keep in mind that the specific words you write here will become the headlines of the first five slides of your PowerPoint presentation, as shown in Figure 4-2. These five slides will determine everything you say, show, and do in the critical first few minutes of your presentation, and they also represent your opportunity to start strong and clear and to guide working memory through the entire presentation.

Inspired by the basics of classical story structure, Act I of the story template includes the specific elements that make up the beginning of a well-crafted story, ensuring that you always have the essential pieces to begin your presentation properly. Once you have a solid foundation established in Act I, you'll have limitless creative options for what you actually do visually and verbally in the presentation. Later you'll look at a range of ideas for creating the words and images for these first five slides. But first you'll write a specific example to see exactly how all the pieces of Act I fit together in a tight and smooth sequence.

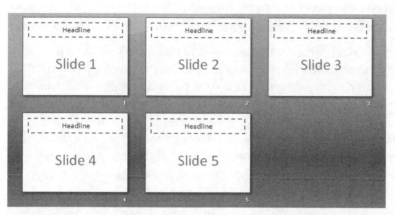

FIGURE 4-2 The five headlines you write in Act I of the story template will become the headlines of the first five slides of your presentation that determine what you'll show, say, and do during the critical first few minutes.

Starting with the Title and Byline

The scenario for this example presentation is that you're in charge of a team that currently manages a line of products and services. Although things have gone well in the past, you see the environment quickly changing and you know you'll run into trouble soon. Your team is savvy and experienced and don't have time to waste, so they expect you to get right to the point. So with that, you start at the top of the story template.

In the top cell above Act I, replace the text *Title and byline* with the title of your presentation—in this example, **A new way of thinking**. Type a byline for the script following the title—in this example, **by Pat Coleman**, as shown in Figure 4-3.

A new way of thinking by Pat Coleman		
Act I		
Setting		
Role		
Point A	**Call to Action**	**Point B**

FIGURE 4-3 Type the title and byline in the top cell of the story template.

Now that you've added a title and byline, the story template is ready for you to start writing Act I.

WHY A BYLINE IS IMPORTANT

The byline of the story template is important because it names the person who is responsible for the story's successful delivery: the presenter. In many organizations, PowerPoint files will pass through many hands as they're being developed, and ownership can easily become lost or unclear. The impact of these presentations diminishes because they are disconnected from the real names and faces of the people who will stand at the podium. Many people can contribute to a presentation, but only one person will ultimately make the presentation. The byline at the top of the story template makes it clear at all times who is behind the slides and whose reputation and credibility are on the line.

Choosing a Story Thread

Act I of the story template lays down the pattern for the headlines of the first five slides in a sequence that will orient the audience, interest them, engage them, motivate them, and then focus them on a path forward. These five headlines will answer the clarifying questions that every audience silently asks every presenter: *where* and *when*, *who*, *why*, *what*, and *how*.

In Act I, you shape the answers to these questions in a creative way that awakens the imagination of your audience, connects with their emotions, and persuades them that they want to participate in your story.

Orienting the Audience with the Setting Headline

The headline of your first slide establishes the context for your entire presentation. In a film or television show, if a scene takes place in the living room of a house in the daytime, you might first see a shot of the exterior of the house in daylight that then fades into a shot of the living room where the action will take place. This film technique is called an *establishing shot* and quickly shows the audience the *where* and *when* of a story.

To begin writing the first headline of Act I, type a headline in the row in the template labeled *Setting* that describes the establishing shot and answers the questions your audience members are silently asking: "*Where* am I, and *when* is it?" *Where* is not necessarily a literal geographic location but could be an abstract setting, such as a profession or a general topic of discussion that establishes the context for the presentation. *When* could be an implied time, such as today, if that's obvious to the audience. For the

Setting headline of Act I of this story, enter **Our team has done well here until now, but the environment is fundamentally changing**, as shown in Figure 4-4.

A new way of thinking by Pat Coleman		
Act I		
Setting	Our team has done well here until now, but the environment is fundamentally changing	
Role		
Point A	**Call to Action**	**Point B**

FIGURE 4-4 Write your first headline of Act I to describe the setting.

The use of "here" in this headline establishes the location for this presentation within this organization, and "until now" indicates the time frame of the past leading up to today. Now that the *where* and *when* have been established, the rest of the headline can say something about the setting that everyone in the room agrees is true—in this example, that "the environment is fundamentally changing." At this early stage in the presentation, the headline should not say something controversial or unclear, or else you'll quickly derail your presentation before you even get started.

The reference to "the environment is fundamentally changing" is an example of establishing the setting at a macro level—presenting the big picture of the situation, to which you'll zoom in with laser-like focus shortly. This makes sense for this audience of executives because they all would know about trends in the industry environment, and this headline affirms what they know to be true—perhaps more succinctly than normally would be said in a presentation.

This first slide is important because when your presentation begins, audiences might have different expectations than you do. The Setting headline invites them to join you at the same location, establishes a common ground, and leaves no doubt about the context for what you are about to say.

THE SETTING HEADLINE

The Setting headline answers the question the audience members are silently wondering: "*Where* am I, and *when* is it?"

When you've written the Setting headline, you've made sure you will orient the audience by establishing the where and when of the story in the first slide of your presentation, as shown in Figure 4-5.

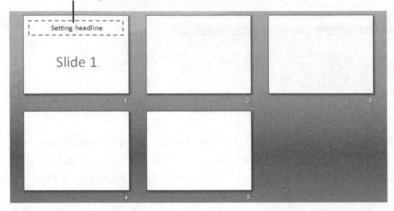

FIGURE 4-5 The headline of the Setting slide orients the audience to where they are and when it is.

After you write a headline for the Setting slide, it's time to add some character to the presentation.

Interesting the Audience with the Role Headline

The headline of your second slide names the role of the main character of the story. Every story is about somebody, and that includes your PowerPoint story. The *main character* of your story is the person who will make a decision to do something or come to believe something by the end of the experience. According to this definition, the main character of every nonfiction presentation is *your audience*.

Establishing your audience as the main character in your second slide makes your presentation personal to them. Because the audience members have a direct involvement and stake in the outcome, they will pay attention. Making your audience the main character also helps you to stay focused on your audience and makes sure that you tailor your presentation to their needs. Many PowerPoint presentations tend to be "all about me," with little if any consideration of the audience. With this single slide, you remind your audience that this is "all about you."

■ **REMEMBER** The main character of every presentation is your audience, and you are a supporting character. This is the crucial spin on crafting stories for live presentations.

The main character of a presentation could be a single person, such as a customer or client, or it could be a group, such as a committee, a team, a jury, a board, or an organization. In this presentation, the executives are the main character because they are the ones who have to figure out what to do in the changing environment.

Now that you have a star for the leading role in your presentation, write a headline that acknowledges your audience's role in the setting you described. In the row labeled *Role*, type a headline that answers the question your audience is wondering: "*Who* am I here in this setting?" In this example, enter **You're here to help us figure out what we're going to do**, as shown in Figure 4-6.

A new way of thinking by Pat Coleman		
Act I		
Setting	Our team has done well here until now, but the environment is fundamentally changing	
Role	You're here to help us figure out what we're going to do	
Point A	**Call to Action**	**Point B**

FIGURE 4-6 Write your second headline of Act I to describe the audience role.

In any particular context, a person could have a number of different roles—for example, the same individual could be the supervisor of one person, the peer of another person, and the subordinate of yet another person. Here you choose the specific role your audience members play in the context of the setting you just established. The subject of this headline, "you," establishes the audience, the executives, as the main character of this story. Now that the *who* of the story is clear, the rest of the headline can simply affirm something about the audience's situation that everyone in the room can agree on. In this case, the executives would concur that they are "here to figure out what we're doing to do."

THE ROLE HEADLINE

The Role headline answers the question the audience is silently wondering: "*Who* am I here in this setting?"

When you have written the Role headline, you've made sure that you'll interest the audience by acknowledging their role in the second slide of your presentation, as shown in Figure 4-7.

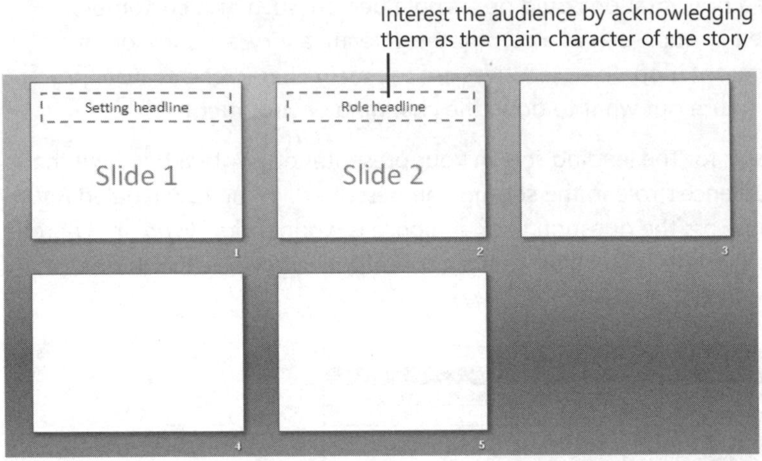

Interest the audience by acknowledging
them as the main character of the story

FIGURE 4-7 The headline of the Role slide interests the audience by making them the main character of the story.

In the next slide headline, it's time to stir things up for the main character.

Engaging the Audience with the "Point A" Headline

The headline of your third slide begins the action and presents your most important opportunity to quickly engage your audience. Because you should make an emotional connection within the first few minutes of a presentation, this is the specific slide where you make that abstract concept a reality.

Stories are about how people respond to something that has changed in their environment. People like stories of how other people handle changes in circumstances and what their choices reveal about their characters. When a main character experiences a change, an imbalance is created because things are no longer as they used to be. This creates a challenge that sets the story in motion. In your story template, you'll define this challenge with the Point A headline. This headline is called Point A because it defines the specific point where your audience begins the action of this story. Later you'll define the specific point where your audience wants to be in light of this challenge—Point B.

The Point A challenge that has brought everyone to the presentation today could be a crisis brought on by an external force that has changed your organization's environment, such as a sudden economic shift or the action of a competitor. It could be the result of an internal change, such as a revised opinion or mindset, a new piece of information, a new research report, or an anecdote from the field.

■ **REMEMBER The Point A headline sets your story in motion by defining a specific challenge your audience faces.**

A DOZEN STORY TYPES

Although the classical story structure of Act I is the foundation for limitless story variations, there is a more limited set of story types that can help you to frame your own stories. In his book *Moving Mountains* (Crowell-Collier Press, 1989), Henry M. Boettinger describes a dozen story types, summarized in the following list, that reflect various situations that people in organizations might face. Many of these story types can help you to refine the Point A and Point B dynamic you set up in Act I:

1. **Historical narrative**   "We have a history that makes us proud, and we want to apply our high standards to the current situation."

2. **Crisis**   "We have to respond to the danger facing us."

3. **Disappointment**   "We made a decision based on the best information we had available, but now we know it wasn't the right decision, so we have to try something else."

4. **Opportunity**   "We know something now that we didn't know before, which presents us with a new possibility if we act."

5. **Crossroads**   "We've been doing fine on the path that we're on, but now we have a new choice and we have to decide which path to take."

6. **Challenge**   "Someone else has achieved something amazing—do we have it in us to do the same?"

7. **Blowing the whistle**   "Although it appears everything is going fine, we have a serious problem we need to fix."

8. **Adventure**   "We know that trying something new is a risk, but it's better to take a risk than to stay in a rut."

9. **Response to an order**   "We've been told we have to do this, so we're here to figure out how to make it happen."

10. **Revolution**   "We're on a path to disaster if we don't radically change what we're doing today."

11. **Evolution**   "If we don't keep up with the latest, we'll fall behind."

12. **The Great Dream**   "If we can only see our possibility, we can make it our reality."

No matter what type of story you have, read through these story types when you start writing your Act I headlines to see whether one of them can help you to find the words you're looking for.

On the upside, a change could be brought on by an inspiration, a new idea, a discovery, or the appearance of a new opportunity that the main character hadn't seen before. On the downside, the challenge could be the realization that a mistake was made, a fall from grace, the loss of market share, declining profits, or a sudden drop in status. Whether positive or negative, all of these challenges are the core reasons why people gather for presentations.

Your Point A headline should establish the challenge that the specific audience faces in this story. Do this by answering, in the cell labeled *Point A*, the question your audience is wondering: "*What* specific challenge do I face in this setting?". In this example, enter the headline **What worked in the past isn't working anymore – and you're feeling the impact**, as shown in Figure 4-8.

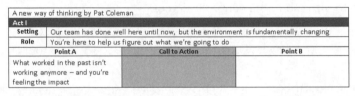

FIGURE 4-8 Write your third headline of Act I to describe Point A—a specific challenge that your audience faces in this setting.

This headline gets right to the point by describing the challenge that starts the emotional engine of your presentation. Here you've moved from the macro view of the Setting headline that presented the overall state of the environment and have now gone to the micro level, where you describe specifically how the big picture is playing out in the audience's lives. In other words, the earlier Setting headline was the big, general problem, and now with Point A, you've made the situation personal and identified the specific challenge the audience faces in the context of the setting. There are many other ways to write your Point A headlines—see Appendix C for a list of many other possibilities.

The point of the Point A headline is to arrive at an emotional touchstone that makes it crystal clear why your audience would want to engage with your presentation. As you're thinking of what to write, answer this question from the audience's viewpoint: "What is it that I would stand to lose if I missed your presentation today?" Or put another way, "What makes me lose sleep at night?" It might be related to sales, an insight, or the opportunity to find clarity or direction. By focusing on what the audience might feel they would lose, or what causes them to lose sleep, you'll find the challenge they really care about that you should address in your Point A headline.

> **Note** It might appear that writing headlines is a straightforward process where you write what you need in the first pass, but in reality it's an iterative process where you'll write a first draft and then make multiple rounds of changes. As mentioned earlier, you'll get the best results if you develop your headlines with a team so that you get multiple perspectives and distill the best of your collective effort.

The challenge of the Point A headline defines your story and helps you to focus. You could tell a dozen stories about any particular topic; focusing on a single challenge helps you to narrow your scope to a single story presented to a specific group of people at a particular moment in time. Selecting one and only one challenge is often a difficult process, but because the capacity of working memory to process new information is so limited, you have to go through a difficult decision-making process and choose the one story thread that is the best fit. To write the best Point A headline, you have to know your audience as well as possible and make your decision based on the best of your and your team's experience, research, competitive intelligence, analysis, and intuition.

THE POINT A HEADLINE

The Point A headline answers the question your audience is silently wondering: "*What* challenge do I face?"

When you've written the Point A headline, you've made sure that you will engage the audience by describing a challenge they face in the third slide of your presentation, as shown in Figure 4-9.

Engage the audience by
describing a challenge they face

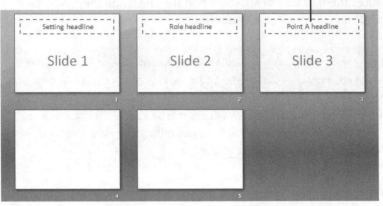

FIGURE 4-9 The headline of the Point A slide engages your audience by describing a challenge they face.

Although you've left your audience with a formidable challenge in the Point A headline, you'll provide them with the resolution they want in the next headline.

Motivating the Audience with the "Point B" Headline

No one likes to remain in a state of discomfort. When you are challenged, you feel unsettled and emotionally uncomfortable until you bring the situation back into equilibrium. The same holds true for the main character in this story or in any presentation.

In the Point A headline, you described a challenge that faces your audience. Now, in the Point B headline, they naturally want to see how things will look when the situation is brought back into balance. To write the headline for this slide, in the cell labeled *Point B* in the template, type an answer to the question your audience is wondering: "*Where do I want to be?*" In this example, enter **You'd like to find a new way to do things**, as shown in Figure 4-10.

A new way of thinking by Pat Coleman		
Act I		
Setting	Our team has done well here until now, but the environment is fundamentally changing	
Role	You're here to help us figure out what we're going to do	
Point A	**Call to Action**	**Point B**
What worked in the past isn't working anymore – and you're feeling the impact		You'd like to find a new way to do things

FIGURE 4-10 Write your fourth headline of Act I to describe Point B, where your audience wants to be when facing the Point A challenge.

This headline concisely affirms what the executives want—namely, to find a better way to do things. This establishes the desired outcome that will bring the main character's situation back into balance.

The Point A headline describes the challenge facing the audience, and the Point B headline shows them a vision of where they want to be in this context. When they see where they want to go, they'll be fueled by their desire to get there with your help.

THE POINT B HEADLINE

The Point B headline of the fourth slide answers the question the audience is asking themselves: "*Where* do I want to be?"

When you've written the Point B headline, you've made sure that you will motivate the audience by affirming what they want in the fourth slide of your presentation, as shown in Figure 4-11.

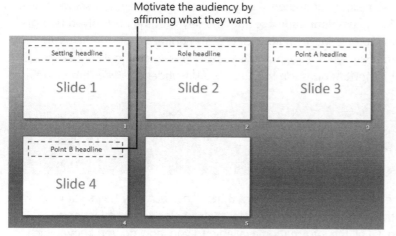

FIGURE 4-11 The Point B headline motivates your audience by defining where they want to be.

Creating Dramatic Tension Between the Point A and Point B Headlines

In the story template, the two cells that hold the Point A and Point B headlines are separated from one another physically, as shown in Figure 4-12, while the cell between them is shaded a dark gray.

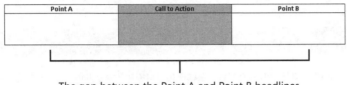

The gap between the Point A and Point B headlines creates the dramatic tension that energizes the story

FIGURE 4-12 The gap between the Point A and Point B headlines is the emotional engine of the entire presentation.

Remember, the Point A headline puts your audience in an emotionally uncomfortable state of imbalance, and the Point B headline describes the state of balance that they want to achieve. These two headlines spark off one another to generate the energy that drives your story forward and makes your audience eager to hear your proposed solution. The gap between A and B engages your audience immediately with the unresolved tension of a story. This timeless storytelling technique of creating dramatic tension helps you quickly engage and motivate your audience and to further an emotional connection. It also answers another important question the audience is wondering: *"Why* am I here?

Tip   An easy way to remember the essence of Act I is to think of the central question the audience is asking at the beginning of any presentation: "A to B, what's in it for me?"

The problem described by the Point A and Point B headlines not only helps your audience engage with your presentation, but later it also helps you to select and prioritize information. Of all the information available to you, how do you know which information to include? The answer is to select only information that specifically helps your audience close the gap between Points A and B. Any other information is unnecessary for this presentation and can be set aside for another story on another day.

CAN I APPLY A STORY STRUCTURE TO AN "INFORMATIONAL" PRESENTATION?

One objection to using Beyond Bullet Points (BBP) is the misconception that a story structure is not appropriate for informational presentations. The thought that people don't need to be engaged or motivated when faced with new information is based on the mythology described in Chapter 3 that assumes that you pour facts into the passive minds of your audience and they will automatically "get it." The research reality is that people need to actively engage new information, so offering them tools and techniques to do so will help them learn better. Why pass up the opportunity to engage your audience when doing so can increase focus and involvement? The Act I technique of creating dramatic tension by creating a gap between the Point A and Point B headlines is thousands of years old and offers a dynamism that still works today when it is applied to any type of presentation.

The problem created by the gap between the Point A and Point B headlines also forms the *purpose* of your presentation, so when you make the problem clear, you make your purpose clear. This problem is central to your entire presentation and forms the singular question that your presentation will try to answer. It creates an emotional center of gravity that focuses your story and makes it cohere across all of its separate parts. The gap between Points A and B defines the problem that you are there to help your audience solve and also answers for the audience another important question: "What's in this for me?"

Whatever way you frame the gap between Points A and B is how you frame the entire presentation going forward. If you get this framing right, your presentation will create a connection with your audience; if you get it wrong, you will create a disconnect. Defining the problem for your audience is probably the hardest thing you'll do in your presentation. You and your team might go through several rounds of drafts and revisions to get the Point A and Point B headlines right, but when you do, the rest of your presentation will fall into place. There are many ways to write the Point B headline—see Appendix C for a list of some of the possibilities.

When you have a clear problem established with the Point A and Point B headlines, it's time to let your audience know how you propose to solve it.

Focusing the Audience with the "Call to Action" Headline

Remember, the Point A headline defines a challenge, and the Point B headline shows your audience where they want to be in light of that challenge. Now you'll literally fill the gap between A and B with your Call to Action headline.

The Call to Action headline defines the reason you're the presenter—you've taken the time to figure out how the main character can solve the problem at hand. To complete the fifth slide, in the dark gray cell labeled *Call to Action*, type an answer to the question your audience is wondering: "*How* do I get from A to B?" In this case, enter **Change your way of thinking to get breakthrough results**, as shown in Figure 4-13.

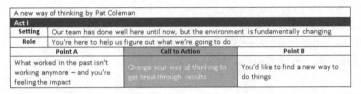

A new way of thinking by Pat Coleman		
Act I		
Setting	Our team has done well here until now, but the environment is fundamentally changing	
Role	You're here to help us figure out what we're going to do	
Point A	**Call to Action**	**Point B**
What worked in the past isn't working anymore – and you're feeling the impact	Change your way of thinking to get breakthrough results	You'd like to find a new way to do things

FIGURE 4-13 Write your fifth headline of Act I to describe the call to action.

In this example, you ask the executives to "Change your way of thinking to get breakthrough results" to close the gap formed by the Point A and Point B headlines. In the context of the first five slides, the audience now affirms a problem they face, and they will be able to solve it if they let you help them in the story that will continue shortly.

Although the phrase "change your way of thinking" may be more direct than you want to be with this particular audience, it does strip down to the essence what you want from them in clear and direct language. If less-direct phrasing is in order, modify the wording to meet your and your audience's needs. In this example, other options include: "Consider a new way of thinking," "Explore new ways to think," or "Uncover new ways to think." Whatever wording you choose, it should be a good fit for both you and your audience. Refer to Appendix D for a range of phrases that you can use to start off your Call to Action headlines.

THE CALL TO ACTION HEADLINE

The Call to Action headline answers the question your audience is wondering: "*How* do I get from A to B?"

The Call to Action headline should describe what your audience should do or believe to solve the problem created by the gap between the Point A and Point B headlines—it is literally the *point* of the presentation. Your final wording is important, because the Call to Action headline clearly defines what you and your audience want to accomplish and offers a clear direction and road map that they will be able to use and follow through the rest of the presentation. As you go through the process of writing Act II in Chapter 5, you will thoroughly develop and test your Call to Action headline and will likely revise its wording.

The Call to Action headline also puts your ideas in a decision-making format that's important to people who want to accomplish something. In a single sentence, the wording of the Call to Action headline defines how you know if you were successful in your presentation, whether that success is a next meeting, a sale, an agreement, or a good grade. If your audience accepts your Call to Action headline by the end of your story, you'll know you succeeded.

I'M STUCK!

What do you do if you get stuck somewhere in the process of writing the headlines for your first five slides? Visit Appendixes C and D for inspiration. Or when you're stuck in Act I, skip ahead to Act II and return to Act I later. Often the process of working through the structure in Act II will help you define and refine Act I.

When you've written the Call to Action headline in Act I of the story template, you've made sure that you will focus the audience by offering them a way to get from Point A to Point B in the fifth slide of your presentation, as shown in Figure 4-14. The Call to Action slide in this illustration now has a dark gray background like the corresponding cell in the story template, making it stand out from the others because it is in fact the most important slide in a presentation. If you had only one slide to show, it would be the Call to Action slide—by the time you have finished with this slide in Chapter 8, it will distill your entire presentation into a single visual accompanied by your verbal narration.

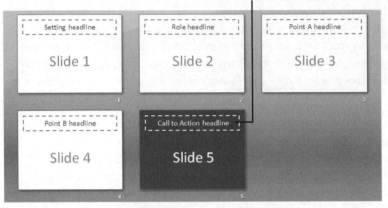

FIGURE 4-14 The Call to Action headline focuses Act I and the rest of the story to come.

Choosing a Pattern to Follow

Now that you have chosen a story thread to help new information pass through the eye of the needle, you increase the efficiency of working memory by introducing a pattern for the story to follow. Do this by adding a *motif*, or recurring theme, to the first five slides. A motif carries your ideas all the way through your story in a coherent way and adds color and interest to your language. It also makes the job of searching for graphics to add to your slides significantly easier because you map the motif to your visuals.

A motif might seem like a "nice-to-have" addition to make the presentation colorful and interesting, but research shows that it can provide much more than just a pretty face for your presentation. Working memory cannot possibly process all of the new information it experiences, and without a clear structure to organize the new information, it has to create a structure from scratch—a very inefficient process.

But with a structure that works, you help working memory select, organize, and integrate the new information much more effectively. The structures that happen to work best are ones the audience already holds in long-term memory—they might take the form of a familiar metaphor, an organizing system like 1-2-3, or any number of familiar story themes.

See Also For more information about metaphor and its impact on the way people think, see George Lakoff's work, including Metaphors We Live By, 2nd ed. (with Mark Johnson; University of Chicago Press, 2002).

For example, most people are familiar with the process of putting together a puzzle, so a puzzle-making structure already exists in their long-term memory. When you apply a puzzle motif to the structure of your story, as shown in Figure 4-15, you increase the efficiency of working memory of your audience so that they can much more quickly make sense of the new information. Introducing a preexisting structure reduces cognitive load because working memory doesn't need to exert as much energy to create a structure from scratch.

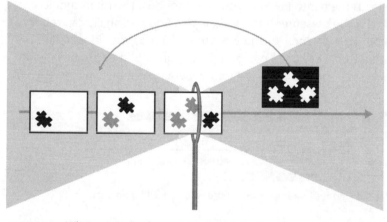

FIGURE 4-15 When you pull a familiar structure from long-term memory and use it to structure a presentation, you make working memory more efficient.

There are many different motifs you are able to apply to your presentation, which are incorporated into some of the example phrases in Appendix D. To apply a motif to your presentation, integrate it through your headlines as in the following variations of the Act I example in this chapter. Keep the following general principles in mind when you search for a motif for Act I:

- **The motif should exist already in your audience's long-term memory.** You need to get into the minds of your audience to find the right motif, because the structure has to exist already in their long-term memories. You need to figure out what they think, and what they know, through your research, interviews, and analysis. In legal trials, lawyers create juror questionnaires designed to find out what potential themes might resonate in a legal presentation. You might need to do similar in-depth research if your presentation is particularly important. If you don't know your audience or can't find enough information about them, choose a general metaphor like the checklist motif shown in Figure 4-16.

A checklist for results by Pat Coleman		
Act I		
Setting	The situation has changed recently, so we've adopted a new strategy	
Role	Now you'd like to know what specifically you need to do to handle the changes	
Point A	**Call to Action**	**Point B**
The situation seems so overwhelming, it's hard to know where to begin	Check off three items to change your way of thinking to get break through results	You'd like an approach that guides you through the process

FIGURE 4-16 The checklist motif is familiar to most audiences.

- **The motif should resonate with your audience.** Your motif needs to be a good match with your audience, and they should be able to easily relate to it. A motif can work against you if the structure is a mismatch, because it distracts your audience or misleads them into thinking you're not serious. The motif should also resonate with you as the presenter—choose one that you personally can relate to so that it draws out your personality and warmth and brings your ideas to life with your natural enthusiasm. Only use a complex or special motif if everyone in your audience shares knowledge of it, as in the formula example shown in Figure 4-17.

A formula for results by Pat Coleman		
Act I		
Setting	What worked in the past isn't working anymore	
Role	You're feeling the impact	
Point A	**Call to Action**	**Point B**
Figuring out what to do seems complex	Follow a simple formula to get breakthrough results	You'd like to cut through the clutter

FIGURE 4-17 The formula motif can resonate with those who deal with numbers.

- **The motif has to be simple.** When you find a motif, simplify it and break it into its essential elements before you apply it to your first five slides. For example, you need a more specific motif than just the general topic of puzzles, so focus the motif by using the phrase "put together the pieces of the puzzle," as in the example shown in Figure 4-18. The motif should be clear and easy to understand, and it should couch and complement your ideas without becoming convoluted or clichéd or making things confusing.

Piecing the puzzle by Pat Coleman		
Act I		
Setting	Our team has done well here until now, but the environment is fundamentally changing	
Role	You're here to help us figure out what we're going to do	
Point A	**Call to Action**	**Point B**
It can be hard to see the big picture so you know what you need to do	Put together the pieces of the puzzle to get breakthrough results	Others have found a new way to gain a new perspective

FIGURE 4-18 The puzzle motif is simple yet effective.

- **A motif is more memorable if it is unexpected.** Introducing a surprising motif in Act I will also increase memorability. Choose a surprising insight, a different way of looking at things, or another unexpected way to introduce your idea, as shown in Figure 4-19. Creatively applying a motif by putting it in a surprising context can heighten interest and stimulate creative thinking and mental participation. The more surprising and interesting and engaging the motif is, the more memorable it will be. But as mentioned earlier, make sure that in every case the motif is a good match with your audience.

Thinking backward by Pat Coleman		
Act I		
Setting	Our situation has changed, but it's not exactly clear what we need to do	
Role	The one thing for sure is that you've got to re-think what you do	
Point A	**Call to Action**	**Point B**
How can you know how to get things done if the situation looks so muddy?	Think backward to move forward	It's possible to find a way to see things clearly

FIGURE 4-19 Telling someone to go backward instead of forward gives a twist to a journey motif.

THE BLOCKBUSTER MOTIF

Some of the most powerful presentation motifs are drawn from popular culture, such as the opening statement of a jury trial using a *CSI* motif inspired by the popular television show. Finding a blockbuster motif that works well for your audience is a blend of science and art—the science of doing thorough research to know your audience and the art of applying an interesting theme in an innovative way to your information.

- **The best motifs are extendable.** The more elegantly a single motif can extend through the presentation, the more impact it will have. Sometimes a motif is straightforward, and other times it will be clever, humorous, or surprising. The deeper and more broadly your simple motif extends through the presentation, the more cohesive and elegant the communication.

You should invest a good amount of time considering your motif and trying on different ones for size, because if you find a good one, it transforms the fiber of your story thread into fiber optics as your new information travels through working memory.

Closing the Curtain on Act I

Now that you have five headlines, you've completed the first draft of Act I. Review your headlines. They might seem simple, but they've helped you to accomplish many important tasks, such as tailoring your presentation to your audience and establishing criteria to narrow down the information you want to communicate. Consider these headlines a working draft as you complete the rest of the story template; you might need to return to them and revise them as you develop the rest of your presentation.

> **Note** When a journalist puts the most important information somewhere else in the article rather than up front, it's called *burying the lead*. The structure of Act I ensures you don't bury your lead by making sure that you always bring the most important information to the top level of attention at the start of every presentation.

If you haven't already done so, take the time now to review your five headlines with your team and anyone else who needs to approve your presentation. These headlines determine everything that will unfold next in your story, so it's important to get other people involved early in this writing process to make sure that you're on the right track.

Never rush through the process of writing your Act I headlines—the words that you write in Act I will make the difference between a strong start and a weak one. It's not uncommon for an individual or a team to completely revise Act I several times until the story is exactly right for the audience. An executive team might spend a great deal of time fine-tuning Act I because, in a bigger sense, these five headlines can define the way the organization understands and relates to its customers. These five simple headlines are in fact a communications strategy and are worthy of whatever resources you normally invest in developing strategic issues.

Review the tips at the end of this chapter to develop and refine your Act I headlines. Here are a couple of ways to test and review the headlines now.

Reviewing the Five Headlines

Read the five headlines aloud to verify that you have the tone, flow, and clarity of language that you want. Check your headlines to make sure that you answer each of the clarifying questions that every audience wants to know: *where* and *when*, *who*, *what*, *why*, and *how*. Here are the questions in their respective headlines:

- **The Setting Headline** *Where* am I, and *when* is it?

- **The Role Headline**   *Who* am I in this setting?

- **The Point A Headline**   *What* challenge do I face in this setting?

- **The Point B Headline**   *Where* do I want to be?

- **(The gap between the Point A and B headlines)**   *Why* am I here?

- **The Call to Action Headline**   *How* do I get from A to B?

> **Tip** ✔
>
> If you ever have to give an off-the-cuff speech, use the five headlines of Act I to start your talk. This is a sure-fire way to answer your audience's clarifying questions and leave them thoroughly impressed.

Appealing to Your Audience's Emotions

The members of any audience, including these executives, are not purely rational beings—they are emotional too. You avoid a strictly rational approach by using your Act I headlines to make an emotional connection with your audience and persuade them that the information is important to them. You achieve this connection by including the most important elements of a strong story beginning, in the form of headlines for the Setting, Role, Point A, Point B, and Call to Action slides. By tailoring each of these elements to your audience and presenting them in Act I, you make your story personal to your audience and ensure that you are off to a strong start.

■ **REMEMBER Your Act I headlines make an emotional connection with your audience.**

Focusing Your Ideas

As you saw in Chapter 2, if the volume of information overwhelms your audience, especially at the start of a presentation, their minds will shut down, and you won't achieve the results you want. Act I of the story template helps you to establish criteria to narrow down all the things you *could* say to only the most important things you *should* say to this audience during this presentation. When you begin writing the Act II headlines in Chapter 5, you'll find that these Act I headlines have set up your story in a way that will limit the quantity of information to only what is necessary and the quality of information to the high standards you expect.

BBP CHECKLIST: PLANNING YOUR FIRST FIVE SLIDES

Do the first five slides of your presentation accomplish the following:

- Orient your audience to the setting of the presentation?
- Interest them by acknowledging their role in the setting?
- Engage them emotionally by describing a challenge they face (Point A)?
- Motivate them by affirming what they want (Point B)?
- Focus them by offering a way to get from Point A to Point B (Call to Action)?

The process of writing the five slide headlines described in this chapter covers the fundamentals that apply to any presentation story and helps you to appeal to emotion and focus your ideas. Once you learn the basics, you'll apply a broad range of creative resources, tools, and techniques to help you adapt this structure to your own style and circumstances.

When you're satisfied with your Act I headlines, it's time to flesh out your story in Act II. Before you move on to Chapter 5, scan through the 10 tips in the following sections to find ideas that might inspire you to improve on Act I after you're comfortable with the fundamentals.

10 Tips for Enhancing Act I

The Act I structure in the story template isn't a strict formula—it's a basic platform with the potential for endless innovation and improvisation based on the specifics of your situation. Just as writers can create endless story variations using this pattern, you likewise have the potential to create endless presentation variations with this tool. After you learn the fundamentals, there's plenty of room to adapt and improvise to suit your personality, audience, and situation.

If you're ready to take your presentations to the next level, here are 10 advanced tips for building on the basic structure of Act I.

Tip 1: Inspiration from the Screenwriters

Spark your creative energy by going back to the past to see the future of presentation stories. All you need to do is consult with the original expert on story structure. Start by picking up copies of Aristotle's classics *Poetics* and *Rhetoric*. For a more recent adaptation of Aristotle's ideas, a number of excellent books on screenwriting can help you with writing your Act I headlines, including Robert McKee's *Story: Substance, Structure, Style and the Principles of Screenwriting* (Regan Books, 1997); Syd Field's *Screenplay: The Foundations of Screenwriting* (Dell, 1984); and James Bonnet's *Stealing Fire from the Gods: The Complete Guide to Story for Writers and Filmmakers* (Michael Wiese Productions, 2006). Any of these titles will help you learn more about the key elements of the first act of every story, including settings, character development, inciting incidents, and plot points. As you read these books for inspiration, keep in mind that your presentation is a specific type of story in which your audience is the main character and you are in a supporting role. Maintaining this focus will ensure that all of your stories align with the specific needs of your PowerPoint presentations.

Tip 2: Varying your Story

After you've mastered the basics of the five Act I headlines, try improvising in your stories. For example, your story structure might involve changing the order of headlines in Act I. You could place the Point A and B headlines first and define the Setting, Role, and Call to Action headlines later. You could begin with the Call to Action headline to grab people's attention and then continue with the other headlines. At times, you might be able to delete a slide if the audience is absolutely in agreement about a situation, although it rarely hurts to clearly restate information to bring everyone to the same starting point.

Tip 3: Your Act I Screen Test

In filmmaking, a *screen test* puts actors in front of a camera to test how they will do on screen. In a PowerPoint presentation, your first screen test is for your Act I headlines, and your first audience is the members of your team. It's important to include other people at this stage of your presentation to get early feedback and fresh perspectives. If you're working on a small or informal presentation, ask a colleague or your boss to look over your Act I headlines.

Once you get the hang of writing an Act I with your group, try applying these techniques to other communications scenarios beyond your PowerPoint presentations. Crafting Act I of a presentation is a problem-solving framework that also helps a group to clarify strategy, develop marketing messages, create project plans, and resolve other challenges. Sharing your Act I headlines with a team is also a great way to kick off a project or orient someone new to a team. By reviewing the five headlines of Act I and the clarifying questions, team members learn the situation quickly and efficiently.

Tip 4: Multiple Stories, Multiple Templates

When it comes to presentations, one size might not fit all.

The beauty of your Act I headlines is that they are finely tailored and tuned to solve the specific problem of a specific audience. But what if your audience has more than one problem? What if you give the same presentation to different audiences that have different problems to solve? For example, you might need to present a marketing plan to different audiences, including the board, your advertising agency, and your sales team. In each instance, the presentation will have a different focus and will need a different version of Act I. If you don't tailor your presentations to your audiences, you won't connect with them.

One way to plan for these different situations is to create several versions of Act I, each of which is tailored to a specific audience. Create a copy of the document that contains the five Act I headlines from your current story template. In the new document, revise the Point A and Point B headlines, which describe the central problem that your new audience faces. When you change these headlines to reflect a new problem, you might find that you need to revise the Setting and Role headlines if a different set of circumstances led to this problem. And you most likely will also need to revise the Call to Action headline because the solution for the new problem will probably be different from the solution to the previous problem. After creating separate versions of Act I, you choose the most appropriate version for your next audience.

This multiple-version approach also works if you find that you have more stories to tell in addition to the one you're working on. If you sense another story emerging, open up a new story template, and keep it open while you're working on your current presentation, adding headlines to your second story as you go. As you develop your second presentation in parallel to the first, you might find that you're able to refine both versions at the same time.

Tip 5: Visualize Your Audience

The more clearly you know your audience, the clearer your communications will become.

When you start writing your Act I headlines, take some time with your team to visualize everything that you know about your specific audience. To do this, open a new PowerPoint presentation, create a blank slide, and insert a picture of a specific audience member or just type a specific name on the screen. If you're speaking to a large audience, consider the slide a composite of the average audience member.

Ask your group questions like these:

- What do we know about this person?
- What have we heard about his personality type?
- How does she make decisions?

- What can we learn from a Web search about his thinking process?

- What can we learn from our social network about how she works with other people?

- How do we effectively fashion an experience that aligns with his interests and personality type?

Type the information on the slide as your group gives feedback so that everyone has all the information captured on the slide. When you do this, you tap into the collective thinking of your group to better understand your audience. And you think more deeply about your audience and your purpose, which will significantly improve the quality of your headlines.

Tip 6: What Problem Is Your Audience Facing?

To accurately define the problem your audience is facing, try putting yourself in the place of the audience.

Your Act I headlines identify a problem that your audience faces and a solution that you propose. But it's not always easy to figure out the problem to be sure you have the right solution. The visualization exercise described in Tip 5 helps you to see into the mindset of your audience so that you'll be in a better position to write the appropriate headlines for them.

Another technique is role playing. When you review the rough draft of your Act I headlines, ask a member of the group to play the role of a decision maker or representative member of your audience. She will review the material you gathered from the preceding profiling exercise to help her get into character.

Request that this person be a devil's advocate during your review session, continually asking questions such as these:

- What's in this for me?

- Why do you think this is important to me?

- Why should I care?

When you hear this critical voice during your review, you'll be able to test your headlines to make sure that you're hitting the mark. It's better to hear the questions from a fictional audience than to have them pop up unexpectedly during your actual presentation.

Once you've identified your audience's problem, don't be surprised if your presentation holds tightly together and your ideas start to emerge into clear meaning.

Tip 7: Strategic Collage

If you have a high-stakes presentation to make, you might need to invest extra effort to get to know your audience in advance. One way to get to know them is to spend a day in their shoes—at least symbolically. Open up a new PowerPoint file, and then create six blank slides. On each of these slides, type one of the clarifying questions: **Where? When? Who? What? Why?** and **How?**

Use a digital camera to take pictures of the objects your audience uses every day or of the environments where they live and work and the people they might see. Your visuals should represent whatever data you have about your audience, whether it's market research, demographics, or focus group information. Go through your organization's photo libraries to find licensed photographs and clip art to show the buildings in which these people work, the products they use, and the places they visit. Use a digital scanner to insert pictures of documents, a pen tablet to make sketches, a video camera to insert video clips, and a microphone to collect sound.

When you've collected these multimedia elements, arrange them on each of the six PowerPoint slides to create six collages. Size the different elements according to how important you think each is to your audience—for example, if mobility is most important, make the picture of a car larger than less important elements.

Present the file to your team as you discuss what it's like to spend a day in your audience's shoes in the context of these six slides. Then open your story template and start working on Act I. Discuss with your team how well the headlines match the collages, and then edit the headlines to provide a good fit. The better your Act I story matches the reality of your audience's lives, the better your presentation.

Tip 8: The Story of Advertising

Some of the most powerful examples of Act I story structure pass right before your eyes every day. If you look for them, you'll find an endless stream of ideas for your presentations. These stories are all around us—in the form of advertising.

Advertisers are well aware of Aristotle's ideas and techniques of storytelling and persuasion, because at its core, every advertisement is a persuasive story. Whether you look up at a billboard, open a magazine, or watch television, you're seeing a mini-story built on the fundamentals of persuasion. Each advertisement has a singular goal in mind: to persuade you to do something—usually, to buy a product.

To persuade you, an advertiser will use the most current and sophisticated blend of multimedia possible. But beneath the media mix are the same classical story elements you've been working with in Act I of the story template: the clarifying questions *where* and *when*, *who*, *why*, *what*, and *how*. As in a PowerPoint presentation, the main character of an advertisement is usually the audience—in this case, you—because the advertiser's goal is to persuade you to buy or think something new.

So if you're watching a commercial for a laundry detergent, compare the questions your audience silently asks of your five Act I headlines with what you see on TV, something like this:

- **Where** **am I, and** **when** **is it?** I'm at home, and it's the afternoon.

- **Who** **am I here in this setting?** I'm a person getting ready to go out for the evening.

- **What** **challenge do I face?** I dropped spaghetti on my favorite shirt.

- **Where** **do I want to be?** I want to impress my date tonight by looking my best.

- **How** **do I get from here to there?** If I buy Product X laundry detergent, my shirt will be clean in time for my date.

There's usually a one-to-one correspondence between your Act I questions and most advertisements because both have the same intent: to make an emotional connection and to persuade. And both creatively interpret the fundamentals of story structure to get the job done. The next time you notice an advertisement, observe the structure that gives it form. Sometimes the story elements might be implied or communicated using a photo, sound, or movement instead of words, but they will usually all be there.

As you begin to see this common persuasive story structure in advertising, you'll be more aware of the range of storytelling approaches, and you'll be able to apply these techniques to your own Act I headlines.

Tip 9: Persuasive Education

Educators and trainers are in the same boat as the rest of us when it comes to the challenges of communicating today. They also are affected by the expectations of audiences who now are fluent in the visual language around them and expect the same level of media sophistication in the classroom.

For example, a university professor who's struggling to find a way to make his architecture course more interesting and engaging is struck by the fact that every one of the architects he'll discuss also struggled with change—economic change, social change, demographic change, and technological change. So he decides to adopt a classical persuasive technique and chooses the singular topic of change as the key theme of his course. The persuasive story in Act I goes like this:

- **Where** **am I, and when is it?** Architects stand at the epicenter of economic change, social change, and technological change.

- *Who* **am I in this setting?** As a new graduate, you will be facing the reality of the situation soon.

- *What* **challenge do I face?** As a new hire, you are most in danger of instability due to the forces of change.

- *What* **do I want?** You'd like to learn the skills to handle the situation no matter what changes occur.

- *How* **do I get from here to there?** Learn three crucial techniques to ensure that you keep a firm footing.

This persuasive Act I structure provides an elegant framework for the entire course. It gives students a way to understand the single theme and follow it through the various events in the complicated history of architecture. And the dramatic and persuasive elements give students a way to relate personally to the material.

Finding a defining structure like this is not always easy, but it can make the difference between a boring lecture and an engaging presentation. Try applying the persuasive model the next time you teach or inform, and see whether you make things more interesting for both yourself and your audience.

Tip 10: Get the Writing Right

Beyond the nuts and bolts of writing down the words, consider ways to apply literary techniques to convey clear meaning across your headlines. Act I is so brief and elegant that you are actually telling a rich but concise story in only five sentences. Using a motif is one powerful technique; look for other techniques from professional writers whose work you admire.

Writers such as poets are extremely good at communicating a great deal of information in a limited number of words. Pick up a book of good poetry, and pay attention to how the author uses words, metaphor, and pacing. Scan through the text in a range of newspapers, and consider how the writers manage to tell a complicated story in only a brief article. Listen to people speak, and try adapting the direct and clear phrases you hear to the words of your Act I headlines. If you have good writers on your team, ask them to help write your Act I headlines, and if you have the resources, hire a professional writer to help. The success of your entire presentation rests on the language you use for Act I, so invest the resources necessary to get it right.

And you can put that in writing.

CHAPTER 5

Planning the Rest of Your Slides

IN THIS CHAPTER, YOU WILL:

- Write the headlines for the rest of the slides of the body of your presentation.

- Distill your ideas to their essence.

- Prioritize your ideas, and put them in a meaningful sequence.

THE HEADLINES you wrote for Act I will prepare the working memory of your audience for the crucial first few minutes of a presentation by orienting, interesting, engaging, motivating, and focusing them. Although you might have made quick work of planning these first five slides, things get much more challenging as you plan the rest of the slides in the body of your presentation.

And Now Presenting...Act II

Although you face difficult challenges and have hard choices to make when you create the body of your presentation, Beyond Bullet Points (BBP) is up to the job of helping you complete Act II of your story template. As in Act I, completing the story template for Act II creates a solid foundation that will help you choose exactly what you will show and say as you present the working memory of your audience with new information. With this foundation in place, you'll have endless creative options to make the crisp and clear underlying story even more powerful.

To begin, go to Act II of the BBP Story Template you've started to write, locate the Zoom toolbar in the lower right of the screen, and click and drag the Zoom toolbar so that Act II fills the screen, as shown in Figure 5-1. Here you see the empty cells where you will write the rest of the headlines of Act II following the three ground rules described in the section "Writing Headlines Using Three Ground Rules" in Chapter 3.

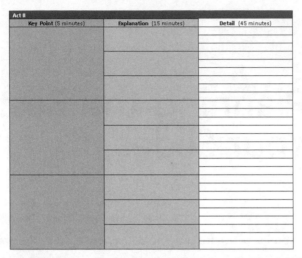

FIGURE 5-1 The cells where you will write the remaining headlines in Act II of the story template.

The specific words you write in these cells in Act II of the story template become the headlines of the rest of the slides of your PowerPoint presentation. But whereas the Act I headlines help you plan only five slides, your Act II headlines will help you plan most of the rest of the slides in the body of your presentation.

A Special Type of Outline

Act II in the story template contains three columns, labeled Key Point, Explanation, and Detail, as shown in Figure 5-2. In the Key Point column, you give the top three reasons your audience should accept your Call to Action headline. The Explanation column contains an additional level of information about the Key Point column headlines, and the Detail column contains the next level of information about the Explanation column headlines.

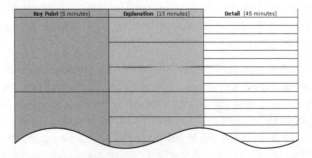

FIGURE 5-2 The three column headings: Key Point, Explanation, and Detail.

One way to understand how Act II works is to see it as a *sentence outline* you might use to write a paper. In a sentence outline, beginning from a single thesis statement, you write out your topic sentences, explanations, and details and organize them by using numbers and letters along with indentation. For example, you write out your first topic sentence and then number it *1*. You then indent and number as *1.a.* the first explanation that follows the topic sentence, and then indent and number as *1.a.i.*, *1.a.ii.*, and *1.a.iii.* the details that follow the explanation, as shown here:

1. Topic sentence (Key Point)
   a. Explanation
      i. Detail
      ii. Detail
      iii. Detail
   b. Explanation

You continue numbering and indenting your sentences in this fashion as you write the rest of the outline.

When you write your presentation outline using your story template, instead of indenting and numbering your headlines, you write them in the corresponding columns of Act II, which are colored according to the levels of indentation. For example, when you view Act II as a sentence outline, as shown in Figure 5-3, your thesis statement corresponds to the dark gray Call To Action cell in Act I (top). Your topic sentences in the first numbered level of your outline correspond to the medium gray Key Point column in Act II (left). The next level of indentation corresponds to the light gray Explanation column (middle), and the next level of indentation corresponds to the white Detail column (right).

OTHER ACT II OPTIONS

Write Act II in a blank Microsoft Word document using a traditional sentence outline if that works better for you—just be sure to write complete sentences as described in the section "Writing Headlines Using Three Ground Rules" in Chapter 3, and discipline yourself to keep your indented headings to three levels. Some BBP practitioners use tools other than Word to write their story templates, including Microsoft Excel, mind-mapping software, and even Post-it notes—visit *www.beyondbulletpoints.com* to learn more.

	Call to Action	
	Thesis statement	

Act II		
Key Point (5 minutes)	**Explanation** (15 minutes)	**Detail** (45 minutes)
Topic Sentence 1	**1.a.**	1.a.i.
		1.a.ii.
		1.a.iii.
	1.b.	1.b.i.
		1.b.ii.
		1.b.iii
	1.c.	1.c.i.
		1.c.ii.
		1.c.iii
Topic Sentence 2	**2.a.**	2.a.i.
		2.a.ii.
		2.a.iii.
	2.b.	2.b.i.
		2.b.ii.
		2.b.iii
	2.c.	2.c.i.
		2.c.ii.
		2.c.iii
Topic Sentence 3	**3.a.**	3.a.i.
		3.a.ii.
		3.a.iii.
	3.b.	3.b.i.
		3.b.ii.
		3.b.iii
	3.c.	3.c.i.
		3.c.ii.
		3.c.iii

FIGURE 5-3 The relationship between the three columns of Act II is similar to the indented levels of headings in a sentence outline.

Built-in Scalability

You'll notice that the column headings in this story template also include time estimates: the Key Point column heading includes the phrase *5 minutes*, the Explanation column heading includes the phrase *15 minutes*, and the Detail column heading includes the phrase *45 minutes*. These time estimates indicate that for any presentation, you choose to complete the columns that correspond to the level of information and length of presentation you want.

The entire story template, including Act I and all three columns in Act II, contains 44 cells, each of which contains a single headline. If you spend an average of one minute per headline, you have enough material for a 45-minute presentation. If you skip the Detail column, you end up with a total of 17 headlines in your story template; if you spend an average of 50 seconds on each, you have enough material for a 15-minute presentation. If you skip the Explanation and Detail columns, you have 8 headlines; if you spend an average of 40 seconds on each, you have a 5-minute presentation.

In this chapter, every cell in the example will eventually contain a headline so that you see how the entire process works.

See Also   The headings in Act II of the story template describe the most common division of levels of information in a presentation. If you want to adapt the headings to align more closely with your profession, see "Tip 3: Tailor Your Act II Column Headings to Your Profession" later in this chapter—it might be worth taking a quick look at these now to keep them in mind as you learn how to use Act II of the story template.

Threading the Eye of the Needle Using a Hierarchy

Act II might look bland and unassuming with its various rows and cells in a Word document, and the idea that it is a form of a traditional sentence outline does not make it seem exceptional. But appearances are deceiving—it is, in fact, a powerful critical-thinking tool that has helped many people in a range of professions to break through intellectual clutter and find a compelling story structure beneath mountains of data, charts, and bullet points. Built into the arrangement of these simple cells is a process that wields tremendous intellectual power to help you get right to the point.

When you use indentations in a sentence outline as described earlier, you are applying a *hierarchy* to your ideas by consciously specifying some ideas (your topic sentences) as more important than other ideas (your explanation), which are in turn more important than other ideas (your details). The relationships between levels of ideas in a hierarchy become clear in a *logic tree*, also called a *tree diagram*—a concept that dates back at least 1700 years. The basic look of the logic tree diagram is recognizable today in the form of an organizational chart. When the logic tree that is built in to Act II of the story template is placed on its side, a triangle drawn around the logic tree shows its shape, as in Figure 5-4. This triangle shape is the powerful tool you will use to distill your ideas to their essence, prioritize them, and arrange them in the sequence in which you will present them in the form of slides to the working memory of your audience.

The concept of a hierarchy illustrated by the triangle in Act II might not be popular these days, with trends moving more toward free-flowing, organic, free-association relationships among people and ideas. But you absolutely need an *idea hierarchy* to help you decide which of your slides are more important than others. You cannot present the working memory of your audience with an unprioritized and unstructured sequence of slides, because you will quickly overwhelm it. A hierarchy breaks up a complex body of information into smaller pieces that are easier for working memory to handle and then prioritizes those pieces and places them in a particular sequence.

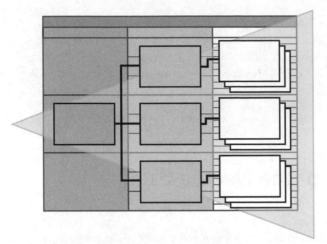

FIGURE 5-4 Act II of the story template is built on the powerful foundation of a hierarchy.

A hierarchy is the natural way people routinely go through a reasoning process—if you are completely new to a topic, you might start with a large amount of unstructured information (bottom of a hierarchy) when you first assemble the many details of the information you want to present. You then apply your reasoning process to sort the information into smaller groups to explain what it means (middle of the hierarchy). Last you develop the key points or conclusion about what you analyzed (top of the hierarchy). You sometimes approach a reasoning process the other way around, as you'll do when you complete Act II in this chapter—if you've already completed the reasoning process by the time you're ready to prepare a presentation, you begin with the key points you want to make, follow those with your explanation, and then follow your explanation with the details. Either approach to Act II is perfectly valid.

Tip   An easy way to remember the essence of Act II is to imagine the audience saying to you as you decide what to keep in your presentation, "1-2-3, show me only what I need to see."

With the hierarchy concept firmly established as the foundation of Act II, it's time to make things practical and apply the hierarchy to the specific slides in the example presentation.

THE POWER OF A PYRAMID

The design of Act II of the story template is inspired by Barbara Minto's book, *The Minto Pyramid Principle: Logic in Writing, Thinking, and Problem Solving* (Minto International, 1996). The book is a sophisticated, thorough, and comprehensive application of a logic tree technique that Minto developed more than 30 years ago to teach management consultants to write business documents more effectively, and she now teaches her approach as an independent consultant to senior executives around the world.

Prioritizing Your Slides

To recap your story so far: Your Act I headlines define the Setting, Role, Point A, Point B, and Call to Action slides. You make your audience's problem clear with the gap between the challenge they face in the Point A headline and where they want to be in the Point B headline. The gap between these headlines forms the dramatic tension for the entire presentation, causing your audience to now pay close attention to find out how they can solve this problem. With this gap wide open, you focus the entire presentation with the Call to Action headline. This makes the headline of the Call to Action slide the top of the triangle, as shown in Figure 5-5, and Act II is the rest of the triangle that will pull your slides through the eye of the needle of your audience's working memory based on a sensible sequence and priority.

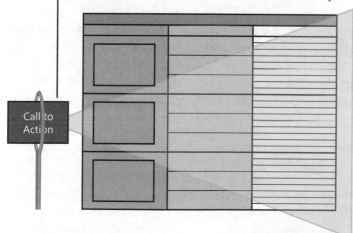

The Call to Action headline focuses all the slides in the hierarchy.

Call to Action

FIGURE 5-5 The tip of the hierarchy is the headline of the Call to Action slide from Act I.

In the example presentation, your proposed Call to Action headline is to "Change your way of thinking to get breakthrough results," as shown in Figure 5-6.

Call to Action
Change your way of thinking to get breakthrough results

FIGURE 5-6 The Call to Action cell from Act I with the headline completed.

Now that your audience knows your recommended Call to Action headline, they're eager to hear why and how it is a good idea, which is what you'll justify next. Focusing exclusively on explaining your Call to Action headline in Act II gives you the criteria you need to reduce the amount of information in your presentation. You'll include only information that supports your reasons for recommending the Call to Action headline and exclude everything else.

> **See Also**   As you work on Act II, refer to the completed story templates available at www.beyondbulletpoints.com. These templates include a range of Act II examples from different types of presentations.

Justifying the Call to Action Headline with the Key Point Headlines

As you begin Act II, your first goal is to write the headlines for the most important slides you will present. If your audience will remember only three key points in your presentation, you need to know specifically where those corresponding slides are in your presentation and allow ample time to show them and speak about them. To create these important slides, you will justify your Call to Action headline. You'll do this by boiling down to only three Key Point headlines the reasons why your audience should accept your recommended call to action or the main steps that describe how they should implement it. You will accomplish that by writing three headlines in the first column of Act II.

> **See Also**   It's always a good idea to limit your ideas to groups of three, as described in "Tip 1: The Power of Three" later in this chapter. But if you need to expand your groupings to four, use the expanded template version that's described in "Tip 2: Make Room for Four." Remember that working memory can hold three to four chunks of new information at any one time, so if you try to present more than that, you'll quickly overwhelm it.

To begin filling in Act II in the story template, position your cursor to the right of the Key Point column heading. If the Call to Action headline recommends your audience do something, they will want to know *why* they should do it. If your Call to Action head-line recommends they follow a set of steps, they will want to know *how*. This is a critical decision-making point, because whether you choose *why* or *how* will shape every slide to follow in Act II.

If you choose *why*, you are giving the entire presentation a persuasive orientation. If you choose *how*, you are giving the entire presentation an explanatory orientation. When the singular focus of the presentation is to persuade someone to do or think something, choose *why*. When the audience already has agreed to the idea and now your singu-lar focus is to explain something, choose *how*. Create a hybrid persuasive-explanatory presentation by choosing *how* for the first column and *why* for the others, or vice versa.

Choose the question that best describes what your audience will want to know next about your Call to Action headline, and type the question to the right of the Key Point column heading—in this case, **How?**—as shown in Figure 5-7.

Act II		
Key Point (5 minutes) **How?**	**Explanation** (15 minutes)	**Detail** (45 minutes)

FIGURE 5-7 The Key Point column indicates the question "How?"

THREE CRITICAL DECISION POINTS

The three critical decision points that have the biggest impact on your presen-tation are these: identifying in Act I the gap between a challenge the audience faces in the Point A headline and where they want to be in the Point B headline; defining in Act I the Call to Action headline that focuses the entire presentation; and choosing in Act II *why* or *how* for your Key Point headlines, which determines whether the rest of your presentation will have a persuasive or an explanatory orientation.

Your Key Point column heading now indicates the question that your audience is won-dering about your call to action—in this case, "*How* do I change my way of thinking to get breakthrough results?" You'll answer their question by explaining the three main ways how they should change their thinking. Follow the three ground rules described in the section "Writing Headlines Using Three Ground Rules" in Chapter 3 to write out your headlines in each of the three medium gray cells of the Key Point column, prioritizing them in descending order of importance. The more concise your Key Point headlines are, the easier they will be to remember, so limit them to a maximum of about two and a half lines, as shown in Figure 5-8.

Your first Key Point headline states "Review what you know"; the second Key Point headline states "Step outside your assumptions"; and your last Key Point headline states "Step back inside to a new way of thinking." These three Key Point headlines are clear, concise, and literally to the point(s), giving your audience a sense of coherence and focus as you develop the details of the information to come. It will be relatively easy for working memory to hold on to these most meaningful visual and verbal pieces and integrate the information into long-term memory.

FIGURE 5-8 Act II of the story template, with the Key Point column cells completed—note the parallel construction of the headlines across the cells.

Your three Key Point headlines might come easily if you've been thinking about these issues for a long time and you simply write them down. Or they might take some work because you're still figuring them out and you need to cluster together related ideas in a single main idea. If you're at a loss for words, try an interviewing technique by asking someone to read the Key Point column question out loud to you. Speak your answers out loud as you formulate them, and then type them in the Key Point column cells.

| Tip ✓ | It is not always easy to boil down complexity to its essence, but it's critical that you do so to reduce the amount of information you present to the limited capacity of your audience's working memory. You simply cannot show and narrate 100 possibilities; rather, the aim is to distill the information to the three most meaningful concepts. Finding the essence is about simplicity rather than simplification; it's about raising the cream of your critical thinking to the top, not the fluff. |

If you're still not sure of your answers, draft a placeholder set of Key Point headlines so that you have a place to start. You will want to spend ample time on writing the Key Point headlines because together with the Call to Action headline, they are the most important information you want your audience to remember and apply.

As you formulate your Key Point headlines, think of how they will read when you present them in their corresponding sequence of slides. After you create a slide from each of these headlines in Chapter 6, you will sketch initial ideas to illustrate each of these headlines, as shown in Figure 5-9. When you imagine your headlines visually as slides like this, you get a better sense of how they will relate to one another as you present them. The goal is to make these three Key Point headlines a neatly coordinated package that flows together from one idea to the next so that it will be easy to illustrate them when you get to your sketches later.

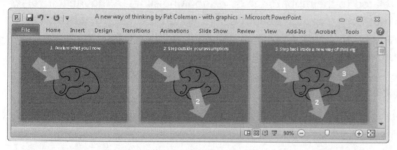

FIGURE 5-9 Keep in mind how your Key Point headlines will become the foundation for a visual story you tell across the corresponding slides in the storyboard.

Improving Your Key Points

Tighten the relationship among these three Key Point headlines, and increase their memorability by carrying your motif from Act I through their wording. Remember, a motif is about much more than being clever—it is about finding a familiar structure from your audience's long-term memory that will ease the introduction of new information into working memory. For example, if you use the puzzle motif in the Call to Action headline *Put the three pieces of the puzzle together to change your way of thinking*, place in front of each Key Point headline the corresponding phrase: *Puzzle Piece 1*, *Puzzle Piece 2*, and *Puzzle Piece 3*. You could use a puzzle motif in two different ways, with the puzzle pieces of the three points either revealing or concealing the final picture.

There are endless ways to lay out the top-level story thread across your Key Point headlines. Whatever you decide depends on what you carry through from the Call to Action headline in Act I. For example, extend a chronology across your Key Point headlines based on the Call to Action headline *Follow the story through the three crucial time periods*, or use a simple list format based on the Call to Action headline *Check off the three items* or *Follow the three parts*. Heighten engagement and suspense through the three Key Point headlines by withholding what will happen, as in *Uncover the three secrets* or *Follow the three clues*—allowing the audience to get involved and fill in the blanks for themselves. A trial attorney might tap into a familiar story structure for an opening statement at a jury trial by following a formula such as *Motive + means = death* or one of its variations such as *Denial + deception = injury*. For inspiration on motifs, review the sample phrases to begin your Call to Action headlines in Appendix D and consider how you could carry the same themes through the language of the Key Point headlines.

Whichever way you decide to go with your motif, make sure you integrate it through the wording of the Call to Action and the Key Point headlines because later you will apply a similar visual design related to the motif to the corresponding slides. Although it is sufficient to integrate a motif only through a set of Call to Action and Key Point headlines, you may want to extend it through the Explanation headlines if it works. Don't stretch a motif beyond its sensible limits, though—remember from Chapter 4 that a motif has to resonate with you audience, and if it starts to sound trite or overused, it will hurt your message rather than help it.

When you've entered your three headlines in the Key Point column, test them by filling in the blanks in this sentence:

> *The three main reasons/ways* (insert audience from Act I) *should* (insert Call to Action headline) *are* (insert Key Point headline 1), (insert Key Point headline 2), *and* (insert Key Point headline 3).

In this presentation example, the completed sentence reads:

> *The three main ways you (the team members) should change the way you think are review what you know, step outside your assumptions, and step back inside to a new way of thinking.*

THE KEY POINT HEADLINES TEST

Test the three Key Point headlines by filling in the blanks in this sentence:

> *The three main reasons/ways* (insert audience from Act I) *should* (insert Call to Action headline) *are* (insert Key Point headline 1), (insert Key Point headline 2), *and* (insert Key Point headline 3).

For this sentence to sound right, each Key Point headline should be written in a similar form and should contain a similar type of information. Just as the Key Point headlines explain the Call to Action headline, the Call to Action headline should also summarize the Key Point headlines.

Your Call to Action and Key Point headlines should neatly distill to the essence what you want to communicate in your presentation and define your measure of success—if your audience can remember and apply these points, you've succeeded in your presentation mission. If your measure for success is not present in the wording of your Call to Action and Key Point headlines, you go back and change the wording so that the core of your message is clear and visible without a doubt.

As you test your three Key Point headlines, you might find that the Call to Action headline isn't exactly what you intended and you need to go back and revise it or entirely rework Act I. Or you might need to revise your three Key Point headlines to make sure that each supports the Call to Action headline in a way that makes your test sentence sound right. You'll probably need to do a couple of rounds of testing and revising before you're satisfied with your results and are ready to move on to the next step.

When you have written your three Key Point headlines, you have made sure that you will justify the Call to Action slide with the Key Point slides that follow it. Your Call to Action and Key Point headlines form the most important information at the top level of the hierarchy, as shown in Figure 5-10, which defines the most important and meaningful information that you want your audience's working memory to engage and integrate into long-term memory.

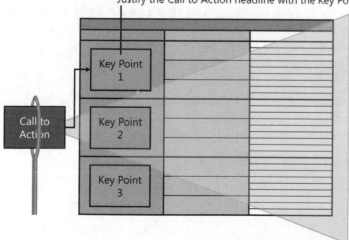

Justify the Call to Action headline with the Key Point headlines.

FIGURE 5-10 The top of your slide hierarchy consists of your most important slides—the Call to Action slide and the three Key Point slides. In a sentence outline, the Call to Action slide corresponds to the thesis statement and the Key Point slides correspond to topic sentences 1, 2, and 3.

Clarifying Each Key Point Headline with Its Explanation Headlines

Now that you've written the headlines for the Key Point slides, the next step is to write the headlines for the second-most important slides—the Explanation slides. Each Act II *scene* in your story template is represented by a horizontal row of cells that begins with each Key Point cell and extends to the right to include all the adjacent cells in the Explanation and Detail columns, as shown in Figure 5-11.

Act II		
Key Point (5 minutes) **How?**	**Explanation** (15 minutes)	**Detail** (45 minutes)
Review what you know		

FIGURE 5-11 Act II, Scene 1, extends horizontally from left to right in the story template.

As in this example, the headline in the single Key Point cell anchors each Act II scene by maintaining a singular focus horizontally across all three columns. The Explanation and Detail columns will flesh out the main idea in increasing depth as you enter the headlines of your scene from left to right, top to bottom. This keeps all the pieces of information related to the single Key Point headline organized and coherent.

To start writing the rest of Act II, Scene 1, position your cursor to the right of the Explanation column heading and type the question (either *why* or *how*) that your audience will want to know next about your three Key Points headlines—in this case, **How?** Reread your Key Point headline, and ask yourself *how* this is true—in this case, "*How* do we review what we know?" As you did in the Key Point column, type your three answers in descending order of importance in the three cells of the Explanation column. When you enter your first reason in the top cell of the Explanation column, your story template should look similar to Figure 5-12.

Act II		
Key Point (5 minutes) **How?**	**Explanation** (15 minutes) **How?**	**Detail** (45 minutes)
Review what you know	We currently follow a 3-step process	

FIGURE 5-12 Act II, Scene 1, with the top cell of the Explanation column completed.

Enter your second answer in the cell below, and enter the third answer in the cell below that, as shown in Figure 5-13. Your Explanation column answers should offer more detailed support for your Key Point headline and cite specific evidence, such as findings from research, case studies, financial analysis, or anecdotes.

Act II		
Key Point (5 minutes) **How?**	**Explanation** (15 minutes) **How?**	**Detail** (45 minutes)
Review what you know	We currently follow a 3-step process	
	But the process isn't working anymore	
	If we stay on this path, we'll be out of business	

FIGURE 5-13 Testing the three headlines in the Explanation column to make sure that they support the Key Point to the left.

Test the three answers in the Explanation column by filling in the blanks in this sentence:

> *The three main reasons/ways* (insert Key Point headline) *are* (insert Explanation column, answer 1), (insert Explanation column, answer 2), *and* (insert Explanation column, answer 3).

In this example, the test sentence reads as follows:

> *The three main ways to review what we know are we currently follow a three-step process, but the process isn't working anymore, and if we stay on this path, we'll be out of business.*

As in your earlier test sentence, for this sentence to sound right, each answer should be written in a similar way and should contain a similar type of information. Apply this test visually by reading the test sentence from the left column to the right. You should also test the headlines the other way, from the right column to the left—after you read your three Explanation column headlines, you should find that the Key Point headline summarizes them.

Just as you thought of the Key Point headlines as a tightly related package of thoughts that you will show over a sequence of slides, think of the Explanation headlines the same way. The headlines from the three Explanation column cells in Figure 5-13 will form the headlines for the corresponding Explanation slides in the storyboard, and the sketches in Figure 5-14 show how the sequence of ideas in this example is the foundation for a three-part visual story.

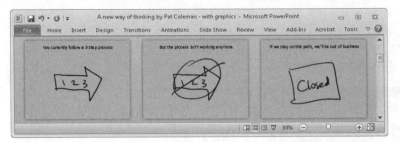

FIGURE 5-14 Keep in mind how your Explanation headlines will become the foundation for a visual story you tell across the corresponding slides in the storyboard.

Breaking up the explanation of each Key Point headline into smaller pieces that you will show and narrate reduces cognitive load across a sequence of slides. This aligns with the research-based *temporal contiguity principle*, which explains that people learn better when animation and narration are presented simultaneously. For example, if you were to show an entire diagram first and then the narration later, you would split the attention of your audience as their working memory struggles to coordinate what it sees and what it hears. The story template ensures that you break up every explanation into digestible pieces, so you end up tightly coordinating what you say and what you show, one idea at a time.

Organize your ideas within the cells of the Explanation column using a "checklist" structure, a chronology, a list, a 1-2-3 sequence, or any other way you might explain an idea in three parts.

THE EXPLANATION HEADLINES TEST

Test the three Explanation headlines by filling in the blanks in this sentence:

> *The three main reasons/ways* (insert Key Point headline) *are* (insert Explanation column, answer 1), (insert Explanation column, answer 2), *and* (insert Explanation column, answer 3).

When you have written your Explanation headlines, you have made sure that you will clarify each Key Point slide with the Explanation slides that follow it. The Explanation slides form the middle of the slide hierarchy, as shown in Figure 5-15, which presents the second-most important informational pieces to working memory—the sub-parts of your Key Point headlines.

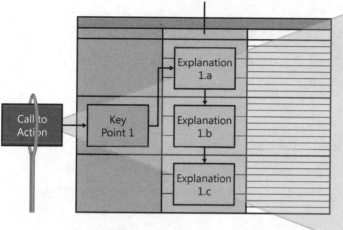

Clarify each Key Point headline with its Explanation headlines.

FIGURE 5-15 The middle of your slide hierarchy consists of your second-most important slides—the Explanation slides. In an indented sentence outline, these slides correspond to outline items 1.a.,1.b., and 1.c.

Backing Up Each Explanation Headline with Its Detail Headlines

Now that you've written the headlines for your Key Point and Explanation slides, the last step is to back up each Explanation headline by writing headlines for its Detail slides. Fill in the Detail column using the same techniques you used for the Explanation column. Position your cursor to the right of the Detail column heading, and type the question (*why* or *how*) your audience will want to know next about your Explanation headlines—in this case, **How?** The questions you choose for your column headings will vary according to your topic, and sometimes they might be all *why*, all *how*, or combinations of the two. Now read each headline in the Explanation column, and ask why or how that headline is true. In this example, you'll be asking the question *how*, as in: "*How* do we currently follow a three-step process?"

As you did in the Key Point and Explanation columns, type your three answers in the three cells of the Detail column in descending order of importance—the cells will expand to hold your text. Keep your headlines limited to about two and a half lines, as you did in the other two columns. The answers you enter in the Detail column should offer more detailed support for the Explanation headline and cite specific evidence that backs it up, as shown in Figure 5-16. This is where you include quantitative information, case studies, charts, graphs, anecdotes, analysis, and any other details that support the Explanation headline in the column to the left.

Act II		
Key Point (5 minutes) **How?**	**Explanation** (15 minutes) **How?**	**Detail** (45 minutes) **How?**
Review what you know	We currently follow a 3-step process	We study the market using our proprietary set of tools
		We build a product based on what we've learned
		We market the product to our target segments
	But the process isn't working anymore	
	If we stay on this path, we'll be out of business	

FIGURE 5-16 Testing the three Detail headlines to make sure they back up the Explanation headline to the left.

As with the Key Point and Explanation headlines, think of the way you will end up presenting these headlines visually in a sequence of slides, as shown in Figure 5-17. As before, you are breaking up the previous column's headline into smaller pieces that you will present visually and verbally across slides. Whatever specific wording you choose for each Detail headline, you will back it up by the appropriate type of visual evidence, whether it is a screen capture, chart, graph, photograph, diagram, or other illustration. And just as you did in the previous columns, organize your headlines in a wide range of formats, including chronological, before-and-after results, 1-2-3 lists, and more.

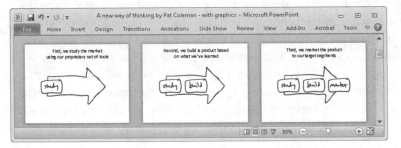

FIGURE 5-17 Keep in mind how your Detail headlines will become the foundation for a visual story you tell across the corresponding slides in the storyboard.

After you've entered three answers in the Detail column, test them by filling in the blanks in this sentence:

> *The three main reasons/ways* (insert Explanation column headline) *are* (insert Detail column, answer 1), (insert Detail column, answer 2), *and* (insert Detail column, answer 3).

In this example, the test headline would read as follows:

> *The three main ways we currently follow a three-step process are we study the market using our proprietary set of tools, we build a product based on what we've learned, and we market the product to our target segments*

After you test your Detail column answers, go to the second Explanation headline and repeat this process for its corresponding Detail headlines. Then go to the third Explanation headline and repeat the process for its Detail headlines. When you've finished, you will have completed Act II, Scene 1, of your story template, as shown in Figure 5-18.

Act II		
Key Point (5 minutes) **How?**	**Explanation** (15 minutes) **How?**	**Detail** (45 minutes) **How?**
Review what you know	We currently follow a 3-step process	We study the market using our proprietary set of tools
		We build a product based on what we've learned
		We market the product to our target segments
	But the process isn't working anymore	Sales dropped last quarter
		Our research shows our products stayed on the shelf longer
		We weren't able to reach our market through traditional channels
	If we stay on this path, we'll be out of business	This is a red flag moment
		The trend is worrisome as you look at it over time
		If we stay on this track, we'll be in the red by the fourth quarter of next year

FIGURE 5-18 Act II, Scene 1, of the sample story template, with all cells completed.

THE DETAIL HEADLINES TEST

Test the three Detail headlines by filling in the blanks in this sentence:

The three main reasons/ways (insert Explanation headline) *are* (insert Detail column, answer 1), (insert Detail column, answer 2), *and* (insert Detail column, answer 3).

As always, it is helpful to think of how your headlines will play out across the slides of your storyboard. In Figure 5-19, the Detail headlines tell the story of the second Explanation headline in the form of an anecdote told chronologically across the three slides.

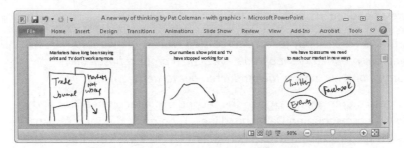

FIGURE 5-19 Sketches showing how the Detail headlines tell a chronological story.

In Figure 5-20, the Detail headlines play out differently, as sketches of charts and screen captures explain the third Explanation headline with a step-by-step sequence of details across the slides.

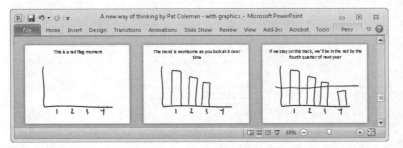

FIGURE 5-20 Sketches showing how the Detail headlines relate quantitative information across slides.

When you have written your Detail headlines, you have made sure that you will back up each Explanation slide with the Detail slides that follow it. This is the bottom of the hierarchy, as shown in Figure 5-21, which presents the third-most important informational pieces to working memory.

Now that you've finished writing the headlines for Act II, Scene 1, it's time to move on to Scenes 2 and 3.

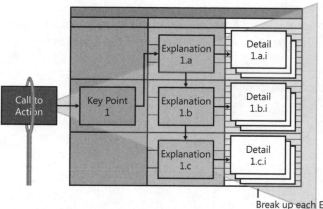

Break up each Explanation
slide with its Detail slides

FIGURE 5-21 The bottom of your hierarchy consists of your third-most important slides—the Detail slides. In a classical indented outline, these slides correspond to outline items 1.a.i., 1.b.i., 1.c.i., and so on.

Fleshing Out the Rest of Act II

With Act II, Scene 1, complete, your final job is to write the headlines for the rest of the slides in Act II. You'll do this by applying the same process to both Scene 2 and Scene 3. Continue to check your reasoning with test sentences at each level, and revise your story template headlines as needed to keep the test sentences clear and consistent.

Act II of the story template is structured using groups of three ideas to make your ideas easier for your audience to understand, but you might find that you don't have exactly three supporting headlines to write at any level in the template. If you want to use only two headlines, simply leave the third cell blank. If you need to add a fourth cell to the Explanation or Detail column, position the cursor in a cell, right-click, and select Insert Row—if the extra row creates extra cells in the Key Point and Explanation columns, merge the new cells into adjacent cells within the column. If you need to create four Key Point headlines, see "Tip 2: Make Room for Four," later in this chapter. If you have more than four Key Point headlines, find a way to reduce that number, either by reworking your ideas or by merging several ideas into one main headline.

If you are having difficulty completing any point of the story template, try tackling it from a different direction. This chapter followed a process of completing Act II working from the top of the hierarchy to the bottom (from left to right in the story template), which you may choose to do if you know your topic well. If you're not completely sure of your message or your Key Point headlines, start first from the Detail column on the right, and work left through the Explanation column and finally the Key Point column.

When you complete the three scenes of Act II, your story template will likely extend across more than one page. In the completed Act II section of this story template, shown in Figure 5-22, the Detail column headlines have been abbreviated to display the three scenes on a single page.

Act II		
Key Point (5 minutes) **How?**	**Explanation** (15 minutes) **How?**	**Detail** (45 minutes) **How?**
Review what you know	We currently follow a 3-step process	We study the market using...
		We build a product based on ...
		We market the product to...
	But the process isn't working anymore	Sales dropped last quarter
		Our research shows our products
		We weren't able to reach our...
	If we stay on this path, we'll be out of business	This is a red flag moment
		The trend is worrisome as...
		If we stay on this track, we'll...
Step outside your assumptions	Assume the market isn't stable	Our marketing consultants ...
		The trends show this will ...
		We have to assume that ...
	Assume products have shorter lives	The average life of a product ...
		Research confirms consumer ...
		We have to assume products...
	Assume marketing isn't working anymore	Marketers have long been ...
		Our numbers show print and ...
		We have to assume we need ...
Step back inside a new way of thinking	Reconsider what a market is	The fixed market is giving way...
		Several market leaders have ...
		Instead of fixed markets, think...
	Reconsider what a product is	Products are one-time efforts...
		Several of our competitors...
		Instead of a finished product...
	Reconsider what marketing is	Social media has opened up ...
		Our competitors have had...
		Instead of 1-way media buys...

FIGURE 5-22 Act II of the sample story template, with all three scenes completed.

Each idea you introduce in the presentation will prompt your audience to wonder, "*Why* or *how* is this true?" Because each column in your story template is set up to answer the question *why* or *how*, you provide immediate answers. In story terms, this creates a steady dynamic of action/reaction—one column is an "action," and the next column is a "reaction" to it. This dynamic structure in Act II helps you to examine all the possible directions for your story. It also helps you to align your information with the way people naturally think and reason, making your story more interesting and engaging.

AN INTELLECTUAL MACHETE

Just as much as you need to identify what you want to include in a presentation, the hierarchy in Act II is equally important for the *potential* slides it leaves out of a presentation. The built-in hierarchy of Act II guides you through a sometimes difficult but disciplined critical-thinking process that forces you to decide what to include in a presentation and what to leave out. The process of completing Act II acts like an intellectual machete that chops away unneeded data so that clarity shines through.

You will find that there is a great deal of information that did not make it into your presentation. If you're missing something important, go back and include it in your headlines. What does not make it into the hierarchy, such as detailed quantitative analysis, can be captured and documented and can then be handed out before, during, or after the presentation.

When you have written the rest of your Act II headlines, you have made sure that you have fleshed out the rest of the slides of your presentation. Now every slide in your presentation will be prioritized in your slide hierarchy, as shown in Figure 5-23.

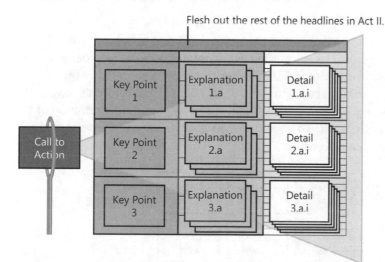

FIGURE 5-23 You determine the rest of your slide hierarchy when you flesh out the rest of your slides in Act II, and in the process you have prioritized every slide.

Don't worry about Act III of your story template at this point—you'll quickly take care of that soon when you add graphics to the storyboard in Chapter 8.

BBP CHECKLIST: PLANNING THE REST OF YOUR SLIDES

Do the rest of your headlines in Act II accomplish the following:

- Justify your Call to Action headline with your key points?
- Clarify your Key Point headlines with further explanation?
- Back up your Explanation headlines with the appropriate detail?
- Put your ideas in a logical sequence and priority?
- Integrate your motif verbally through your headlines?

Pulling Through What's Most Important First

Now that you've completed the story template, you have accomplished what you set out to do at the start of the chapter—that is, prioritizing your ideas and finding the right sequence in which to present them. The three columns of Act II established the priority of your ideas from Key Point headlines at the top of the informational hierarchy, to Explanation headlines in the middle, to Detail headlines at the bottom. The process of creating Act II helps you write out information in complete thoughts, rather than lists and fragments that the audience has to sort through. Now there is a clear flow that connects each idea to the next in a logical way.

When you next import your headlines into Microsoft PowerPoint to become your storyboard in Chapter 6, your slides will automatically appear in the same order you wrote them in Act II, as shown in Figure 5-24. In your storyboard, you will cue the audience to the levels of the hierarchy with the slide layouts and backgrounds as you present each idea in the sequence you wrote them. This is an important innovation of the BBP approach that has both prioritized your ideas with a hierarchy and prepared them for a logical sequence in your storyboard.

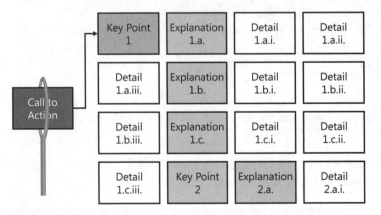

FIGURE 5-24 The hierarchy provides both a priority for your slides and a proper sequence in which to show them.

As described earlier, writing your slide headlines using the Act II columns has now given your presentation an important scalability that will play out when you work in PowerPoint. When you create a presentation with three columns, you are prioritizing your ideas in order of importance, from left to right. If you have a 45-minute presentation, you'll present all your slides in Act II. If your time is unexpectedly cut to 15 minutes, you'll skip the Detail slides, and if your time is cut to 5 minutes, you'll also skip the Explanation slides. Because you have applied the power of a hierarchy to prioritize your ideas, you scale up or down to the level of information appropriate to the time you have, without sacrificing the integrity or the clarity of your thinking at any level.

But perhaps most important, what you've done in Act II reduces cognitive load by easing working memory into new information by presenting what is most significant first. Typical PowerPoint presentations show the details first, then the explanation of the details, and finally the key points—the recommendations or conclusions—at the end. Other presentations simply display lists of detail without any explanation or key points at all to provide context or a framework for understanding the detail. Either way, this approach tries to jam the wide bottom of the hierarchy through the eye of the needle, as shown in Figure 5-25. If you present all the details first, the working memory of your audience has to struggle to retain that information until it knows where your presentation is going.

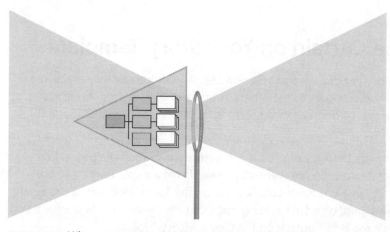

FIGURE 5-25 When you present the details first, you quickly overwhelm working memory.

With BBP, you always pull through the eye of the needle what's most important first, as shown in Figure 5-26. That's because Act II of your story template flips the typical outline around, presenting the most important information first and the supporting information after. By presenting the tip, and the top, of the hierarchy first, you reduce the cognitive load on your audience by focusing first on what's essential and leaving out extraneous information that could overwhelm the eye of the needle.

Now, instead of the details and data driving the presentation, the proper management of the working memory of your audience is driving the presentation, which aligns with the three research realities described in Chapter 2.

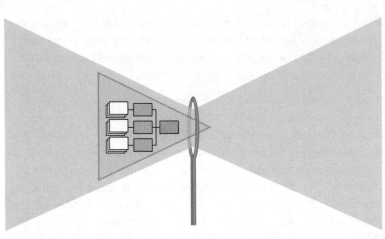

FIGURE 5-26 When you present the most important information first, you properly manage working memory and provide a framework for the rest of the explanation and details to come.

Lowering the Curtain on Your Story Template

One benefit of your story template is that you now see all your ideas in one place and quickly grasp how each idea relates to the others. A printout of your story template at this point will guide you through an initial reading of your story to make sure that everything sounds right.

Review your story template before you print it. If it extends over multiple pages, you might need to split Act II into separate scenes that each fit on a page. To do this, position the cursor in any cell in a Key Point column, and on the Table Tools tab, click Layout; and then in the Merge group, click Split Table to split that row from the row above. If you change your mind, click the Undo button on the Quick Access Toolbar.

As this book describes, the story template is the hard-working intellectual and structural engine that makes everything in your PowerPoint presentation work, or not. It is the battleground that determines whether your presentation is a success or failure. If you have an elegant infrastructure, the more time you spend on the presentation, the simpler it will get. If you don't have a solid structure, the more time you spend on it, the more confusing it will get.

If you get the headlines right, they will clarify and expand understanding; but if you get them wrong, you will lead your audience in the wrong direction, in a fruitless, frustrating waste of time. That's why it's important to spend as much time as possible editing, tightening, and clarifying your words.

Just as you use your story template to see and manage all your headlines at a glance, other people can use it to review your story too. If you're working with only a few people, display the story template on your computer screen and make edits together. If you're working with a larger group and want to call a meeting to review your headlines, send a copy of the story template Word document through e-mail to all the members of the team in advance.

■ **IMPORTANT** Don't move forward from this stage of the process until you finalize your story template and get agreement from everyone who has a stake in your presentation.

Get agreement on the story template from anyone who has a stake in the presentation. This includes the members of your team, people in other departments of your organization, and anyone who needs to give clearance and approval for what you'll say.

Using your story template as a review document, make quick adjustments to your wording or structure and invite others to contribute their expertise and take ownership in the success of your presentation. Getting approval for your story template allows everyone to focus on your ideas instead of on design issues, which would prove distracting right now. When you get final approval of the structure and sequence of your story up front, you'll reduce the likelihood that you'll need to spend unnecessary time and effort later, after you've invested time in the design process.

Tip
✓ When you meet with others in person, either project the story template on the wall or print copies of your story template and bring them to the meeting. Talk through the ideas in the order in which you rehearsed them, and discuss the options you have to scale down the story if your presentation time is reduced from 45 minutes to 15 or 5.

Before you move on to the next major step in the BBP approach—storyboarding your script—read through the following 10 tips to find ideas that might improve your story template.

10 Tips for Enhancing Your Story Template

With your story template in hand, rest assured that you have a focused tale to tell at your next presentation. When you're comfortable with the basics of completing your template, try improvising on the concept using these 10 tips.

Tip 1: The Power of Three

As much as you might want to load up your PowerPoint slides with data, the quantity of new information that people can understand is always constrained by the limitations of working memory. As mentioned in Chapter 2, you help your audience to understand information better by presenting new information to working memory in groups of three.

Your story template helps you to organize your ideas in groups of three in multiple ways. The essence of your story consists of your Call to Action headline and your three Key Point headlines. Each Key Point headline has three supporting headlines, listed in the Explanation column. Each Explanation headline has three supporting headlines as well, listed in the Detail column. It might be challenging to boil down your headlines to groups of three in this structure, but your hard work will pay off: your audience will more easily absorb, remember, and understand your ideas.

Tip 2: Make Room for Four

Although three is a powerful number, you might find while working in Act II of your story template that you have four points to make in a column. As described earlier in this chapter, if you have fewer points to make in any section than you have cells, simply leave the cells blank; if you want to add another cell, you insert one. If you'd like to try other versions of story templates with four columns across, or four rows per Act II scene, visit *www.beyondbulletpoints.com*. The disadvantage of using a template with four levels of information is that the number of cells might significantly increase the size and complexity of your presentation. Keep in mind that the more headlines you have, the more time you need and the more information people need to process. To avoid long and complicated presentations, try to stick to three points rather than four.

Tip 3: Tailor Your Act II Column Headings to Your Profession

The headings of the three columns of Act II are based on the most common categorization of information in a hierarchy. But there are many other ways to look at these columns—if one of the alternatives shown in the following list works better for you in your profession, simply type over the existing headings in your story template to replace them with new headings.

The most common categories for the three columns are Key Point, Explanation, and Detail:

Act II		
Key Point	Explanation	Detail

If you're a market researcher, your column headings might be Recommendation, Explanation, and BackupData:

Act II

Recommendation	Explanation	Backup Data

If you're a lawyer, your column headings might be Main Point, Explanation, and Evidence:

Act II

Main Point	Explanation	Evidence

If you're an analyst, your column headings might be Conclusion, Analysis, and Fact:

Act II

Conclusion	Analysis	Fact

If you're an executive, your column headings might be Summary, Breakdown, and Backup:

Act II

Summary	Breakdown	Backup

If you're a salesperson, your column headings might be Benefit, Feature, and Demonstration:

Act II

Benefit	Feature	Demonstration

If you're a writer, your column headings might be Act, Scene, and Action:

Act II

Act	Scene	Action

If you're a journalist, your column headings might be Lead, Body, and Detail:

Act II

Lead	Body	Detail

If you're a teacher or an instructor, your column headings might be Lesson, Explanation, and Detail:

Act II

Lesson	Explanation	Detail

Tip 4: Story Templates for Teams

Act II works well for teams and organizations that have multiple points they have to make to different audiences. For example, most groups have a finite set of Key Point headlines they might want to write about a topic, so someone in the group can create additional Act II scenes to cover those. When you are ready to present, you display only the scenes you choose and hide the rest. This can also be done with Act I variations as you create a range of story template "shells" from frequently used story structures.

Tip 5: The Story Nugget

A *story nugget* is a telling detail that encapsulates, distills, and frames the entire story—for example, the $6,000 shower curtain represented to most people the excess of company executives found guilty of taking money from a large, international corporation as reported in the news. Place a story nugget in one of the headlines in Act I as an encapsulation of the whole story, or place it as a detail in a strategic place in the Detail column. If the information is truly important and you want to be sure it's remembered and applied, integrate it into the Key Point headlines. If your points are already clear, place the story nuggets somewhere in your presentation for your audience to discover and remember.

Tip 6: BBP Beyond PowerPoint

People have reported using the BBP Story Template for a wide range of purposes beyond PowerPoint presentations, including to structure e-mail messages, curriculum design, radio spots, ads, and classroom outlines. When you're at a loss for words or are bogged down or frustrated with writing or communicating, open up a story template. The reliability and simplicity of the structure can break an intellectual or creative logjam by providing clarity and focus. Give it a try, and see what clarity it can help you uncover beyond PowerPoint.

Tip 7: Build an Outline in a Brainstorm

Your Act II headlines have to come from somewhere. If they don't flow easily from your imagination, you might need to loosen things up with a little brainstorming. A number of excellent books and online resources such as *www.innovationtools.com* are available to help you to brainstorm new ideas either on your own or with your team. Whatever technique you decide to use, you need to understand the relationship between the fruit of your brainstorming labor and the story template process you undertake in Act II.

Brainstorming is the art of generating ideas for a particular purpose; it supports an environment of free-flowing thinking without constraints. *Presentation development* is the art of selecting and prioritizing ideas; it calls on a different set of skills, including critical thinking, selection, prioritization, and reasoning.

When you've finished your brainstorming exercises, the story template helps you select the ideas that best support the focus of your presentation. As you begin to work on Act II, gather all the brainstorming ideas you might have on hand, whether they're in the form of lists, note cards, whiteboard diagrams, or other formats. Then apply the process of writing your Act II headlines described in this chapter.

At times, you might need to switch back into a brainstorming mode when you're stuck on a headline or if your Act II structure isn't working. But when you've generated fresh ideas, it's time to switch back into story template mode to select appropriate ideas that support the focus of your presentation.

Brainstorming and using the story template are different but complementary techniques, and when you alternate the two, you have the best of both worlds—the correct selection of the freshest ideas that support your singular story.

Tip 8: Tap Your Team's Talents

Consider working with your team to structure your ideas in Act II. By connecting a projector to your computer, you are able to display a number of software tools that allow you to work with your team to develop your Act II headlines. Or build your own tables or logic trees using Microsoft Visio, Microsoft OneNote, or the PowerPoint organization chart feature.

If you don't have a projector or you prefer a hands-on approach, use a sheet of paper, a flip chart, or a whiteboard to draw your logic tree. Or write your draft Act II headlines on sticky notes and affix them to a wall to build a logic tree, as described in David Straker's *Rapid Problem Solving with Post-it Notes* (Fisher Books, 1997). Experiment with a range of techniques and tools until you find what works best for you and your team to focus and prioritize your ideas. When you've finished, return to your Word document and enter your headlines in the story template.

Some people think clearly and quickly at the top level, others at the detail level. If you're caught up in the detail, step back and ask a top-level thinker/organizer to help.

When it comes to creating the story template, you'll probably find that tapping into the talents of your team will build the best presentation possible.

Tip 9: Take the Express Elevator

When entrepreneurs begin to approach investors to raise money for a venture, they're expected to have something called an *elevator pitch*. The idea is that they pitch their company within the length of time of an elevator ride. Even if you're not trying to raise money for your company, you might need to give your own version of an elevator pitch if you get a call from your boss before you give your presentation and she says, "I'm sorry, but I can't make it to your presentation—can you tell me quickly what you're going to say?"

In every case, you'll be clear about what you're going to say after you complete your story template. To respond to your boss, give your own elevator pitch by first summarizing your Act I headlines and then describing each of your Key Point headlines in Act II of your story template. This sets the context for the presentation and covers the high-level points. If your boss is interested in knowing more about any particular point, elaborate more as needed by providing more supporting information from the Explanation and Detail columns.

This handy technique is not just for elevator pitches and verbal summaries. If you have to write the marketing description for your talk, you've got the outline already written in the story template in the form of your Act I and Act II Key Point column headlines. If you want to let other people know the structure of your talk in advance, summarize it in the same way in an e-mail message. In all these situations, your story template keeps you speeding along with effective communication.

Tip 10: The Hierarchy in Your Mind

There are many reasons why the ancient concept of hierarchy still holds such power today. Some researchers believe that the mind uses hierarchical structures to store information in and retrieve information from long-term memory. For example, the idea of *chunking* is based on the idea that long-term memory applies a higher category to smaller pieces in working memory to bring them together and make them easier to handle. Some experts believe that a part of the brain called the neocortex retrieves information in a hierarchical way. And certainly the organizational technique of hierarchy is fully a part of most outlining systems, as well as many computer languages.

When you write your Act II headlines, you tap into hierarchical power by bringing the structure itself from long-term memory and applying it to the organization of your slides, as shown in Figure 5-36. A hierarchy turns out to be a deep and memorable way to help you and your audiences get right to the heart of the matter.

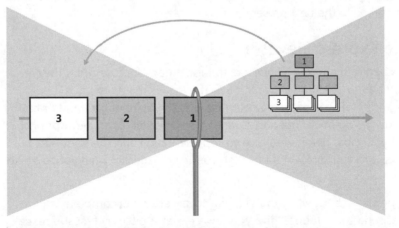

FIGURE 5-36 Applying a familiar hierarchical structure from long-term memory to your slides helps make them easier to prioritize and put in a proper sequence.

CHAPTER 6

Setting Up Your Storyboard and Narration

IN THIS CHAPTER, YOU WILL:

- Transform your script into a storyboard with preliminary backgrounds.

- Write out the words you'll speak during the presentation.

- Review the three ground rules for storyboarding.

WHEN YOU COMPLETE the Beyond Bullet Points (BBP) Story Template, you have in hand a complete and coherent story that sets the foundation for all your slides. Your story is so clear that even if your technology fails during your presentation, you have the security of knowing that you are able to present using only a printout of the story template as your guide. But of course you'll want to use graphics in your Microsoft PowerPoint presentation, because research indicates that people learn better when you add graphics to your narration in a multimedia presentation.

In Chapter 4, you used a story thread to prepare new information for the eye of the needle of your audience's working memory, and in Chapter 5, you used the sharp tip of a triangle of hierarchy to determine the sequence and order of information along that thread. Now in this chapter you will focus on the two strands of that story thread that represent the two essential elements you have to coordinate in any multimedia presentation—the visual and verbal channels, as described in Chapter 2.

You'll learn how to guide these visual and verbal strands through the rest of this book. Your challenge in this chapter is to set up your PowerPoint presentation in specific ways that don't split the attention of the audience or create redundancy. In Chapter 7, you'll explore the wide range of options you have to plan and sketch the graphics for your storyboard; in Chapter 8, you'll add the final graphics based on the sketches you choose; and in Chapter 10, you'll see the BBP approach applied to a range of presentations types for inspiration.

Expect that it will take some time to learn and apply the techniques described in these chapters, but as you develop your skills, the process will go faster and BBP will become a handy tool for rapid visual prototyping of creative concepts. As you build presentations over time, you'll develop a personal library of styles to review for inspiration on future projects.

What Will You Show, Say, and Do During Every Slide?

The prospect of managing everything you show, say, and do during every slide in a presentation can seem daunting at first. Even if you have written a clear and coherent set of headlines, as shown in Figure 6-1, how can you possibly fill all the empty slides you will create from the story template with graphics, narration, and interaction in a quick and efficient way? And at the same time, how can you seamlessly integrate all these complex elements during a live presentation? The answer lies in a different way of looking at PowerPoint—as a visual storytelling tool.

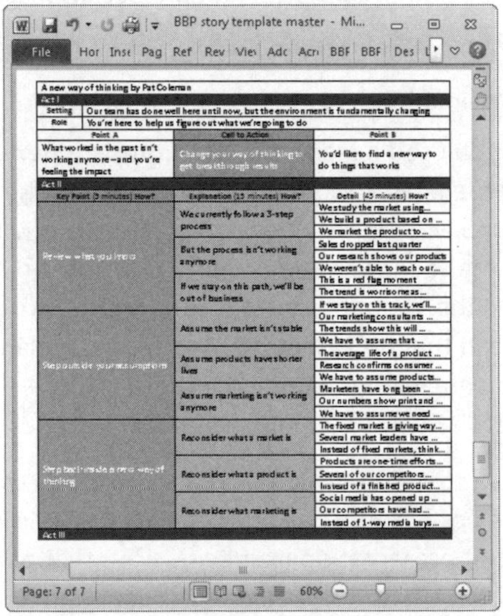

FIGURE 6-1 Your completed story template.

As mentioned in Chapter 3, if you were a filmmaker with a finished script, you'd probably hire a storyboard artist to sketch frames of selected scenes from your script. These initial sketches enable everyone on the production team to begin to see how the film will look so that they can start to turn the words from the script into spoken words and projected images. A storyboard is a powerful tool because it lets you see many frames from a story in a single view and consider how those frames relate to one another through a narrative. Without this important perspective, you would find it hard to see how the parts link together to become a coherent whole.

You won't need to hire a storyboard artist to create your storyboard; instead, you'll adapt the basic techniques of creating a storyboard to your PowerPoint presentation to help you organize the visual and verbal pieces of your story. This approach will shift your thinking of a PowerPoint presentation from individual slides toward frames in a strip of cinematic film. By setting up a new PowerPoint presentation in this way, you'll use the storyboard not only to plan your words and visuals but also to present them to the audience using a single media document that works across projector, paper, and browser.

Preparing the Storyboard

As you complete the story template in Chapters 4 and 5, you're actually also formatting your information in a specific way that prepares it for a PowerPoint storyboard. The concise headlines that communicate each act and scene in the story template are the same concise headlines that will communicate clearly to the audience on your PowerPoint slides. Writing headlines for both the story template and the PowerPoint slides is the powerful fulcrum that allows you to leverage PowerPoint software beyond bullet points into a new world of visual storytelling. This process embeds your script in a storyboard and ensures that everything you say and show maps back to the structure and sequence of a story. It also ensures that you have broken up your ideas into bite-size pieces so that working memory can easily digest them.

Although you're finished with the story template for now, it's a good idea to print a copy and keep it handy while you set up and work on your PowerPoint storyboard. The story template gives you the significant benefit of seeing your entire story on a single page or two, but when you import your headlines into PowerPoint, you will break the link between story template and storyboard. If you make changes to the headlines or the presentation structure later in PowerPoint, it's always a good idea to update your story template so that it continues to serve as an organizing tool.

Reformatting Your Story Template Manually

To prepare the headlines in your story template to become the headlines of your PowerPoint slides, you need to do some prep work on the story template. First save the Microsoft Word document, and then on the Home tab, in the Editing group, click Select; then choose Select All to select all of the headlines in the template, and then press Ctrl+C to copy them. Next create a new Word document and save it on your local computer in a familiar folder, adding the word *Formatted* to the end of the file name. Position the cursor in this new document, and then on the Home tab, in the Clipboard group, click the Paste button, and on the drop-down menu, click Paste Special. In the Paste Special dialog box, select Unformatted Text, and then click OK. The resulting new document should look similar to Figure 6-2.

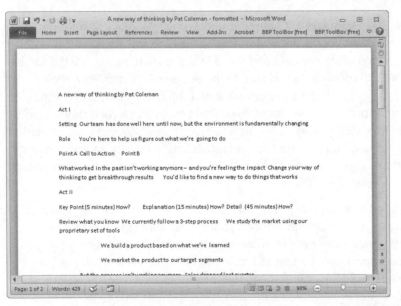

FIGURE 6-2 Initial view after pasting headlines from the story template into a new Word document.

Delete the line containing the column headings and any extra text so that only your headlines remain. Remove any extra spaces between words and add new line breaks where needed so that you end up with only one headline per line. Last select your Call to Action headline, and click and drag it to the line after your Point B headline—your final document should appear as shown in Figure 6-3. After you save the document, close it.

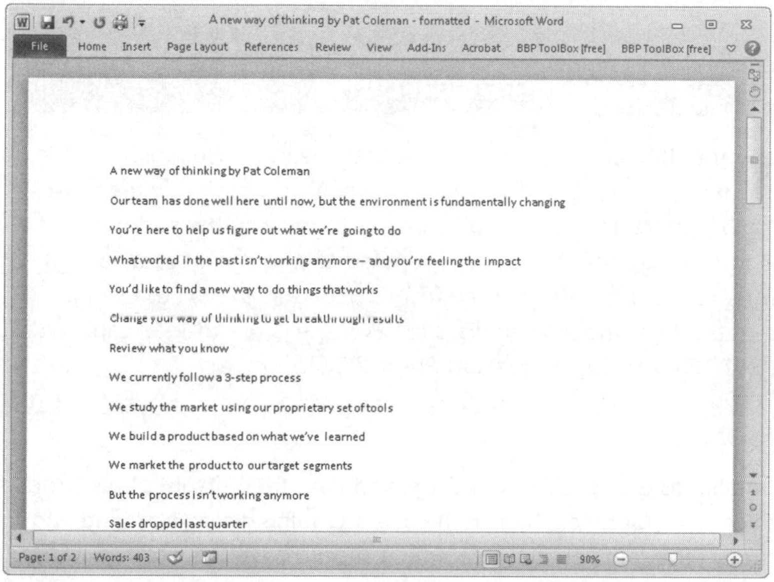

FIGURE 6-3 Word document with extra spaces between words removed, new line breaks added, and only one headline per line.

Using the BBP Storyboard Formatter

Now that you've reformatted your story template, the next step is to import your headlines into PowerPoint. You'll do that with the BBP Storyboard Formatter—a specially formatted PowerPoint file that takes care of a number of technical steps for you so that you don't have to take the time to apply them manually.

> **Note** If you choose not to use the BBP Storyboard Formatter, manually apply the settings as described in the sections "Tip 1: Set Up the Slide Master Manually" and "Tip 2: Set Up the Notes Master Manually" later in this chapter.

Download the BBP Storyboard Formatter file from *www.beyondbulletpoints.com* to a folder on your local computer. Locate the BBP Storyboard Formatter on your local computer, and double-click it. Because the file format is a PowerPoint Design Template, as indicated by the .potx file extension, double-clicking the file will open a new presentation based on the template's formatting. Your PowerPoint file contains one blank slide and is now shown in Slide Sorter view. Name and save the new PowerPoint file on your local computer.

WORKING IN NEWER VERSIONS OF POWERPOINT

If you're new to PowerPoint 2007 or 2010, you'll notice that the interface looks completely different from earlier versions. The Ribbon at the top is probably the most noticeable new feature, but there are many other changes to the way the software works. This book aims to give you only the basics you need to know to get started with BBP in PowerPoint—to learn more about the technical details of how to use the software, refer to one of the many how-to books, such as Joyce Cox and Joan Lambert's *Microsoft PowerPoint 2010 Step by Step* (Microsoft Press, 2010).

On the Home tab, in the Slides group, click New Slide, and near the bottom of the drop-down menu, select Slides From Outline. Then, in the Insert Outline dialog box, find and select the formatted story template you just created—it should have the word *Formatted* that you added to the title—and then click Insert. (If you get an error message, you likely have your formatted Word document still open—in that case, return to the document and close it.)

This last click of the mouse produces a result that amazes most people when they see it happen before them on the screen—it creates a PowerPoint storyboard. You have now created a single slide for each of the headlines you wrote in the story template, with each headline now placed at the top of a slide, as shown in Figure 6-4. It's a storyboard because you literally have a story embedded into your slides—the story you wrote in your story template, which now reads from one slide to the next. You'll unlock the tremendous power of your storyboard shortly.

But first, take a tour of your new storyboard. If there are any blank slides in the presentation without headlines, delete them. At the lower right of the PowerPoint window on the status bar is a View toolbar with three buttons—when you click them from left to right, you will see the storyboard in Normal, Slide Sorter, and Slide Show views. Click and drag the handle on the Zoom toolbar to the left to decrease magnification of your current view and to the right to increase magnification. The indicator to the left of the Zoom toolbar displays the exact percentage of magnification—click this value to open the Zoom dialog box and make more precise adjustments.

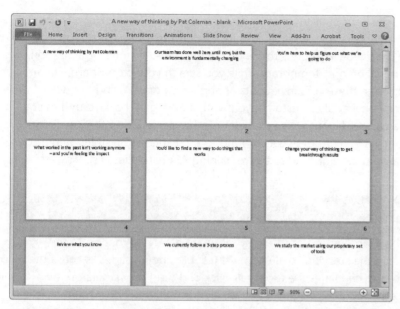

FIGURE 6-4 Slide Sorter view of all your headlines imported into the BBP Storyboard Formatter.

> **Note**
> After you master the fundamentals of the BBP approach, customize the settings of the BBP Storyboard Formatter according to your needs. Save the template to your local computer to make it easily accessible when you create a new presentation; for details, see the section "Tip 3: Install the Storyboard Formatter on Your Local Computer" later in this chapter.

Cuing Working Memory with Preliminary Slide Backgrounds

One of the big benefits of using the BBP Story Template is that you easily see how all your ideas relate to one another in the Word document. The story template is a particularly effective organizing tool for the Act II scenes because it shows you a visual hierarchy of your ideas. In each column, you write out the headlines in descending order of importance from top to bottom and add columns of information from left to right.

But when you transform the story template into a storyboard, you lose the template's ability to show you the hierarchy of your ideas. Every slide you see in Slide Sorter view looks as though it carries the same visual weight, and each slide follows the next in an undifferentiated sequence.

To be able to quickly see your built-in informational hierarchy in Slide Sorter view and begin to address the need to provide visual cues for working memory, you'll apply custom layouts with special backgrounds that indicate the presentation's organization. These custom layouts will be only temporary while you sketch your storyboard—later, in Chapter 8, you'll change these custom layouts or apply new ones. Using the BBP Storyboard Formatter, you'll apply a custom layout with a dark gray background to your Call to Action slide, a custom layout with a medium gray background to the Key Point slides, a custom layout with a light gray background to the Explanation slides, and a custom layout with a white background to the remaining Act I and Detail slides.

FINDING YOUR SLIDES

Keep a printout of the Word version of the story template handy as you locate the corresponding slides on the storyboard. If you have trouble finding slides because the slides are too large or the headlines are too small, click and drag the handle on the Zoom bar to increase or decrease magnification of Slide Sorter view. Try counting slides to find the slides you're seeking—for example, once you have located a Key Point slide, you know that an Explanation slide follows directly after it, and you count three Detail slides after that one to find the next Explanation slide, and three Detail slides after that to find the third Explanation slide.

To color-code these slides in Slide Sorter view, click Ctrl+A to select all the slides in the presentation. On the Home tab, in the Slides group, click Layout, and on the drop-down menu, click the layout titled Detail Sketches, as shown in Figure 6-5. Now select the Call to Action slide, click Layout, and on the drop-down menu, click the layout titled CTA Sketch. Next select the first Key Point slide, hold down Ctrl and click to select the second and third Key Point slides, and then click Layout again, and on the drop-down menu, click the layout titled Key Point Sketches.

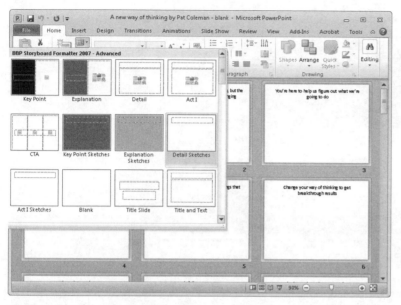

FIGURE 6-5 Applying the Detail Sketches custom layout to all the slides in Slide Sorter view using the custom layouts included in the BBP Storyboard Formatter.

Next click the first Explanation slide, hold down Ctrl and select the rest of the Explanation slides, and then click the Layout button, and on the drop-down menu click the layout titled Explanation Sketches. Finally, click the first Setting slide, hold down Shift and select the Point B slide, and then click the Layout button, and on the drop-down menu click the layout titled Act I Sketches.

> **Note**   If you choose to not use a storyboard formatter at all, follow the steps in the section "Tip 5: Apply Slide Backgrounds Manually" near the end of this chapter.

Scroll through your slides as you read the headlines, and check them against the printout of your story template to make sure you have applied the layouts properly. If you made a mistake, select the slide, click the Layout button, and select the correct layout to apply it. Your storyboard should now look like Figure 6-6.

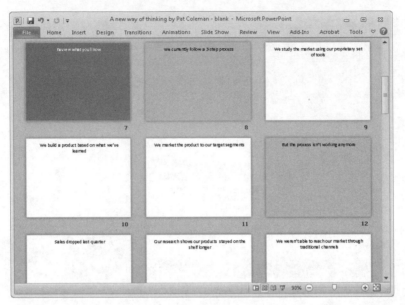

FIGURE 6-6 Slide Sorter view, showing the Call to Action slide with a dark gray background, the Key Point slides with medium gray backgrounds, the Explanation slides with light gray backgrounds, and the Detail slides with white backgrounds.

As you scroll through the slides of the presentation in sequence, the change in color of the backgrounds from dark gray to medium gray to light gray to white indicates you have made a transition to a new point that corresponds to Act I or the three columns in the storyboard. This transition should also be reinforced by your spoken words when you deliver the presentation.

Even though the shaded backgrounds are only temporary, already the contrast of the different shades of color calls attention to the three levels of hierarchy—the dark gray color calls attention to the most important Call to Action slide, the medium gray to the Key Points slides, the light gray next to the Explanation slides, and the white color to the Detail slides. Stick with these backgrounds for now so that you'll be able to sketch over the backgrounds as you work in the storyboard. In Chapter 7, you'll review and sketch a range of color backgrounds, layouts, and graphics to call attention to the different levels of information, and in Chapter 8, you'll apply them to the slides in their final form.

Practicing Scaling to Time

As you saw in Chapter 5, if you complete all three columns of Act II, you have enough Key Point, Explanation, and Detail slides to fill about a 45-minute presentation. However, at the last minute, you might need to scale down your presentation from 45 minutes to 15 or even 5 minutes. Now practice how easy it is to do that with only a few clicks of the mouse. Follow these steps in Slide Sorter view to scale the storyboard to time by hiding the slides you don't need to use in the presentation:

- If you're giving a 45-minute presentation, do nothing—all your slides will appear to your audience.

- To prepare a 15-minute presentation, hold down the Ctrl key and click the white Detail slides throughout the presentation. With all the Detail slides selected, right-click any Detail slide, and then select Hide Slide. Now only the Act I, Key Point, and Explanation slides will appear when you give the presentation; the Detail slides will be hidden. View the result by pressing the F5 key to start the slide show from the first slide. Press the Esc key to return to Slide Sorter view.

- To prepare a 5-minute presentation, complete the tasks for a 15-minute presentation, but in addition to selecting the white Detail slides, select the light gray Explanation slides, and then right-click any Explanation or Detail slide and select Hide Slide. Now only the Act I and Key Point slides will appear during the presentation; the rest of the Act II slides are hidden. Test the result by pressing the F5 key. Press the Esc key to return to Slide Sorter view.

When you use the Hide Slide feature, a hidden slide icon containing the slide number is displayed in the lower-right corner of each slide in Slide Sorter view. To reset the hidden slides to make them viewable again during a presentation, select the hidden slides, right-click any slide, and click Hide Slide again—the hidden slide icon will disappear. Keep in mind that hidden slides don't appear on screen when you run a presentation, but they will be printed unless you clear the Print Hidden Slides check box in the Print dialog box.

When you hide the slides as you scale to time, you maintain a single presentation file that has the flexibility to accommodate different-length presentations. Because of the hierarchy of ideas you wrote into Act II, you can scale your presentation up or down to time without losing the core integrity of the story—with only a few clicks of your mouse.

Editing Your Headlines If Needed

As you practiced scaling to time in Slide Sorter view, you might have noticed that some of the headlines extend beyond the two-line limit or have text that is unevenly balanced between the two lines—to fix that, you need to master the basics of editing headlines, described in the section "Tip 4: Edit the Headlines" later in this chapter. In Normal view, scroll through all the slides, and when you find a headline that exceeds the two-line limit of the title area, edit it down to size. Sometimes you reduce a headline's length simply by deleting a word or two, without affecting its meaning. At other times, you might have to revise and restructure the wording of a headline to make it fit. To force a headline to break to the next line so that the two lines are evenly distributed, position the cursor after any word in a headline and then press Enter. Always stick with the two-line limit for headlines to maintain consistency in the presentation, to leave ample room for visuals, and to challenge yourself to be as concise as possible.

Reviewing the Storyboard

Congratulations! You have now officially moved beyond bullet points. Even before you've added a single visual, the PowerPoint file is embedded with a strong story, meaningful headlines anchoring every slide, preliminary backgrounds that indicate the presentation's structure, and a basic layout designed to hold graphical elements in the main area of the slides instead of bullet points.

Your new PowerPoint storyboard is inspired by the idea of a filmmaker's storyboard, but it's actually a much more sophisticated tool than its namesake. What you've created is the foundation for a complete, integrated, and coherent media document that manages both the words you speak and the visuals you show on screen.

Planning for the Verbal Channel by Writing Down What You'll Say

No PowerPoint slide is an island, because it always exists in the context of your spoken words. To create a coherent presentation, you need to plan not only each slide but also the words you speak while you project the slide on a screen. Your primary objective in writing out your narration is to seamlessly integrate the soundtrack of your voice with the visual track of your slides so that you avoid splitting the attention of your audience between the two. To ensure that you properly manage what you say with what you show on screen, click the View tab on the Ribbon, and in the Presentation Views group, click Notes Page. Scroll through all the slides in the presentation, which will each look similar to Figure 6-7—starting in this view reinforces the concept that you're designing an experience consisting of both projected visuals and spoken words.

FIGURE 6-7 Reviewing both projected visuals and spoken words in Notes Page view. (An outline has been added to the slide area to make it visible in this illustration.)

As described in Chapters 2 and 3, the top half of the page shows what you see on the slide, and the notes area below shows your spoken words. (You won't see an outline around the slide as in Figure 6-7—it has been removed in the BBP Storyboard Formatter settings so that your printed notes pages handouts will look better.) The headline of the slide does double duty in Notes Page view—not only does it summarize the main idea that will appear on screen during the presentation, but it also summarizes the meaning of the entire notes page. If you're used to having a great deal of written information on screen, writing out your verbal explanation in the notes area gives you confidence that you will cover the bulk of the information through the verbal channel, which in turn gives you the freedom to keep the visual channel simple, focused, and to the point.

Tip ✓ An easy way to remember the essence of storyboarding is to imagine the audience saying to you, "Synchronize what you say with what I see."

To unlock the power of Notes Page view, review the slide headline in the top half of the page, position the cursor in the text box in the bottom half of the page, and then write out what you plan to say about this headline, as shown in the magnified view of the notes area in Figure 6-8. The text you write in the notes area represents what you'll say while the slide is displayed on the screen, normally for a period of less than a minute. If you find that you have more to say and your narration extends past the limits of the text box, go back to the story template and break up your ideas across more slides.

FIGURE 6-8 A magnified view of the notes area in Notes Page view, displaying an idea being described in complete sentences and paragraphs.

Fully writing out your ideas in the notes area fleshes out the ideas and increases your confidence in the topic. It also helps you to develop a close connection with the headline, which will aid you later when you speak. During the presentation, the headline will show the audience in a glance the idea of the slide, and it will also prompt you to improvise on the detailed written explanation, with a relaxed voice that comes from knowing the topic so well.

If you're used to having text on screen as a reminder of what to say, you also have full confidence in knowing that whatever you write in the notes area now is also viewable to you alone as the speaker in Presenter view, as described in Appendix B. After you have completed the notes area of one of your current slides, it will look like the slide shown in Figure 6-9 in Presenter view—during a presentation, the text you wrote in the notes area now will be visible to you in the speaker notes pane on the right.

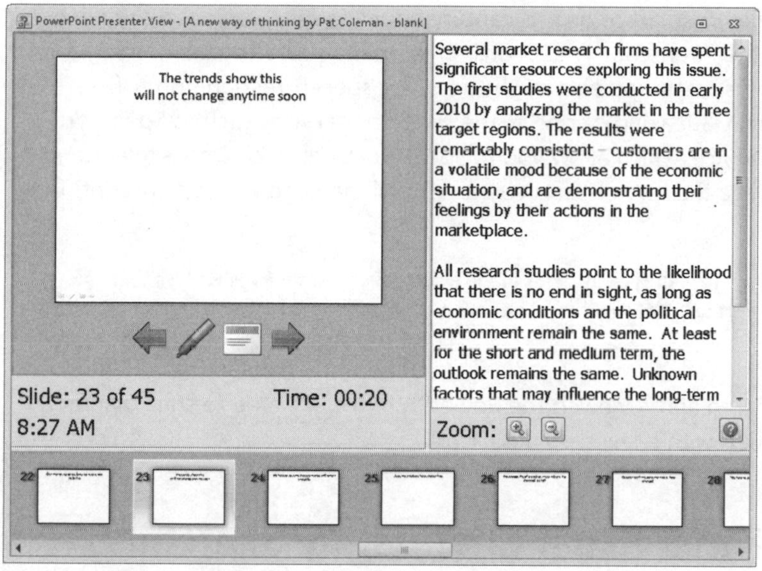

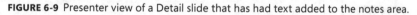

FIGURE 6-9 Presenter view of a Detail slide that has had text added to the notes area.

A valuable byproduct of starting to design in Notes Page view is that at the end of the design process, you have not only well-designed slides but also a useful handout. If you plan to share the presentation with your audience or others who were not present, it is important to write out what you'll say about the headline in complete sentences and paragraphs in the notes area so that your handout is complete and accurate when you print out both the slide and text box together. Don't worry about the formatting of Notes Page view now—you will adjust that in Chapter 8, and you'll also have the option to place additional graphics in the notes area if you choose.

| Note | You also have the option to add text to the notes pane when you are in Normal view by positioning the cursor in the notes pane below the slide view window and typing—it's a common mistake to think that you're in Notes Page view when you use the notes pane in Normal view this way. The disadvantage to using Normal view to write out your notes is that you lose track of how each slide will look as a handout. |

For a quick presentation for which you don't plan to print handouts, write short notes to yourself in the notes area of the slides of the storyboard. For now, spell out as much of your explanation as possible at this stage of the presentation—if you're pressed for time, write what you have at this point and then expand on your text in more detail later.

Or use a digital recorder or smart phone to capture your thoughts as you're speaking about each slide and then transcribe the recording later and paste the text passages into the corresponding notes areas. You also might try using speech-recognition software such as Dragon Naturally Speaking or one of the dictation services such as SpeakWrite Voice-to-Document Service, which allow you to speak your narration into a telephone or smart phone and have the service send you an e-mail message with a transcription a short time later.

■ **REMEMBER Start writing out your spoken words in the notes pane in Notes Page view so that you establish the complete context for what you'll say. Continue to add notes in this view, as well as in the notes area in Normal view.**

Now that you've prepared and reviewed the PowerPoint file, it's time to start planning the presentation's visuals with a few sketches.

Planning for the Visual Channel by Sketching Your Storyboard

Just as a filmmaker would, you should start getting visual in your storyboard by sketching what you would like on each slide before you go looking for the actual graphics you'll use. Creating sketches of the slides accelerates the design process because it keeps you from getting distracted amidst the many visual possibilities you'll find when you search through photo and graphics libraries. A series of sketches can also help you to select a consistent style, because you see all the slides together and can consider a design for all the slides at once.

Note If you've never sketched your PowerPoint slides before, this might seem like an extra step that you don't have the time to take. But the investment you make in taking the time to sketch will actually save you time in the long run. Often, the frustration that comes from developing PowerPoint presentations, especially in an organizational context, comes from endless revisions to graphics. When you sketch your slides first, you get everyone involved to sign off on the sketches to make sure they're what everyone wants. By getting agreement on the visual concepts now, you avoid frustration, inefficiency, confusion, and unhappiness later.

You have two ways to go about sketching your slides—either on a computer or on paper. By far, the best way to sketch ideas for your slides is using a Tablet PC, because it allows you to draw directly on the PowerPoint slides and easily edit and erase the "ink." There is tremendous value to having your sketches in electronic format, because you have a record of what you did that you e-mail to others to review. If you use a Tablet PC, connect your computer to a data projector and project your PowerPoint storyboard on a screen as you sketch ideas with your team—this is a particularly powerful way to tap into the collective visual intelligence of the group, and into the visual creativity that is likely lying dormant within your coworkers.

If you have a Tablet PC, to start sketching your storyboard, open a slide in Normal view, click the Review tab on the Ribbon, and in the Ink group, select Start Inking. The Pens tab that appears gives you options for types of pens, colors, and weights. Read the headline of your slide, and think of the simplest way to illustrate it. Now place the Tablet PC stylus on the screen below the headline (or use your finger or fingernail if you have a Tablet PC with a touch screen), and draw your illustration directly in the slide area as you would with a regular pen and paper, as shown in Figure 6-10. The Tablet PC lets you create your sketches using electronic ink, which you easily erase, recolor, resize, copy, and paste.

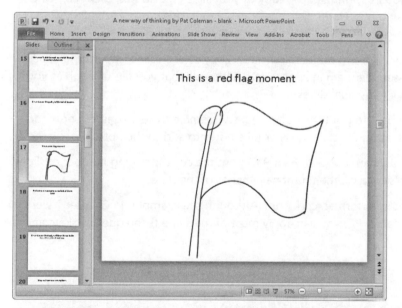

FIGURE 6-10 Slide showing a sketch made on a slide with the stylus of a Tablet PC.

Like the person who drew the sketch in this example, don't worry if you're not an artist—just do your best to capture the general idea of what you're looking for, even if it means drawing the simplest stick figures, shapes, and arrows. In Chapter 8, you'll turn these simple sketches into professional, simple, and clear photographs, illustrations, and diagrams. If you can't draw even a stick figure, just sketch out the words to describe what you want on the screen. Don't try to make everything perfect at this point—you want to apply your more creative side here, and you will likely find that you develop a sense of surprise, cleverness, and a visual sense of humor in your sketches to make sure the presentation doesn't get too stiff and impersonal. On the Slides tab in the Overview pane on the left, view the sketch you just drew in thumbnail size—the first illustration in the sequence of slides of your storyboard.

> **Tip**
> ✓ Even if you don't have a Tablet PC, you are able to sketch on your PowerPoint slides using your computer and a mouse by using the presenter tools available in Slide Show view, as described in Appendix B—the limitation is that your sketching will not be as smooth or natural with a mouse as it is with a Tablet PC stylus.

If you don't have access to a Tablet PC, the next best thing to use is paper. To sketch your complete storyboard, print a paper copy of your slides. To do this, click File, Print, to open the Print dialog box. Under Settings, Print Layout, select one of the following options:

- Select Full Page Slides to print an individual copy of each slide. Tape these pages to a wall or assemble them in a loose-leaf notebook that you flip through as you sketch ideas for individual slides.

- Select Notes Pages to print the notes pages. Assemble these pages in a notebook and sketch visuals in the slide areas or take notes to add to the notes areas later.

- Select Handouts; click 1, 2, 3, 4, 6, or 9 to print the corresponding number of slides per page; and sketch on the thumbnail images of the slides.

When you have selected a format, click Print. Although the examples in Chapter 7 were all sketched using a Tablet PC, you can apply most of the same techniques by sketching a paper storyboard.

> **Tip**
> ✓ To make sketching your paper storyboard more convenient by printing more than nine slides on a single page, see the section "Tip 8: Print Full-Page Storyboards" later in this chapter.

Storyboarding Using Three Ground Rules

Whether you have an electronic or paper version, as you review and work with your new storyboard, three ground rules can help you and your audience to stay connected to the big picture.

Rule 1: Be Visually Concise, Clear, Direct, and Specific

You wrote the headlines for your story template following the procedures in the section "Writing Headlines Using Three Ground Rules" in Chapter 3. Just as you strive to be concise, clear, direct, and specific with your words, you should strive to be the same with your visuals. Whether you use words or visuals to communicate, your singular goal should be to get across the most meaning in the most efficient way possible. When you sketch your storyboard, use the simplest illustration possible without any excess detail. Not only does a simple illustration help you make your visual point quickly, it also will guide you to avoid the extraneous detail that would otherwise clog the eye of the needle of working memory of your audience.

As you sketch, always pay special attention to the wording of the headlines as you read through them in Slide Sorter view to reword them and tie them together more tightly. As you reword a headline in PowerPoint, go back and edit the headline in the story template as well. If you find that you start making many changes to slide headlines, go back to the story template directly to work out the structural issues you are having before returning to the storyboard.

Rule 2: In Act II, Sketch Consistency Within Columns and Variety Across Columns

When you work with the storyboard, keep in mind that in Act II, *it's all about the hierarchy*. Act II of the story template is your disciplined guide that helps you make the tough decisions about whether to include or exclude ideas and automatically prioritizes for you every slide from the most important to the least. When you apply preliminary layouts with color backgrounds to indicate the levels of importance of your slides, you clearly see in Slide Sorter view how the hierarchy fits into the specific sequence of the slides of the presentation. And now you'll build on the rock-solid verbal foundation of Act II by using visual techniques to keep the hierarchy at the top of the minds of both you and your audience.

When you begin to sketch, the Act II structure will help you decide exactly what you want to accomplish visually on your slides, as shown in Figure 6-11. As you learned in Chapter 5, you want the audience to remember and apply your Call to Action and Key Point slides above all—if they walked away and remembered nothing else, these slides carry the most important information. You'll sketch on these slides the most memorable things you say, show, and do to make these points stick—here you'll use striking photographic icons, illustrations, or visual elements from your motif.

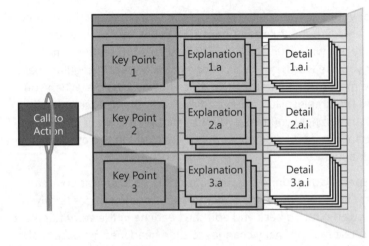

FIGURE 6-11 Act II hierarchy, indicating the relative importance of the slides.

Next you'll sketch the second-most important Explanation slides, which the audience will likely remember—here you might use diagrams, charts, or other illustrations. And then you'll sketch the third-most important Detail slides, which the audience might not remember—here you'll include graphs, charts, screen captures, and other visual elements.

As you sketch the slides that correspond to the three columns of Act II, you want to keep a consistent look in terms of similar layout, style, and placement of headlines and graphics within each column, as shown in the slides that correspond to the headlines from the Explanation column in Figure 6-12. By sketching the slides from a single column together, as you'll do next in Chapter 7, you avoid concentrating exclusively on only single slides; instead, you focus on what is happening *across* slides. This makes sure that you approach the design of any slide by its context and relationship to other slides within its column, not as individual slides in isolation.

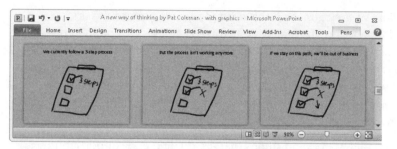

FIGURE 6-12 Telling a visual story across three slides from the Explanation column.

In addition to sketching variety across slides from the same column of Act II, you also want to sketch variety *across the columns* of Act II of the story template. You don't have to worry about how you'll do this—it will happen automatically as a result of the way you approach the sketching process in Chapter 7. But it's important to know what's happening in terms of variety as you sketch your storyboard. For example, the Explanation slides shown earlier in Figure 6-12 will not appear in direct sequence in the storyboard because they will be broken up by their subsequent Detail slides.

However, you do still want to tell this visual story across these Explanation slides even when they are broken up by the Detail slides, as shown in Figure 6-13.

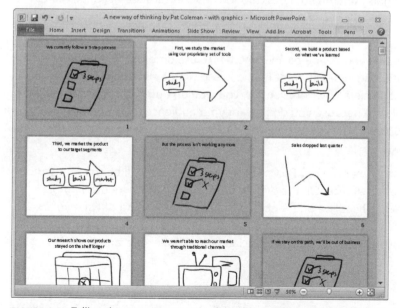

FIGURE 6-13 Telling the story across each of the three slides from the Explanation column, even though they are separated in sequence by the slides from the Detail column.

In the sequence of slides as they appear in this example, you introduce the first Explanation slide and then follow the idea with its three Detail slides. You then present the second Explanation slide and follow the idea with its three Detail slides. This back-and-forth technique is helpful to your audience because with the first Explanation slide, you summarize what you are about to tell them, and then with the Detail slides, you do the actual telling. As you write out the narration in the notes area on the Explanation slides, you likewise should summarize the Detail slides to follow.

Think of the slides as cognitive stepping stones that are guiding and supporting the working memory of the audience along their path of understanding.

Rule 3: Sketch Outside the Screen Too

You have in your PowerPoint file a powerful planning tool, with each slide representing one idea that you will convey at one point in the presentation as summarized by the headline. You will probably add graphics to most of these slides to illustrate the head-lines, but you don't have to limit yourself to showing information on a slide exclusively with a graphic; you have many other media tools and techniques at your disposal. For example, use a physical prop that you hold in your hands or pass around to audience members to communicate an Explanation slide, as shown in Figure 6-14. You might switch to a different software application on your desktop to communicate the headlines across three Detail slides. Or you might use a brief video clip to illustrate each of your three Key Point slides.

The storyboard will guide you as you decide whether to use different media—you will specifically choose to include different media based on the slide's headline and its location within the Act II hierarchy. For example, you wouldn't use your most memorable video clip on a Detail slide because you don't want your audience to remember the Detail slides over the Key Point slides—you would integrate and use the clip through the Key Point slides instead.

Even when you use other media, your PowerPoint storyboard will still be the foundation that guides the entire experience. On the slides where you use other media, in most cases, you'll keep just the headline on the screen to keep the meaning of what you're doing clear and in the context of the overall presentation. Or you may use a photo as a physical prop to ensure that everyone sees it clearly. You'll see an example of this technique shortly in Chapter 7.

FIGURE 6-14 Holding a physical prop while displaying a photo of it on the screen.

THREE GROUND RULES FOR STORYBOARDING

Inspired by a filmmaker's storyboard, your PowerPoint storyboard helps you manage both the words you speak and the images you show. Follow these three ground rules to keep your storyboard coherent:

Ground Rule 1. Be visually concise, clear, direct, and specific.

Ground Rule 2. In Act II, sketch consistency within columns and variety across columns.

Ground Rule 3. Sketch outside the screen too.

BBP CHECKLIST: PREPARING THE STORYBOARD

Does your storyboard:

- Include backgrounds that cue the Key Point, Explanation, and Detail slides?
- Provide you with the ability to quickly scale your presentation up and down to time?
- Contain notes in the notes area of what you'll say during each slide?

Now that you have an operational storyboard, here are 10 advanced things to do with it.

10 Tips for Enhancing Your Storyboard

Your storyboard is a versatile tool to prepare and plan both your spoken words and your projected visuals during the presentation. Once you've mastered the basics, try using these 10 tips to enhance the storyboard.

Tip 1: Set Up the Slide Master Manually

If for some reason you decide not to use the BBP Storyboard Formatter, follow these steps to set up the basic formatting you'll need to start sketching the storyboard:

1. Open and save a blank PowerPoint presentation, and as described earlier in this chapter, import the formatted story template headlines into PowerPoint following the New Slide, Slides From Outline sequence.

2. In Slide Sorter view, on the Home tab, in the Editing group, click Select, Select All, and then in the Slides group, click Layout, Title Only.

3. On the View tab, in the Presentation Views group, click Slide Master. In the Overview pane on the left, click the Office Theme Slide Master.

4. In the Slide pane, right-click the Title box, and on the formatting shortcut menu, select Calibri for the font (or a different font if you prefer), select 32 for the font size, and make sure that Centered is selected.

5. Right-click the Title box again, and on the second shortcut menu below the formatting menu, select Format Shape.

6. In the Format Shape dialog box, select Text Box; on the Vertical Alignment drop-down menu, choose Middle Centered; in the Autofit area, select Do Not Autofit; and then click Close.

7. On the Slide Master tab, in the Close group, click Close Master View to return to the previous view of the slides.

Tip 2: Set Up the Notes Master Manually

Just as the Storyboard Formatter uses the Slide Master to set the formatting for all the slides, the Notes Master sets the formatting for all the notes pages. By making a few adjustments to the Notes Master, you'll be able to use the notes pages to effectively plan both your slides and your spoken words.

To format the Notes Master, follow these steps:

1. Continue working on the same PowerPoint file you started in the section "Tip 1: Set Up the Office Theme Slide Master Manually," and on the View tab, in the Presentation Views group, click Notes Master. Right-click the Slide Image placeholder in the top half of the page, and on the drop-down menu, click Size And Position.

2. In the Size And Position dialog box, on the Size tab, make sure that the Lock Aspect Ratio check box is selected, change the Width setting to 6" (the Height setting will be automatically adjusted to 4.5"), and then click Close.

3. Right-click the border of the Body placeholder in the lower half of the page, and on the drop-down menu, click Size And Position. If the notes area doesn't already have these settings, clear the Lock Aspect Ratio check box, make sure that Height is set to 4.5" and Width is set to 6", and then click Close.

   On the Notes Master tab, in the Placeholders group, delete or add any other Notes Master placeholders, including Header, Date, Footer, and Page Number.

4. Hold down Shift while you click both the Slide Image placeholder and the Body placeholder, and on the Home tab, in the Drawing group, click Arrange, point to Align, and click Align To Slide. Click Arrange again, point to Align, and click Align Center. Then drag the two placeholders to position them one above another. If you want to align any placeholders on the Notes Master more precisely, right-click the slide background, and on the shortcut menu, choose Grid And Guides, and then configure the settings of the grids and guides according to your needs, and click OK.

5. Select the Slide Image placeholder again, and on the shortcut menu, click the Line Color down arrow, and then in the drop-down list, select No Outline.

6. On the Notes Master tab, in the Close group, click Close Master View to return to the previous view.

Tip 3: Install the Storyboard Formatter on Your Local Computer

To make the BBP Storyboard Formatter available on your local computer every time you create a new PowerPoint file, save it in your PowerPoint Templates folder by following these steps:

1. Double-click to open the BBP Storyboard Formatter that you saved to your computer earlier in this chapter.

2. Click File, Save As, and then in the Save As dialog box, click the Save As Type drop-down arrow, and choose PowerPoint Template.

3. PowerPoint automatically selects the location on your local computer where the default PowerPoint template is stored. To create a new presentation, click File, New, and then My Templates. In the New Presentation dialog box, you should see the template you just saved—select it and click OK to create the presentation.

Tip 4: Edit the Headlines

PowerPoint provides two ways to edit your headlines. The first method is to click the View tab and, in the Presentation Views group, click Normal. In this view, click in the title area of the slide, insert the cursor, and then start editing. The second method is to view the presentation in Outline format. In Normal view, the leftmost pane of the PowerPoint window contains an Overview area with two tabs: Outline and Slides. Click the Outline tab to see a list of headlines and, to the left of each headline, a number and a small icon of a slide. Click in the text of the headline you want to edit. As you make changes to a headline on the Outline tab, the corresponding text in the title area of the slide to the right is updated. Drag the vertical line at the right side of the Outline pane to increase or decrease its size to accommodate the width of the headlines. The Outline tab is useful for reviewing all the headlines of the slides in a list that you read from top to bottom. Print this outline later to use as speaker notes.

Tip 5: Apply Slide Backgrounds Manually

If you do not use the BBP Storyboard Formatter, you will not be able to use the built-in custom layouts to format the Key Point, Explanation, and Detail slides, but you can still format them manually. To quickly do this, follow these steps:

1. In Slide Sorter view, right-click the Call to Action slide, click Format Background on the shortcut menu, and in the Format Background dialog box, click Fill and then select Solid Fill.

2. On the Color drop-down menu, click More Colors, select dark gray, and then click OK. Make sure that the Transparency bar slider is set to 0%, and then click Close.

3. Click the first Key Point slide, and then hold down Ctrl and click to select the second and third Key Point slides.

4. Now right-click one of the slides, click Format Background on the shortcut menu, and in the Format Background dialog box, click Fill and then select Solid Fill.

5. On the Color drop-down menu, click More Colors, select medium gray, and then click OK. Make sure that the Transparency bar slider is set to 0%, and then click Close.

6. Next click the first Explanation slide, and then hold down Ctrl and select the rest of the Explanation slides.

7. Now right-click one of the slides, click Format Background on the shortcut menu, and in the Format Background dialog box, on the Fill tab, select Solid Fill.

8. On the Color drop-down menu, click More Colors, select light gray, and then click OK. Make sure that the Transparency bar slider is set to 0%, and then click Close.

Do nothing to the Act I and Detail slides.

Be sure to change only the background colors for now and otherwise leave the slides blank except for the headlines. If you were to include logos, other slide backgrounds, and other graphics on your storyboard at this point, they would constrain your design decisions and interfere with the way you will use backgrounds in this chapter to purposefully cue the working memory of your audience.

Tip 6: Set Up Custom Layouts and Themes Manually

The BBP Storyboard Formatter includes built-in layouts that you apply to your Key Point, Explanation, and Detail slides. These were built using the custom layouts feature in PowerPoint, which is described in more detail in Chapter 8—you'll be able to modify the current custom layouts at that point, or add new ones and apply them to your slides. Learn more about modifying and creating themes manually by referring to a PowerPoint 2010 book that covers the topic in more detail.

Tip 7: The BBP Storyboard Sketchpad

Visit *www.beyondbulletpoints.com* to download a blank BBP Storyboard Sketchpad to print and use to sketch ideas for the Act I and Key Point slides, as shown in Figure 6-15.

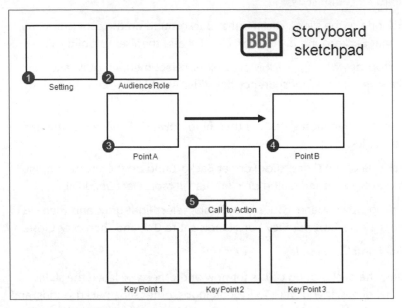

FIGURE 6-15 The BBP Storyboard Sketchpad.

Tip 8: Print Full-Page Storyboards

Although PowerPoint allows you to print up to nine slides per page on a handout, an add-in for PowerPoint called the Handout Wizard allows you to print many more slides per page. This is particularly useful if you plan to sketch your storyboard on paper. For example, fit groups of 20 slides from your storyboard on 8½-by-11-inch sheets of paper by using the Handout Wizard to arrange them five slides across and four slides down, as shown in Figure 6-16. Fit even more slides per page if you use 11-by-17-inch sheets of paper. The add-in places all the slide thumbnails on a single PowerPoint slide that you then print. For more information about the Handout Wizard add-in, visit *http://skp.mvps.org/how.*

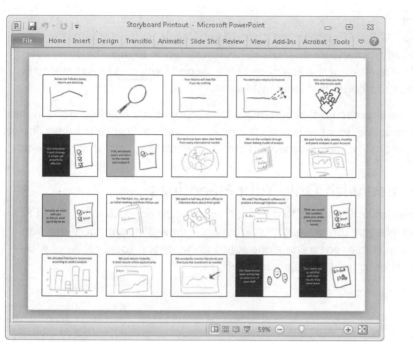

FIGURE 6-16 A 20-slide storyboard ready for printing, created with the Handout Wizard.

Tip 9: Create Nested Storyboards

What if you're not certain which of two stories you want to present until you're standing in front of the audience? The section "Tip 4: Multiple Stories, Multiple Templates" in Chapter 4 explored the possibilities of developing two related story templates in parallel. Both stories presumably relate to the same topic, so they should share the same Setting slide because this is a general statement about the context that everyone should agree is true. Use this single slide as the starting point for whichever story you choose to present from that point forward.

To do this, create a separate PowerPoint file from each story template, and then copy and paste all the slides from the second presentation to the right of the last slide in the first presentation. This creates a "nested" storyboard in which the second story sits in the same file as the first. Note the number of the slide that begins the Role slide of the second story.

When you present the Setting slide, ask the audience a question such as, "Which option do you prefer, 1 or 2?" Based on their responses, if you decide to stay on path 1 with the first story, you advance the slides as usual. But if you decide to take the alternative path 2, type the number of the Role slide of the second story and press Enter to go directly to that slide and begin that story instead.

The drawback of this approach is that you might have more than a hundred slides in the PowerPoint file to manage, so when you try it out, you'll need to balance the flexibility of a nested storyboard against the management challenges that large storyboards create.

Tip 10: Rehearse with Only Your Headlines

Before adding sketches and graphics to the slides, which you'll do in Chapters 7 and 8, it's a good idea to rehearse the presentation with only the headlines on the slides. You might be more comfortable rehearsing alone at this stage, or you could rehearse with your team if you prefer to get some early feedback.

CHAPTER 7

Sketching Your Storyboard

WHEN YOU PUT stylus to screen or pencil to paper to sketch your slides, it's a revolutionary moment in terms of Microsoft PowerPoint approaches. Think of the way you use PowerPoint according to the conventional approach—you open up a slide with a predesigned background, type a category heading such as Our Company in the title area, and then type a list of facts about the company below, maybe adding a small photo of your company building to spice things up.

But now you are doing something completely different. As described in Chapter 6, you've printed out copies of your slides and you have the paper version of your slides before you. There are no words to type anywhere—the headline already on the slide summarizes your point, and the off-screen text box holds the words you'll speak aloud. With just a clear headline on the printout of the slide before you, the only thing left to do now is tap into your visual thinking skills to illustrate the headline.

What Do I Sketch on Each Slide?

Sketching literally puts you in a different frame of mind, especially if you spend most of your day working with words and numbers. If sketching is completely new to you, you might find it difficult at first, and the prospect of sketching your entire blank storyboard, as shown in Figure 7-1, might be daunting.

But just take it one slide at a time—this chapter guides you through the sketching process and shows you a range of specific sketches to draw on any one of your slides or across several of them. The sketches in this chapter relate to the specific example from the story template, but they also work on many types of presentations. Be patient as you practice your new visual thinking skills—as you tackle the first few slides, your creativity will start to flow and you'll get the hang of sketching in no time.

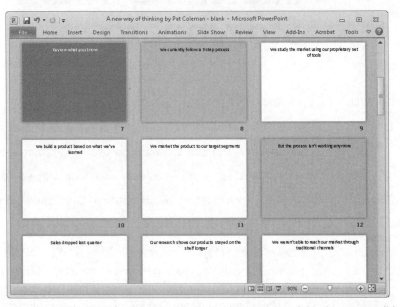

FIGURE 7-1 This chapter will guide you through the process of sketching every slide in your storyboard.

Just as you wrote the verbal essence of your presentation in the story template, your focus now is to sketch the visual essence in the storyboard. Again, don't worry about the artistic quality of the sketches—they are only temporary placeholders for the graphics you'll add to each slide later.

So let's get started at the start, by reviewing a range of sketching possibilities for your Act I slides.

Sketching the Act I Slides

As you saw in Chapter 5, the first five slides of your presentation accomplish the crucial work of orienting the audience to your story and making the experience personal and relevant to them. When you import your headlines into PowerPoint, an additional slide is inserted in front of these five slides—a Title slide is automatically created from your title and byline, as shown in Figure 7-2. Now you will sketch illustrations for the Title slide along with the Act I slides to powerfully complement the clear and coherent flow of ideas you set in motion in the beginning of your story.

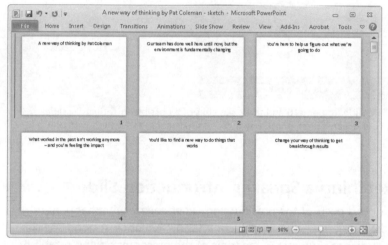

FIGURE 7-2 The Title and Act I slides in the storyboard.

Arrange the printouts of the Title and Act I slides in front of you. If you're using a Tablet PC, review the slides to sketch in Slide Sorter view first, then click on an individual slide to sketch it in Normal view, and then return to Slide Sorter view to review your work.

Sketching the Title Slide

The Title slide will be the first thing to appear on the screen as you begin your talk, so it should intrigue the audience and set the visual tone of the presentation to come. In this instance, sketch a light bulb to illustrate "thinking," as indicated in the title, "A New Way of Thinking." As shown on the upper left slide in Figure 7-3, sketch your organization's logo in the corner and perhaps add a note to use your company's colors on this slide.

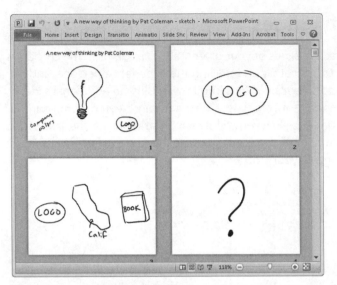

FIGURE 7-3 A sketch of a Title slide (upper left) and three sketches of a possible Introductory slide: one with only the logo of your organization, another with three small icons, and a third with only a question mark.

Adding and Sketching a Speaker Introduction Slide

One of the most overlooked parts of the presentation experience is what happens directly before you start speaking—your introduction to the audience. A good speaker introduction raises an audience's interest in the topic of the presentation and establishes the speaker's authority to give the talk in the first place.

To make sure your presentation gets off to a solid start, plan the way you'll be introduced by adding an optional speaker introduction slide. In Slide Sorter view, position the cursor to the right of the Title slide in the presentation, and on the Home tab of the Ribbon, in the Slides group, click New Slide, and then select Blank on the drop-down menu.

What you sketch on this new speaker introduction slide depends on who will be introducing you. If someone else from your organization will introduce you, sketch your organization's logo on the slide, as shown on the upper right slide in Figure 7-3. In this case, only the logo will appear on screen while that person introduces you. If you're an expert in your field, sketch a photo of the cover of a report or book you've written.

In the notes area of this slide, write the introduction you would like the person who introduces you to read. Keep it brief and informal, and include your relevant credentials for the topic of the presentation. This isn't about boosting your own ego—to be in the right frame of mind to listen to the presentation, the audience needs to know that you're the right person to be giving this talk. When you meet with the person who will introduce you, provide a printed Notes Page version of this slide to show what will be displayed on the screen along with the script of the introduction you would like that person to read. You're not being controlling if you ask the person doing the introduction to read it verbatim—many a presenter has gotten off on the wrong foot when they were introduced with incorrect facts, inappropriate comments, or off-color humor.

If you will introduce yourself at the start of your presentation, sketch three visual icons that symbolize who you are in the context of the presentation. For example, as shown on the lower left slide in Figure 7-3, sketch the logo of your organization, which will appear as you describe what you do there; then sketch the shape of the state of California, which will appear while you describe your upbringing in the state to your California audience; and then sketch the cover of your favorite book or movie, which will appear as you describe how that book or movie shaped who you are today. These three simple images will prompt you to speak naturally, unlock your personality, and connect with your audience. When you add graphics later, animate the images so that they appear in sequence as you click your remote control.

If you're speaking to a small group or conducting a workshop, consider inserting an additional introductory slide asking your audience members to introduce themselves—to illustrate it, simply sketch a question mark, as on the lower right slide in Figure 7-3. When the question mark appears on screen, ask the audience members to introduce themselves and state one thing they would like to accomplish at the event. As each person speaks, use a flip chart or a Tablet PC to write the names and responses on paper or the screen. This approach demonstrates to the audience that you will listen to them, that you agree to accomplish certain tasks over the course of the presentation, and that you have created a record of the conversation. Review the same flip chart or screen again at the end of the presentation to make sure you covered everything.

Sketching the Setting Slide

Now you'll sketch the Setting slide, which orients the audience to the context of the presentation.

Picture a Strong Start

As you probably remember from Chapter 4, the first five slides work their magic by appealing primarily to emotion. To enhance your appeal to emotion, add a full-screen photograph to the slide. If that's the way you want to go in this example, sketch a photo of a magazine cover with a headline about the changing environment, as shown on the upper left slide in Figure 7-4.

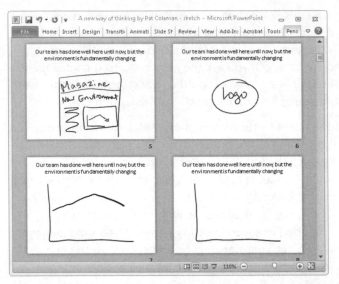

FIGURE 7-4 Four ways to sketch the same Setting slide: a photograph of a magazine cover, a brief anecdote with a black screen, a chart, and only the axes of the chart—the line will be drawn by hand.

> **Tip** ✓
>
> To explore more than one sketch option for any slide in your storyboard, select the slide in Slide Sorter view, and then click Ctrl+D to duplicate it. Try a different sketch on the duplicated slide, or create several slides and compare them side by side before you decide which sketch you like best.

Start with an Anecdote

Another way to start strong is to tell an anecdote—a brief story—while you display a simple graphic. In this case, the anecdote should communicate the point of the headline of the slide—be sure that your story lasts no more than a minute or two, because you have many more slides to present. To illustrate your anecdote, think of the topic of your story—perhaps it is about a competitor who has encountered similar struggles in the environment and has successfully overcome them. In that example, sketch the logo of the competitor's organization on the slide, as shown on the upper right slide in Figure 7-4.

When you advance past the Title slide to the Setting slide, say something like, "I know you're expecting me to start with bullet points, but I'm going to start with an anecdote instead. Let me tell you a story about a company you know well—our main competitor..." Your spoken words and the simple graphic work together to create a sense of surprise, focusing attention intensely on you and what you say next—a good example of a strong way to start.

Start with a Chart

When you decide what to sketch, choose the visual elements that are the best fit for an audience. For example, if you're presenting to executives in the financial industry, it might not be a good fit to start with a full-screen photograph on the Setting slide. A better fit would be to sketch the meaningful visuals these executives are more accustomed to seeing—charts and graphs. When you sketch a chart that everyone in the audience instantly recognizes (as in the example shown on the lower left slide in Figure 7-4), you quickly connect with the audience because you're speaking the same visual language.

Start with a Simple Line

To make the chart concept even more powerful, integrate other media in the Setting slide to increase engagement and make the experience more interesting. For example, sketch only the two axes of a chart on the slide, as shown on the lower right slide in Figure 7-4. When you show the chart axes, say something like, "I know you all are familiar with what is happening in our business environment." After a pause, position the stylus on the screen of your Tablet PC and draw a line traveling upward and then downward as you say, "Things have been good, but now they are turning in another direction." Since people don't usually write directly on screen during a presentation, this technique is sure to be memorable and catch everyone's attention. If you don't have a Tablet PC, do something similar by drawing the chart axes on a flip chart before your talk and then placing the chart near the podium. When you're ready, move to the flip chart and draw a similar line there.

Start with a Video

Using a video is a great way to capture everyone's attention at the start of a presentation, especially when you present to large groups. If you have the resources to license or produce a brief video clip to illustrate the headline on the Setting slide, sketch a note to indicate you'll use a video on that slide.

Sketching the Role Slide

Next, on the Role slide, sketch something that engages the audience in the setting and puts them in the middle of the action. If you sketched a photograph on the Setting slide, as shown earlier on the upper left slide in Figure 7-4, use the same sketch on this slide and sketch a circle around the headline as shown on the upper left slide in Figure 7-5. This indicates that you'll add a circle shape using the PowerPoint drawing tools. When you arrive at the slide during the presentation, say, "Although the environment is changing, you're here to help us do something about the situation." If you have a Tablet PC, write directly on the photograph using the stylus of your Tablet PC, circling the headline.

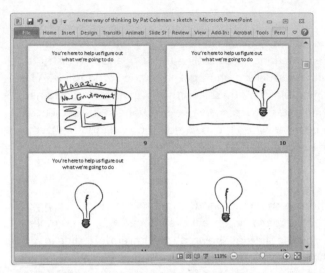

FIGURE 7-5 Four ways to sketch the Role slide: using the Setting slide's photograph and updating the headline, using the Setting slide's chart and adding a magnifying glass, showing only the headline and the magnifying glass, and hiding the headline.

In a similar way, if you sketched a chart on the Setting slide, as shown on the lower left slide in Figure 7-4, use it again on the Role slide. Sketch a light bulb over the chart to illustrate the "new thinking" theme of the presentation, as shown on the upper right slide in Figure 7-5. Carrying over the same graphical element from the preceding slide helps to tell the story visually across the two storyboard frames. Your verbal explanation will keep the story flowing too, as you transition between the two slides by saying something like, "We all agree that the environment is changing, and we must do something." Advance to the Role slide, and say, "You play a crucial role in figuring out what's next."

Create a Simple Visual Prompt with a Photo

Try something a little different by sketching only a light bulb on the Role slide, as shown on the lower left slide in Figure 7-5. This turns the slide into a visual prompt in which a photograph alone prompts you to unlock your natural voice. If you keep the photograph simple, the audience members will use their imagination and see themselves in the role and in the setting you verbally and visually describe.

Hide the Headlines

To unlock even more visual power from the light bulb in the last example, hide the headline, as shown on the lower right slide in Figure 7-5. When the headline is not visible on the screen, you increase the audience's reliance on you to explain why you are showing this image. To sketch this slide, simply draw a line through the headline. Or go ahead and take care of this now: in Normal view, click on the outer edge of the headline box and drag it off the slide into the gray area above the slide. The headline now will be hidden from the audience when you show the slide in Slide Show view. When you're working on the slide in Normal view, you'll still be able to view the headline above the slide area.

Tap into the Power of Paper

Although you use a projector to show your slides on the screen, consider what paper does for you too. Especially for an audience that likely wants to see detailed data, quickly establish credibility by referring to a detailed, printed handout when you display one of the Act I slides. Here say something like, "We crunched the numbers and they're all here, but out of respect for your limited time, we've pulled out what we thought would be most relevant to your situation, which will be the focus of this presentation." Print a handout in PowerPoint Notes Page view, Microsoft Excel spreadsheets, or whatever other format your data is in. Generally, wait until the presentation ends to provide handouts so you keep focus on your topic and avoid the handouts becoming a distraction.

Sketching the Point A and Point B Slides

As described in Chapter 4, the Point A slide engages the audience by describing a challenge they face, and the Point B slide motivates the audience by affirming what they want in light of the challenge. This gap between Point A and Point B forms the dramatic tension you propose to resolve in the rest of the story. Just as the wording you choose for the Point A and Point B headlines spells the difference between hitting or missing the mark with your audience, what you choose to sketch here will make a difference too.

Because these two slides are so critical to the entire presentation, sketch them as a pair, as shown in Figure 7-6, as you carefully consider how to connect with the emotions of the audience and confirm that they care about the problem that exists in this gap between A and B.

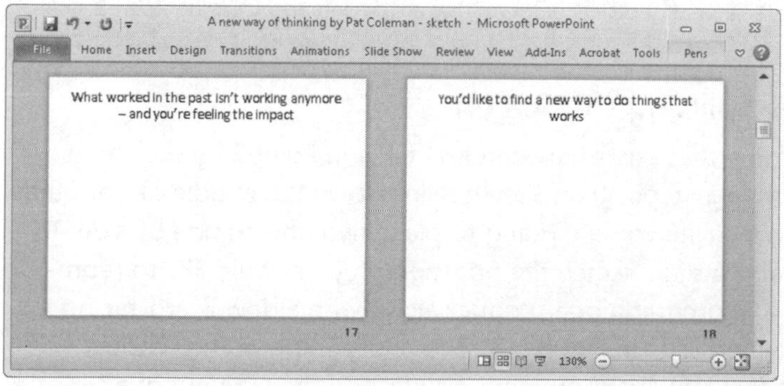

FIGURE 7-6 It's critical that you hit the mark of the Point A and Point B slides, both verbally and visually.

Use an "Emotional" Chart

Just as with the Setting slide, it might be a good match with your audience to use a chart on these two slides. Sketch a bar chart showing the organization's declining monthly product sales on the Point A slide, as shown on the upper left slide in Figure 7-7. On the Point B slide, sketch several more bars showing possible improved sales, as shown on the upper right slide in Figure 7-7. Although charts are normally considered purely objective displays of information, this chart is sure to stir up emotions if the audience members are unhappy with the numbers at Point A and would like to get to Point B. The use of this particular chart in this context makes an emotional connection with this audience, although in other contexts and to other audiences, the same chart might not work.

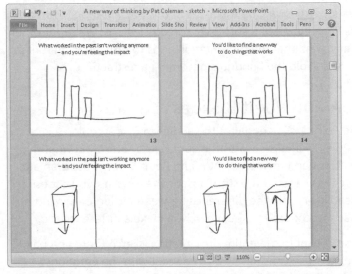

FIGURE 7-7 Two ways to sketch the pair of Point A and Point B slides. Top row: Sketch a chart on the Point A slide showing declining monthly sales, and then sketch additional bars showing improving sales on the Point B slide. Bottom row: A split-screen layout starts with a photo of a product with a downward-facing arrow on the Point A slide; a second photo includes an upward-facing arrow on the Point B slide.

Double Your Impact by Splitting the Screen

Emphasize the dramatic tension that exists between Point A and Point B by sketching two contrasting photographs in juxtaposition. Sketch a line down the middle of both the Point A and Point B slides to indicate you are going to place two photos side by side. To the left of the line on the Point A slide, sketch the photograph you would like to represent Point A—for example, a photograph of a product along with a downward-facing arrow, as shown on the lower left slide in Figure 7-7. The photograph of the product brings the reality of the product into the room on the slide, and the addition of a downward-facing arrow indicates declining sales. Sketch the same graphic on the left of the Point B slide, and then to the right of the midline, sketch a contrasting photograph—in this case, another photograph of a product, except this time featuring an upward-facing arrow. When you show the slides in sequence, the Point A slide introduces the first photograph as you explain it, and then on the Point B slide, the second photo appears directly next to the first. This pair of contrasting images communicates the tension between A and B more powerfully than words ever could.

Interact at Points A and B

Of all the places in your storyboard where you plan to interact with your audience, the Point A slide is a particularly good one. When you interact with your audience here, open a conversation to get the critical information you need to confirm you are on track. If you hear from your audience that you are off track with your Point A slide, adapt your verbal narration or follow a different track through the material. (See "Tip 9: Create Nested Storyboards" in Chapter 6 for more information about creating a range of possible pathways through a presentation.)

Take a Poll

To engage your audience using the Point A slide on the upper left in Figure 7-7, try one of the oldest and simplest techniques to prompt interaction: ask a question. Sketch a question mark on the chart. The Point A headline is "What worked in the past isn't working anymore—and you're feeling the impact." When you show this slide to a smaller group, ask an open-ended question such as, "What sort of impact have you personally felt?" and then have a conversation about it. When you show the same slide to a larger audience, ask the question, "How many of you agree?" and then hold up your hand to signal the audience to raise their hands. Quickly count the number of hands and tell the audience the results of the poll as you move on to the next point, "It looks like about two-thirds of you agree. Well, today we're going to talk about..."

Taking a quick poll like this makes the audience feel like they're part of the conversation and also gives you a gauge of where the audience stands in relation to the topic. Vary this technique with larger audiences by providing the audience with interactive polling devices, which some companies build specifically for PowerPoint. When you ask the audience a question, the results of the poll are displayed directly on your Point A slide in the form of a chart that summarizes the polling results. The same thing can be accomplished using Twitter and other social media tools—to find out how, search the Web for the terms *Twitter* and *presentations* and you'll find many resources.

Introduce the Motif

So far, you've focused on numbers and charts to start off strong with your audience. Another way to go is to sketch out a motif as it plays out over the Point A and Point B slides. If you chose to incorporate a motif through the headlines of your story template, now you'll extend this recurring theme from your written words to the sketches of your slides.

For example, if you use a puzzle motif in the story template, the Point A headline might read, "The pieces we've use in the past no longer fit together—and you're feeling the impact" and the Point B headline might be "You'd like to find a new way to put the puzzle together." As shown in Figure 7-8, sketch three puzzle pieces on the upper left Point A slide to visually refer to the "pieces." Sketch the pieces coming together on the upper right Point B slide to "put the puzzle together."

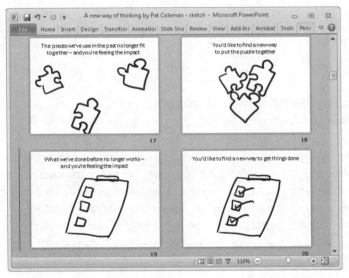

FIGURE 7-8 Two ways to sketch the pair of Point A and Point B slides. Top row: Introduce the motif of scattered puzzle pieces, and then show the pieces coming together to form a picture. Bottom row: The Point A slide shows a clipboard with empty check boxes, and the Point B slide shows the check boxes selected.

An alternative motif might have a Point A headline that reads, "What we've done before no longer works..." and a Point B headline that reads, "You'd like to find a new way to get things done." As shown in the bottom row in Figure 7-8, sketch the clipboard with empty check boxes on the Point A slide, and then sketch check marks in the same boxes on the Point B slide.

Later add simple animation to the elements on the Point A and Point B slides because these slides serve the important function of capturing the audience's attention in Act I. In the examples on the top row in Figure 7-8, sketch a note to animate the puzzle pieces to appear separately on the Point A slide and then come together to form the picture on the Point B slide. On the slides in the bottom row, make the check boxes appear on the clipboard on the Point A slide, and then make the check marks appear one by one on the Point B slide.

Unlock Information with a Visual Prompt

To use interaction to obtain useful information from your audience, sketch a simple photo object that relates to your topic on one or both of the Point A and Point B slides, and then use the photo to prompt conversation about specific topics. For example, if your Point A headline reads, "What worked in the past isn't working anymore—and you're feeling the impact," sketch graphics that indicate the various possible impacts, for example a dollar sign for money lost or a clock for wasted time. Hide the headline on the slide, and when the graphics on the slide appear, say, "There are many ways the situation is impacting us—what are the ones that are most important to you?"

Link the Act I Slides with a Single Chart or Photograph

To tie together even more tightly the slides in this example, sketch a single unifying image across all of Act I to make it a backdrop. Figure 7-9 shows how to do this. The Title slide includes a sketch of a light bulb indicating new thinking to set up the presentation. The Setting slide shows a chart of the monthly product sales declining, and then the Role slide shows the chart with a question mark indicating the audience wants to figure out what to do about the situation. The Point A slide uses the chart but now adds sketches of simple graphics indicating the impact of the declining sales—lost money and wasted time. The Point B slide adds a dotted upward arrow indicating the desired point—increasing monthly sales. The final Call to Action slide adds the light bulb directly over the chart indicating that a new way of thinking will get the results the audience wants.

This is a good example of how your PowerPoint slides are no longer like pieces of paper filled with lists of facts. Now your slides are like frames in a filmstrip, moving at a pace of about one frame per minute, with your voice providing the soundtrack to a clear and compelling story. Although to the audience, your presentation is a single smooth and seamless experience, in fact you have packed a great deal of information into these first five slides and have covered the essential elements that ensure you always start strong, as described in Chapter 4: orienting, interesting, engaging, motivating, and focusing your audience.

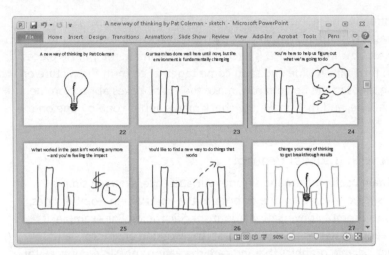

FIGURE 7-9 Telling a visual story using a single chart across all the Act I slides.

> **Tip** ✔
>
> Build the same sort of visual story across the frames of Act I by sketching a single photograph, copying it to each slide, and then sketching additional elements on each slide. If you present using a Tablet PC, sketch graphical elements directly on the photograph for more impact.

To increase the visual impact of these Act I slides, sketch a note on the slides reminding you that you plan to hide the headlines so that only the graphics are visible to the audience. As described earlier, when you present slides without headlines, the simple graphics make the audience rely on you to describe the slides' meaning, which creates an engaging interdependence between speaker and audience. This is an effective technique to use on your Act I slides while you make an emotional connection with your audience. Later, on the Act II slides, you'll usually want to keep your headlines visible to your audience to guide their attention through the much larger volume of information.

Although in this example the Call to Action slide shown in Figure 7-9 was sketched as part of the group of Act I slides, be sure you visually integrate it with the important Key Point slides, as you'll do next.

TABLET PC SKETCHING TIPS

The best way to sketch a visual story across slides using a Tablet PC is to work backward from the last slide to the first. For example, in the sequence of slides shown in Figure 7-9, first sketch all the elements you want to include on the lower right Call to Action slide. On the Review tab, choose Start Inking, and on the Pens tab, click Select Objects, hold down the Ctrl key while you click to select the Ink objects you want to include, and then right-click and select Copy. Go to the preceding slide, right-click and paste the Ink objects, and then on the Pens tab, click Eraser and move the mouse pointer over the parts of the sketch you don't need. Then copy this sketch, and follow the same steps as you work backward through the slides. Designing the last slide in the sequence first ensures that the final slide is organized and composed in a way that works—if you were to build from the first slide to the last, you would probably end up making changes to the last slide's layout. Working backward through the sequence also saves time because you don't need to sketch the same elements on the different slides in the sequence. Unfortunately, inking on your Tablet PC works only in Normal view and not in Slide Sorter view, so you'll need to switch back and forth between the two views to see how the story is flowing visually across slides.

Sketching the Call to Action and Key Point Slides

Your next job is to sketch the most important group of slides in the presentation—the Call to Action and Key Point slides. If you're working on paper printouts, gather these slides together. If you're using a Tablet PC, to see the Key Point slides together, zoom out in Slide Sorter view, and then locate the Key Point slides. Drag each one in sequence so that they follow the Call to Action slide, as shown in Figure 7-10. When you've finished sketching, you'll drag these slides back to their original positions. You don't have to do this every time you sketch, but it is helpful as you're honing your storyboarding skills. It's important that you see and work with these four slides together as a visual package because when each slide appears in its sequence in the storyboard, it should cue the audience that these are the most important slides in the presentation.

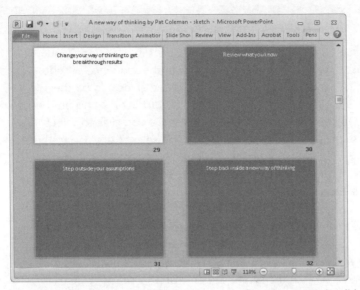

FIGURE 7-10 The dark gray Call to Action and medium gray Key Point slides should be the most visually memorable in the storyboard.

The Call to Action headline summarizes the Key Point headlines, and in turn the Key Point headlines summarize the Explanation headlines, and the Explanation headlines summarize the Detail slides. Because the Call to Action headline sits at the top of the informational hierarchy, as described in Chapter 5, it is really the verbal summary of the entire presentation. Likewise, what you sketch on the Call to Action slide should be a visual summary of the Key Point slides and of the entire presentation—if you had only one slide to show, this one would be it.

This group of slides formed by the Call to Action and three Key Point slides (referred to in shorthand as *CTA+3*) is very important—sketch them using the most creative, memorable, and powerful techniques you can come up with. If you have a marketing background, on these slides, you will apply the most powerful "branding" techniques you know—the set of techniques to visually distill a message and integrate it through an experience. The only difference here is that you're not applying these techniques to your corporate identity; instead, you're applying them to the highest level of ideas in your presentation.

Following are a range of techniques to "brand" the top level of your thinking on your CTA+3 slides. These sketching ideas are some of the basics—as you become comfortable with sketching, try out your own ideas, or invite a graphic designer to give you a hand.

Tripling Your Impact with Three Panels

A simple yet effective visual technique is to sketch full-screen photographs to illustrate each of the Key Point slides. Full-screen photographs are a good fit on the CTA+3 slides if they function to make the ideas of the headlines memorable. In the example shown on the upper right slide in Figure 7-11, the first Key Point slide refers to "what you know," so the sketch of the photograph is a simple illustration of a brain. The second Key Point slide, on the lower left, refers to stepping outside, so that sketch illustrates a door open to the outside. The third Key Point slide refers to the clients stepping back inside, so the sketch is of a photo of a doorway open to the inside.

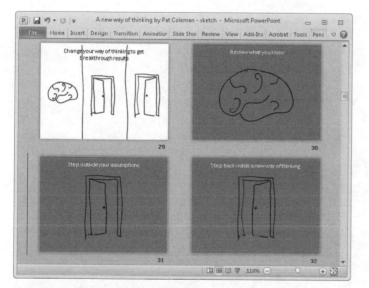

FIGURE 7-11 Sketches of the Call to Action slide with a three-panel layout and the Key Point slides with full-screen photographs.

Now that you've sketched three photographs on the Key Point slides, use these elements to sketch a *triptych*, or a single slide with three vertical graphical elements placed side by side. To create a triptych on the Call to Action slide (upper left), draw two vertical lines on the slide to create three panels, and then sketch in each of the three panels a key visual detail from each of the three photographs that were sketched on the Key Point slides. As you present them in sequence, these sketches on the Call to Action slide form a tight, crisp visual package and provide a preview of the material you're about to cover.

Adding It Up with Icons

Another approach related to the three-panel photographs is to sketch simple icons that represent the essence of your idea in a basic visual form. For example, add a sketch of "1-2-3" on the Call to Action slide that illustrates you'll cover three ways to "change your thinking." Then sketch a simple icon that illustrates the headline of each Key Point as in Figure 7-11, except now create a "build" of the three icons across the slides. Sketch a brain on the first Key Point slide, copy it to the second Key Point slide in addition to a door opening to the outside; and then copy both of these and add it to the third Key Point slide in addition to a door opening back to the inside, as in Figure 7-12.

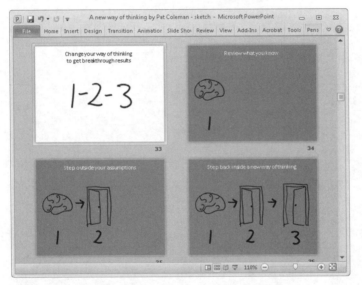

FIGURE 7-12 CTA+3 slides with icons in a diagram format.

As shown here, you build a simple *3-step visual process diagram* out of the icons by adding the numbers 1-2-3 below each icon and adding an arrow between each icon on the second and third Key Point slides to indicate the sequence.

Propping It Up

A classic technique in oral presentations is to show a physical prop and explain how the object relates to the presentation. The CTA+3 slides are a good place to integrate a prop, especially when you tie in that prop with your motif. For example, hold up a numbered puzzle piece when you present each Key Point slide to carry through a puzzle motif. Or better yet, pass out to your audience their own numbered puzzle pieces to hold—they will literally carry the main message of the presentation out of the room in their hands, and undoubtedly in their long-term memories too. If you plan to use a physical prop, sketch a photograph of it on the CTA+3 slides—during the presentation, you'll show the photo of the prop on the screen while you display the prop physically in the room.

Using Video, Sound, or Motion Graphics (Carefully)

If you plan to use video, audio, or motion graphics in your presentation, these forms of media stand out so significantly from your slides that you want to use them carefully and strategically. Before you use them, consider the research study described in Chapter 2 that found when you remove extraneous information from a multimedia presentation, you increase learning.

Remember, in Act II it's all about the hierarchy in your storyboard, and your measure of success is if your audience recalls and applies the information on your Key Point slides. If you plan to use video, sound, or motion graphics to illustrate the Key Point headlines, go ahead and sketch these elements on the Key Point slides. Be very careful about using these types of media in another part of the presentation if you don't use them on your Key Point slides—you would be unsuccessful in your presentation if the audience remembered your trendy video on the Detail slides but not the message of your Key Point slides.

Blacking Out the Screen

Consider fading to black to emphasize the Key Point slides. Visuals projected on a screen are spellbinding, but when you break that spell by blacking out the screen, you focus the audience's attention completely on you and your ideas at a specific moment. This creates an abrupt shift in the presentation with dramatic effect that works well to emphasize important points.

The best way to black out a screen is to change the background of your slide to black: Right-click the slide, and then select Format Background on the shortcut menu. In the Format Background dialog box, click Fill in the left pane, click Solid Fill in the right pane, and in the Color drop-down list, click Black. Make sure the Transparency control is set to 0%, and then click Close. Making the background of any slide black in your storyboard ensures that when you review the presentation in Slide Sorter view, you see exactly where among the sequence of slides you will fade to black and what happens on the slides immediately before and after.

An alternate way to black out a screen without changing the background of your slides is to use the B key. When you present your slides in Slide Show view, press the **B** key on your keyboard, or the appropriate button on your remote control, to turn the screen to black. Then, as all eyes turn to you, you'll emphasize verbally the key point. When you've finished, press the **B** key again to return to the same slide. (Alternatively, press the **W** key to turn the screen to white.)

Raising Interest with Your Layouts

A striking way to set up your CTA+3 slides is to use a distinctive layout to make them stand out among all the other slides in the storyboard. In Chapter 6, you set up a preliminary medium gray background on the Key Point slides when you set up the storyboard. Change those placeholder backgrounds to something more striking—for example, by using a split-screen layout on the Key Point slides. This layout style, shown in Figure 7-13, is a quick and easy way to set up these slides for sketches, and it's a particularly good fit for using icons as described earlier in this chapter.

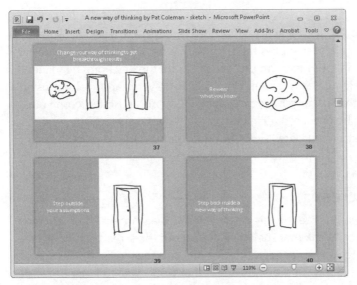

FIGURE 7-13 Sketches of the CTA+3 slides with a split-screen layout on the Key Point slides.

In Chapter 8, you'll explore PowerPoint features to set up and apply different layouts to the different levels of the storyboard. For now, if you want to quickly set up these slides to see how they look when you sketch on them in split-screen layout format, go to Normal view for the first Key Point slide. On the Insert tab, in the Illustrations group, click Shapes and then select Rectangle. Position the cursor in the upper right of the slide, click and drag until the rectangle fills half the screen, and then right-click the box and add a white fill. Then click and drag the headline to the left and click and drag the sizing handles to fit the headline, as shown on the upper right slide in Figure 7-13. Copy and paste the rectangle to the other two Key Point slides, and adjust the headlines. On the Call to Action slide, add a horizontal white rectangle to the middle of the slide to distinguish this slide from the Key Point slides, as shown on the upper left slide in Figure 7-13. Once you have the temporary layouts in place on the CTA+3 slides, sketch on the slides as usual.

Keeping the Motif Flowing

Your sketches will start to really strengthen your visual story if you have used a motif throughout your story template. For example, carry the puzzle motif from the Act I slides to the Call to Action slide, as shown on the upper left slide in Figure 7-14. Beginning with the third Key Point slide on the lower right, sketch three puzzle pieces together with the numbers *1-2-3*, then put the first two puzzle pieces on the second Key Point slide on the lower left, and then put the first puzzle piece on the first Key Point slide on the upper right. Then add photos that illustrate the headlines, as in the upper right and bottom row of Figure 7-14.

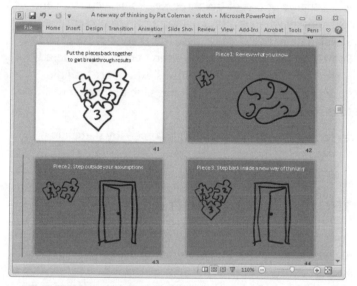

FIGURE 7-14 Sketches of the CTA+3 slides with a puzzle motif.

The photos in this example might be full-screen photos or simple photo objects with the backgrounds cut out. Or if you want to get really creative, bring the puzzle motif and the photos together by sketching each photo inside a puzzle piece.

Pausing at the End of Each Key Point Section

Just as the Point A and Point B slides are good places to ask questions and prompt dialog, other good places to do that are just before the second and third Key Point slides. To plan for audience interaction at these points, go to Slide Sorter view after you sketch your Key Point slides, select Key Point 1, and then press Ctrl+D to duplicate the slide. Drag the duplicate Key Point 1 slide to just before the Key Point 2 slide. Now select Key Point 2, duplicate it, and drag the duplicate to just before Key Point 3.

After you present the Explanation and Detail slides that follow Key Point 1, you'll see the Key Point 1 slide again, and there you'll pause to ask your audience for questions. When you've finished, advance to the Key Point 2 slide. Pause again after the Key Point 2 slide, and then advance to Key Point 3. You also might choose to duplicate these slides in Chapter 8, after you've added graphics to visually reinforce the Key Point slides at the end of the first and second Act II scenes.

Presenting with More than One Speaker

Some organizations feature multiple speakers during a presentation—if you plan to do that, put each of three speakers in charge of one of the three Key Point sections. Hand over the microphone to the next speaker when it is that person's turn to present the assigned section of Key Point, Explanation, and Detail slides. The change of speaker adds emphasis to each of the Key Point slides, but because the presentation is constructed from a single underlying story template, the audience members experience a single story that makes sense to them. Make a note on each Key Point slide of the name of the assigned speaker if you plan to do this.

Next you'll explore a visual way to link the rest of the slides to come—by sketching a navigation bar.

Sketching an Optional Navigation Bar

Tie together the slides of the presentation even more tightly with a visual navigation bar at the bottom of the screen. In the conventional PowerPoint approach, the space at the bottom of a screen usually contains the presenting organization's logo. Sketch your own organization's logo to illustrate the point of any single slide in the storyboard if the headline calls for that, or sketch the logo on the Introductory slide, as described earlier. But don't place your logo on every slide because doing so adds extraneous visual information for working memory to process, which impairs learning, as described in Chapter 2. (Besides, putting your logo on every slide sends the wrong visual message that every slide is all about you, when it is really all about the audience.)

A much better way to use the small space at the bottom of the Explanation and Detail slides is to visually cue your audience to the organization of, and current location within, the presentation. For example, if you use a puzzle motif through the presentation, after you sketch the first puzzle piece on the first Key Point slide, add a small horizontal bar at the bottom of the subsequent Explanation and Detail slides, and then sketch a small puzzle piece throughout these slides, as shown in Figure 7-15. You'll learn how to set up and apply navigation bars using custom layouts in Chapter 8.

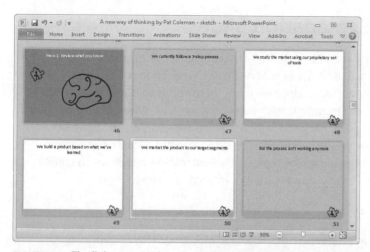

FIGURE 7-15 The light gray Explanation slides and white Detail slides now include a navigation bar with a single puzzle piece.

After you add a second puzzle piece to the second Key Point slide, add a similar puzzle piece to the navigation bar through the rest of the Explanation and Detail slides in this section, as shown in Figure 7-16. Then, after you add a third puzzle piece to the third Key Point slide, add three similar puzzle pieces to the navigation bar through the rest of the Explanation and Detail slides in that section.

As the audience views the slides in sequence, the navigation bar appears the same, until you reach the slides in the subsequent Key Point section, when they see a new puzzle piece appear to cue them that they are in a new section.

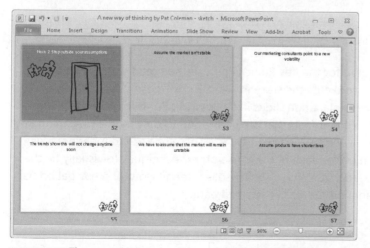

FIGURE 7-16 The second Key Point slide and the Explanation slides and Detail slides with a navigation bar with a second puzzle piece added.

Sketching the Explanation Slides

Your next job is to sketch the second-most important slides in the presentation—the Explanation slides for each scene of Act II. In Slide Sorter view, zoom out to locate the light gray Explanation slides, and then drag each one in order to follow their corresponding Key Point slide to see them together, as shown in Figure 7-17. When you've finished sketching, you'll drag these slides back to their previous positions. As with the CTA+3 slides, it's important that you see and work with these four slides together as a package—just as each Key Point headline summarizes the Explanation headlines to come, each Key Point slide should visually summarize its Explanation slides.

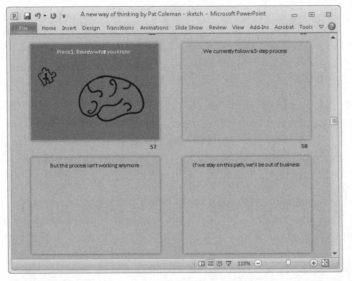

FIGURE 7-17 The first medium gray Key Point slide and its corresponding light gray Explanation slides.

Look at the sketch you created for the Key Point slide, and then read your Explanation headlines and imagine how to sketch the story forward across these slides. Sketch a single visual story across the Explanation slides if it's possible. But it might be that the Explanation slides are independent facts that are tied together only by the preceding Key Point slide and not to one another. If the Detail slides stand alone as independent ideas, sketch a standalone illustration for each one and use other techniques to visually tie the Explanation slides together, such as using a similar split-screen layout or a navigation bar running through the Explanation slides, as described earlier.

Tip	If you have difficulty sketching the Explanation slides, sketch the Detail slides first and then return to the Explanation slides. This approach is helpful because the Explanation slide summarizes the Detail slides to come, and if you sketch the Detail slides first, use them to come up with a visual summary for the Explanation slide.

Sketching a Visual Organizer

Earlier in Figure 7-8, the sketch of a clipboard with check boxes served to visually carry an idea across the Point A and Point B slides. Try a similar concept using check boxes to visually organize your ideas across your Explanation slides. On the upper left in Figure 7-18, the Key Point slide features a sketch of a piece of paper with three empty check boxes to illustrate what we will review. Sketch the first Explanation slide (upper right) with only the top box checked and the phrase *3 steps* from the headline, and then on the second Explanation slide (lower left), add a second checkmark and an *x* to indicate "isn't working" from the headline. On the third Explanation slide (lower right), add a third checkmark with a downward-facing arrow showing "we'll be out of business" from the headline.

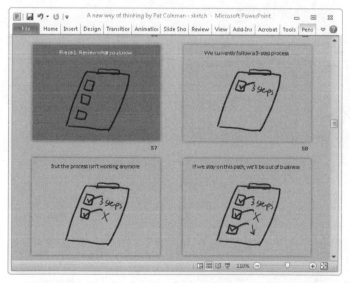

FIGURE 7-18 Sketches of a Key Point slide and Explanation slides using a checklist to visually tie them tightly together.

As they appear in sequence, the Key Point slide introduces the simple visual concept of the three check boxes, the first Explanation slide introduces the concept of 3 steps from the headline, the next slide builds on the preceding one and adds the concept of the process not working, and then the third slide builds on the preceding slide and adds the concept of going out of business. When each Explanation slide is dragged back to its position in the storyboard, it introduces another layer of meaning to the visual checklist story and at the same time ties together the Detail slides that follow.

Sketching Headline-Only Explanation Slides

When you deliver a 15-minute version of your presentation, you will spend the bulk of time on your nine Explanation slides that back up your three Key Points. But when you deliver a 45-minute version of your presentation, you won't spend much time on the Explanation slides because they only serve as a quick summary of what is to come in the Detail slides. If that's the case, and if you're pressed for time to find graphics, plan to use the headline alone—sketch a downward-facing arrow that notes you will move the headlines down to the center of the slide, as shown in the upper right slide in Figure 7-19. If you think a headline alone will be too stark, sketch on the slide a shape you would like to add to the Explanation slides to add to the background, as shown in the lower left slide. And if you have the time to find the graphics, sketch a small graphic that illustrates the headline of the Explanation slide, as shown in the lower right slide.

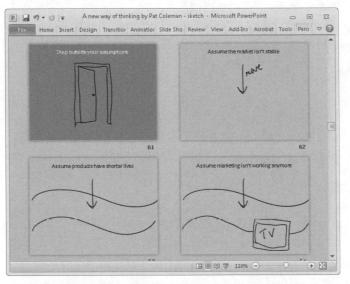

FIGURE 7-19 Sketches of a Key Point slide and Explanation slides that show headline only, headline with a background, and headline with a background and graphic.

Using a Screen Capture

For a quick illustration, consider sketching a screen capture. Anything viewable on a computer screen can be captured and displayed on a slide, including pictures of your desktop, Web pages, documents, and more. For example, use a screen capture to convey more detailed quantitative information available in other documents. Each dollar amount or other piece of quantitative information included in a headline is likely derived from an Excel spreadsheet or another data source that reflects the detailed analysis that produced it. You could probably spend an hour discussing the details of any single figure, but if you did that, you wouldn't have time to cover any of the other points in the presentation.

Instead, sketch a screen capture of a close-up of a spreadsheet that you will add to the slide, and when you display the slide, explain that the detailed data is contained there. Sketch a note on the slide that you will also bring printouts of the spreadsheet providing the detailed financial analysis and explanation that support the headline. Now the headline communicates the main idea you want to get across, the tightly cropped screen capture of the spreadsheet indicates you have backup for your point, your verbal explanation conveys what you intend, and the printouts hold the detailed information you will have readily available.

When you've finished sketching the Explanation slides, in Slide Sorter view, drag each slide back to where it belongs in the sequence of the storyboard. Now look at the storyboard and see how these slides guide your audience across the sections of the storyboard—with a Key Point slide, Explanation slide and then Detail slides all carrying the visual story forward.

Sketching the Detail Slides

Your last job is to sketch the third-most important slides in the presentation—the Detail slides that follow each Explanation slide. In Slide Sorter view, zoom in to see a set of Explanation and Detail slides together, as shown in Figure 7-20. It's important that you see and work with these four slides together as a package, because when you write out an Explanation headline in Act II, it summarizes the Detail headlines that come next. Similarly, each Explanation slide should be a visual summary of the Detail slides.

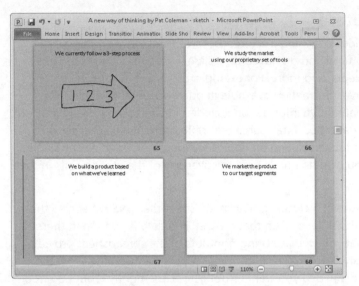

FIGURE 7-20 A light gray Explanation slide and the following three white Detail slides.

Look at the sketch of the Explanation slide, and then read the following Detail headlines and imagine how to sketch the story forward across the Detail slides. Sketch a single visual story across the Detail slides if it's possible. But it might be that the Detail slides are independent thoughts that are tied together only by the preceding Explanation slide—in that case, sketch standalone illustrations for each Detail slide.

Explaining Ideas by Building a Diagram

A common problem in conventional PowerPoint presentations occurs when a diagram or chart is too complex to be understood—or at least not understood all at once on a single slide. If your audience is new to the information in any diagram or chart, you will easily overwhelm the limited capacity of their working memory and impair learning if you show too much at once. You address the underlying root of this problem by breaking down Key Point headlines in the story template into smaller pieces as you write the Explanation and Detail headlines, which later become the foundation for individual slides that appear on screen for less than a minute while you narrate each slide.

Because you have used this approach, instead of explaining a great deal of information in a diagram on a single slide for many minutes, you will explain the same information in smaller pieces for less than a minute each, across a series of slides. This ensures you present new information evenly over the sequence of slides of any explanation, showing and saying only the correct information at the correct time to ensure you do not overload or split the attention of the working memory of your audience between what you are saying and showing at any moment.

Building a diagram across the corresponding series of Detail slides is an effective way to illustrate your ideas if you are describing a process or how the parts of something relate to the whole. For example, sketch on your Explanation slide a simple diagram with an arrow and the numbers "1-2-3" to illustrate the "3-step process," as shown on the upper left slide in Figure 7-21. Carry through this simple structure by sketching three similar arrows across the three Detail slides. On the first Detail slide, shown on the upper right slide, sketch a box with the word "study" to illustrate "first, we study the market." On the second Detail slide, sketch an additional box with the word "build" to illustrate "second, we build a product", as shown lower left; and then on the third Detail slide sketch a box and the word "market" to illustrate "third, we market the product," as shown lower right.

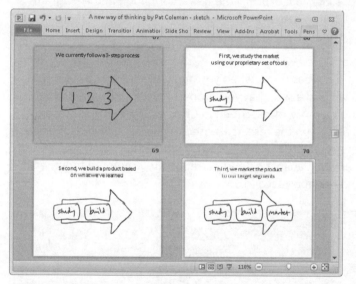

FIGURE 7-21 Sketches of a Key Point slide and Explanation slides showing a diagram carried across the slides.

Review these four slides. You first show a simple 1-2-3 illustration that introduces and summarizes the topic. Then you show and narrate the first headline with the first part of the diagram and build the diagram over the next two slides. Notice that the third Detail slide has more detail than the Explanation slide. You want the Explanation slide to be as simple as possible so that you don't overwhelm the working memory of your audience with too much new information too quickly. As you develop the diagram over the three Detail slides, the final slide is easy to understand because each element has been appropriately introduced both verbally and visually, piece by piece.

MY DIAGRAM DOESN'T FIT!

If you have a diagram you've used in other presentations and you'd like to fit it into your new BBP presentation, go to the story template and figure out where the pieces of the explanation of the diagram fit into the overall story. If the diagram contains information that is new to the audience, you need to break it up into smaller pieces to ease the new information through the working memory of your audience. As you use the story template to explain the diagram, think of the three main parts of the diagram and describe them in the Key Point headlines. Then complete the story template as before, breaking up each Key Point piece into smaller pieces in the Explanation headlines and then breaking each Explanation sub-piece into smaller pieces in the Detail headlines. When you return to the storyboard to revise the storyboard headlines, you'll have laid the groundwork for a series of slides that explains the new information in the diagram piece by piece, slide by slide—rather than all at once.

Although this example diagram is a basic one, when you apply the same approach to other types of diagrams, you will make sure that you properly synchronize the verbal and visual channels of working memory, as described in Chapter 2. When you present your slides this way, you also align with the research-based *temporal contiguity principle* described in Richard E. Mayer's research, which is based on studies that show that people understand information better when animation and narration are presented together rather than animation first and narration second.

Tip ✓	If you find that your headlines don't quite map to the sequence in which you want to present information, return to the story template and adjust the headlines there first. Then return to PowerPoint to edit the headlines accordingly.

Building a Chart Across a Series of Slides

After you have broken up an idea into smaller pieces across a set of Detail headlines in the story template, build a chart across the corresponding series of Detail slides to illustrate quantitative information. With the sequence of headlines in place in the storyboard, you'll know exactly what you want to communicate before you start building the chart. Again, this is where the wording of the headlines in the story template will define what you sketch. Build a chart across a series of Detail slides if the headlines contain specific quantitative explanation, such as "The industry average returns are 20%" and "Your average returns are 10%" and then "We can help you close the gap." If your headlines don't explain a chart but you would like them to do so, return to the story template to see how to revise the headlines to make the chart work.

Completing the Explanation Slides

You should be getting the hang of things by now, because you've already sketched many of the elements that you also sketch on the Detail slides. Here are some of the techniques to use to sketch the Detail slides:

- **Use photos, screen captures, or other graphics.** As in the previous levels, sketch photographs for your Detail slides such as a scan of the covers of trade journals, as shown on the upper right slide in Figure 7-22, or sketch logos of companies that illustrate the headline as shown on the lower right slide. If a photo alone doesn't work, you might include additional informational elements that you will add to the photo such as the circle with the line through it, indicating advertising no longer works, on the upper left slide.

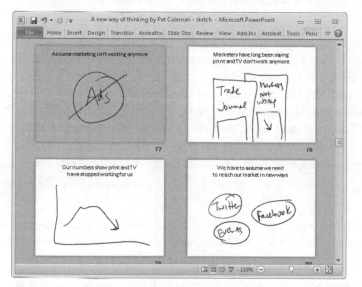

FIGURE 7-22 An Explanation slide with part of a diagram and Detail slides with a photo and added arrows, a photograph, and a screen capture.

- **Use a chart, graph, or diagram.** Sketch a chart, graph, or diagram on a single slide or across three Explanation or Detail slides, depending on what your head-lines say, as shown in a single Detail slide on the lower left slide in Figure 7-22.

Switching to Other Media

Plan to switch out of PowerPoint and into another software application to demonstrate an activity that you plan to cover in your Detail slides. For example, an instructor would switch over to Excel to demonstrate how to use one of its features, or to Word to show how to edit a document. During the presentation, when you arrive at an Explanation slide, verbally explain the point of the headline. Then switch over to the other application to demonstrate the points you covered on the Detail slide. Then return to the PowerPoint slide when you're finished. Before the presentation, hide the Detail slides because you will cover those points during the live demonstration.

HOW TO SWITCH BETWEEN APPLICATIONS DURING A PRESENTATION

Hold down the Alt key and press the Tab key, and then press the Tab key again until you select the corresponding software application that is open on your desktop, and then release the Alt key. After you've shown what you need to illustrate the headline, press Alt+Tab again until you select the software application that is open on your desktop that corresponds to the second hidden slide (lower left).

After you've shown the demonstration, press Alt+Tab again until you select the software application that is open on your desktop that corresponds to the third hidden slide (lower right). (If you have the Microsoft Aero color scheme enabled on a Windows Vista computer, instead of using Alt+Tab, hold down the Windows key and repeatedly press Tab to use a 3-D interface to select applications.) When you've finished with the third application, press Alt+Tab and return to PowerPoint, where you'll see the Explanation slide again. The headline here summarizes the point you made during the demonstrations; from here, advance to the next slide, which will be the following Explanation slide.

With this technique, you're using PowerPoint as a tool to manage what's happening on screen and off screen as well. As always, the headlines of the slides establish the ideas you want to communicate at any and every point in the presentation.

In a similar way, switch over to other non-PowerPoint media to provide variety in the presentation, including the following:

- A flip chart, whiteboard, or chalkboard
- A document projector
- Video clips, audio, or motion graphics
- A physical prop
- Paper handouts

Adapting Your Sketches to Your Profession

As you're thinking about what other sketches to include on your Detail slides, review the optional Act II headings in the section "Tip 3: Tailor Your Act II Column Headings to Your Profession," in Chapter 5. For example, if you're a market researcher, your Detail slides will probably include sketches of screen captures that illustrate your analytical tools, brief video clips from focus groups, and of course charts, graphs, and diagrams. If you're an attorney, your Detail slides will contain sketches of your specific evidence, such as screen captures of your "hot documents," photographs, short clips from video depositions, and scientific drawings. If you're selling a software product, your Detail slides will include sketches of the various sections of your product demonstration.

Sketching Your Story Template

It might take some time to learn the new skills of sketching your slides across frames and across levels. If you're having a tough time figuring out how to sketch diagrams, charts, and other Explanation or Detail slide elements, leave PowerPoint for a few minutes and review a printed copy of your story template. Read through the headlines from top to bottom in the Explanation column, and sketch directly over the column how you want to illustrate each Explanation slide—for example, with a diagram, as shown in Figure 7-23. Then read through the headlines in the Detail column, and sketch how to illustrate each Detail slide—for example, with a diagram, chart, or video clip. Here it might be easier to see that the sketch of each Explanation slide should be a summary and introduction of the adjacent Detail headlines to the right.

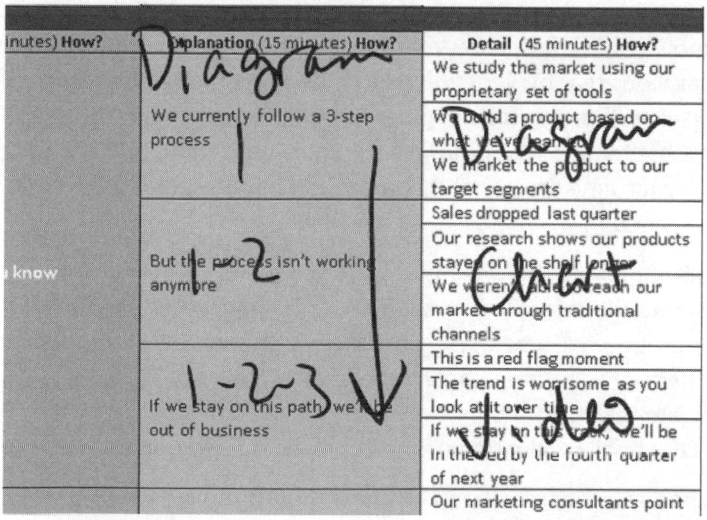

FIGURE 7-23 Sketch what you want to illustrate directly on a printout of the story template.

Tip   Sketching directly on the story template connects you back with the verbal story you wrote and helps you see what you're trying to accomplish from a different perspective. To sketch directly on the story template while you work with a team, place a screen capture of the story template on a PowerPoint slide and mark it up with Presenter Tools while it is displayed on a screen in the room.

Keep this technique in mind when you're writing the story template for the first time and as you go forward with your sketches in the storyboard.

BBP CHECKLIST: SKETCHING THE STORYBOARD

Do your storyboard sketches clearly show

- Where your Act I, Key Point, Explanation, and Detail slides are?
- How you tell your story across frames, at each level of the storyboard?
- Which graphics that you'll use?
- Where you will use interaction, props, and other media?

Ready, Set, Sketch!

Now that you have a range of techniques in mind, sketch the rest of your storyboard. Sketch each and every slide in the entire storyboard first, even if you already have some finished graphics that you know you want to use—that way, you don't get caught up in the visual details of individual slides that prevent you from spending time on the rest of the slides. After you have a sketch for every slide in place, you'll review the entire storyboard in Slide Sorter view in Chapter 8 to assess how much time you have to add graphics, where you need to spend your time first, what resources you have to get things done, and who to ask for help if you need it.

This process might seem challenging now, but the more you storyboard, the more skilled you'll become. Just as with writing the story template, it helps to bring in other people to collaborate with you on the storyboard. If you're using a Tablet PC, project the storyboard on a screen and sketch together; if you're using paper, tape printed copies of individual slides on the wall and collaborate that way. And just as you do when you verbally edit the story template, look for ways to visually edit, tighten, and improve your storyboard.

When you have a fully sketched storyboard in hand, it's time to turn the sketches into finished graphics as you complete your final PowerPoint storyboard in the next chapter.

CHAPTER 8

Adding Graphics to Your Slides

IN THIS CHAPTER, YOU WILL:

- Review the three ground rules for adding graphics.

- Apply custom layouts to the different sections of the storyboard.

- Add graphics to every slide of your storyboard.

TURNING WORDS into visuals can be a daunting task for anybody, especially if you're used to putting mostly bullet points on your slides. Fortunately, you've already done significant work to prepare the way for this moment—you have in hand a storyboard that includes all the slides in your presentation, and each slide includes a sketch that indicates the specific graphic you want to add. As always with the Beyond Bullet Points (BBP) approach, your focus is on helping your audience effectively understand new information. So your next task is to add the specific graphics to the storyboard that help make your visual point on each slide, without overwhelming the working memory of your audience with excessive new visual information.

Which Graphics Do I Add to Each Slide?

Like completing the story template, adding final graphics to your storyboard is both easy and hard. It's easy because all you need to do is use your sketch as a guide to "fill in the blank" below the headline on each slide with the graphic that the sketch describes. But it's also hard because you have a potentially unlimited range of graphics and styles to choose from, and you have to find the ones that are the best match with both you and your audience. Especially if working with graphics is a new skill for you, this project might feel daunting right now. But think of approaching this task just as you would any other project—by first assessing the current state of the project, then figuring out what needs to be done, and then making a plan for how you're going to accomplish that. This chapter will help you through the process of adding graphics to your storyboard step by step, helping you to break up the project into smaller, more manageable tasks.

Defining Your Design Constraints

Every design project has constraints—as much as you might want to take your time creating a work of art, the reality might be that you have only until this afternoon or tomorrow to create a PowerPoint masterpiece. It's important to know up front what limits you're facing so that you can plan your project accordingly. Do that by asking a few questions:

- **What is the scope of the project?** Look at your presentation in Slide Sorter view, as shown in Figure 8-1, to get a sense of the number of graphics you'll need to find. You should first identify where you will *not* need graphics and eliminate those slides from your count. For example, if you're giving only a 15-minute version of your presentation, you will hide the Detail slides, as described in Chapter 6, and focus your efforts on the other slides you need. Likewise, if you'll be switching over to another software application to present the ideas on some of the Detail slides, you won't need to add graphics to those slides either because you'll hide those slides as well.

- **How much time do you have?** Next determine how much time you have to get the job done. If your presentation is a report you need for this afternoon, you'll have to do your best with the resources at hand; however, if it's a presentation for a new product launch in three months, you obviously have more time to invest and to bring other people in on the project. Consider whether you have any additional deadlines before you need the final version of the PowerPoint file, such as marketing or legal approval. All of these factors will determine whether you have a couple of hours, a day, a couple of days, a week, a month, or longer to get the project done.

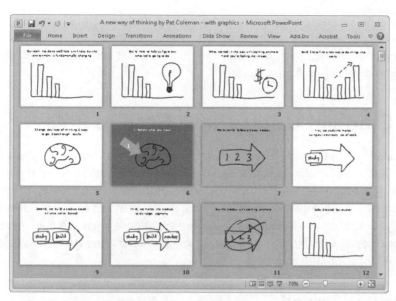

FIGURE 8-1 Review the fully sketched storyboard.

- **Where can you get graphics?** This chapter will show you a wide range of ways to get graphics for your slides, but one of the most useful resources you'll use is a stock photography Web site. These sites feature a database to search to locate photographs, illustrations, motion graphics, and video. Always properly obtain a license or otherwise get permission to use graphics if you do not already hold the rights to use them. Stock photography Web sites are set up to make the licensing process fast and easy, usually charging a few dollars per photo. This chapter features stock photography from *www.iStockphoto.com*, which has a database of millions of images for licensing. Locate other stock photography Web sites by doing a Web search for terms such as "stock photography presentations."

- **What's your budget?** If you have a budget of $0, you will be limited to only free graphics, screen captures, and any graphics you create yourself. If you have a budget of $30, license 10 photographs from a stock photography site for an average of $3 each; if you have $500, hire a freelance graphic designer for 10 hours at $50/hour; and if you have $10,000, commission a video that you integrate into your Key Point slides and elsewhere throughout the storyboard.

- **What other resources do you have available?** If you have the skills, create original illustrations yourself in another software program, or shoot your own photographs and edit them with image editing software. If you don't have these skills, consider other people to ask for help, such as an in-house design team or your coworkers.

Whatever constraints you have, you don't need design training to produce effective results with your new PowerPoint storyboard. This chapter will introduce and demonstrate a number of new tools and basic design techniques to start applying to your PowerPoint presentations today.

Adding Graphics Using Three Ground Rules

The most important thing to keep in mind when you add graphics to your storyboard is that you're not just designing *slides*; you're designing a complete *experience* that manages the visual and verbal channels for the working memory of your audience. It's easy to become absorbed in the details of fonts, graphics, and animations on the slides while losing track of your spoken words and how the entire experience helps the audience to understand your message. To make sure you stay on track, keep three ground rules in mind while you're working with graphics.

Rule 1: See It in Seconds

In Chapter 7, you sketched your storyboard across adjacent slides and sketched the hierarchy across levels. This process ensures that when you view the entire presentation in Slide Sorter view, you see exactly how you manage the attention of your audience *across time*. Within that context, you then focus on the individual slides to see how to best manage your audience's attention in any particular *moment of time*, both visually and verbally. The best place to understand the design of your slides is in its complete context of screen and narration—that is, in Notes Page view. As illustrated in Figure 8-2, the Notes Page view composition is built on three levels of information hierarchy.

The top of the information hierarchy is the on-screen headline, which summarizes the point you make at this moment; the second level of the hierarchy is the on-screen graphic, which visually explains the headline; and the third level of the hierarchy is the off-screen narrative explanation in the notes area, which further explains both the headline and the visual element with your spoken words. Although you'll be working on individual slides in Normal view, you should return frequently to Notes Page view during the process of adding graphics to view the slides in the context of their verbal narration.

Keeping in mind how your voice will seamlessly integrate with the graphics you add to each slide, look at Figure 8-3, which shows the built-in hierarchy of the default layout for your slides in Normal view. When you display any layout on the screen, you want your audience's eyes to go first to the most important information on the slide—the headline that summarizes your point. The headline communicates the topic clearly to the audience, reminds you as a speaker what you want to say, and keeps both parties focused on a specific topic.

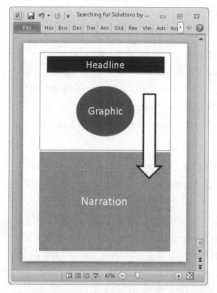

FIGURE 8-2 Information hierarchy seen in Notes Page view.

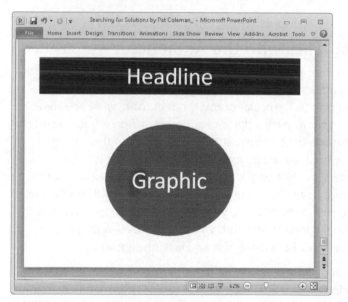

FIGURE 8-3 Slide hierarchy seen in Normal view.

Next you want your audience's eyes to move to the second-most important element on the slide—the graphic. Whatever graphic you add here should illustrate the headline and help your audience literally see your point by using the power of the visual channel of working memory. The graphic should pack as much meaning as possible into visual form and still be simple enough to be quickly digestible.

On the default layout when you first import your headlines into PowerPoint slides, the position for the graphic is centered on the screen, where it is easy to see and understand—adjust this layout according to what you sketched for each hierarchical level of the storyboard. If you do adjust some of the slide layouts later, keep them simple and include white space to give your audience visual breathing room to easily process the new information.

Although the basic layout for the slides is simple in style, it is sophisticated in its effect because the audience scans the headline and graphic and quickly understands the idea. This "verbal-visual reading" of the slide should get your point across in seconds so that the working memory of your audience can then pay attention to you and what you're saying. The goal is to help your audience quickly digest the slide—even if you display the slide for only a few seconds and then black out the screen, your audience should be able to articulate the main point of that single slide as you intended. After the slide initially sets the stage this way by quickly conveying the meaning of the headline, the slide shifts in function to a reinforcing backdrop while you verbally explain the point in more detail over the next minute.

Rule 2: Align the Aesthetics with the Audience

Life would be easy if you could choose any graphics to add to your slides, but there is the matter of *aesthetics*—how your audience thinks your graphics look. You might personally prefer the style or composition of a particular graphic, but in truth, what you think doesn't matter as much as what your audience thinks. For better or worse, your aesthetic choices can present a major obstacle to communication if you don't get them right. If people are paying attention to what they see as your bad choice of graphics, they're not paying attention to your message. Not only is effective learning at stake, but also your credibility. In the days before PowerPoint, you established credibility through your verbal introduction, your ideas, your authority, and your physical appearance. Now, with PowerPoint, you have an additional need to establish *visual credibility*—without it, you and your presentation will be perceived as amateurish and lacking substance.

Because the beauty of the graphic is in the eye of the beholder, you really need to know the beholder of your presentations—your audience. As you research your audience to determine how to focus your presentation across the first five slides of Act I, you also want to find out as much as possible about their aesthetic preferences as well. If you've been in a particular profession or industry for a while, you probably already have a sense for what is perceived as acceptable aesthetics. For example, if you're presenting to corporate executives, you'll take your aesthetic cues from a company's marketing materials, annual report, and office environment. But if you're presenting to a jury, you'll take your cues from the juror questionnaires, popular culture, and the local area. Choose the graphics appropriate to the group so that your graphics do not stand in the way of your message. As a secondary consideration, you also need to be personally comfortable with the aesthetics to deliver the material confidently and naturally.

Although the general aesthetic preferences of your audiences and their cultures might vary, when you work with BBP, you'll use a minimalist style because adding anything extraneous places an unnecessary cognitive load on the working memory of your audience. That said, even if something is simple, it can be an aesthetic mismatch with your audience.

As you search stock photography databases for graphics that are a good aesthetic match with your audience, scan through as many as time will allow so that you get a full sense of the spectrum of possibilities. For example, the headline from the storyboard shown on the upper left in Figure 8-4 reads, "You'd like to find a new way to get things done," and the sketch from Chapter 7 indicates that you'd like to use a clipboard image. When you visit a stock photography Web site such as *www.iStockphoto.com* and search for "clipboard," you'll get more than 7,271 results—which presents you with thousands of potential graphics you could use for this slide. Many of the graphics here might work—or possibly, none of them will.

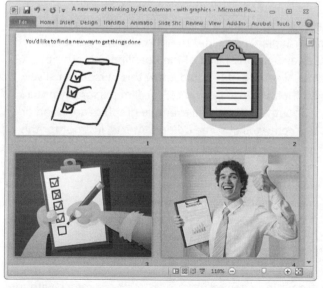

FIGURE 8-4 Aesthetic mismatches for a clipboard.

Tip The general guidelines for choosing graphics are to keep things as simple and unadorned as possible, and when in doubt, take it out. Review the graphics with other people on your team and gather their opinions to get a range of perspectives to help you choose which graphics work best aesthetically for both you and your audience.

When you're searching for an aesthetic match between a graphic and your audience, your focus should not be on whether you think a particular graphic is good or bad, but rather on whether a specific graphic will do the job of communicating the point of a specific headline to your specific audience. Scrolling through the search results reveals that many of the graphics probably are an aesthetic mismatch for the audience of the sample presentation in this book. For example, the clip art example of a clipboard on the upper right is done in a cartoon style that might make your message come across as not being as serious as the topic at hand. The clip art example on the lower left includes hands that are marking up the clipboard, but it's an aesthetic mismatch because the image also is in a cartoon style and comes across as too playful and not aligned with the aesthetic style the audience expects.

Using a photograph of someone holding a clipboard is in the realm of possibility, but this example on the lower right is too whimsical for the context, and it's also hard to see the clipboard because it is such a small percentage of the screen area. This is a good example of why you need to be careful when using a photograph that has a person in it, especially on a Key Point slide or an Explanation slide. The photo of the person in this example will distract attention away from the point of the headline and prompt thoughts in the viewer's mind such as, "I wonder if I should know this person," or "I've never seen anyone walk around with thumbs up in our office," or "I'm personally not a fan of his haircut." Again, this is not about whether these example graphics are good or bad, because they all would work perfectly well in some other contexts, just not for this audience.

Tip An important consideration when you're using graphics from commonly used sources is to be careful not to use images you've seen used in many other presentations. If an image is perceived as trite or overused, it will distract from your headline as well.

Although none of these examples from the search results are an aesthetic match with the audience you'll be presenting to in the book example, there are others that could work. For example, the photograph of the clipboard on the upper left in Figure 8-5 is simple enough to serve as the basis for a graphic in the presentation. A design constraint of this chapter includes not working with photo manipulation software, but you can still do simple things to make this image work if all you have is a preexisting photograph such as this one. Add three square boxes using PowerPoint drawing tools to create the check boxes (upper right), and then add the check marks (lower left). Apply the Explanation layout from the storyboard formatter to provide another variation (lower right).

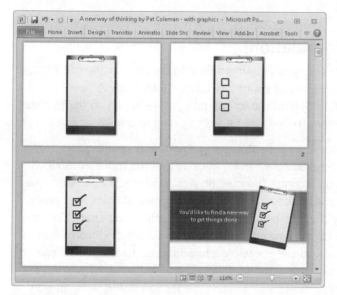

FIGURE 8-5 A closer aesthetic match of a clipboard for the example audience.

The final slide on the lower right is a closer aesthetic match with a financial services audience than the clip art and photo examples shown earlier in Figure 8-4. A professional designer might do an even better job with this slide. But accepting the constraints of doing it yourself and using only existing photographs and PowerPoint drawing tools, you can adapt and improvise like this to make the best of what you have.

Note   Choosing an unpolished aesthetic style can be a savvy and sophisticated strategy at times. If everyone presents the same slick, polished, and flawless style, everyone's presentations will look the same. If you choose something simple to contrast with the norm, you could break through the visual boredom and succeed at making a memorable impression. There is, of course, a risk that using a technique like this might not work if your audience expects the same aesthetics as they see everywhere else. So you need to be confident that you can make this choice work for both you and your audience.

Definitely, considerations related to your innate taste, talent, and skill come into play when you find, create, or add graphics. You might find you are naturally good at choosing graphics that align with the aesthetics of your audience. But you also might discover that your talents lie elsewhere—if so, it's best to enlist the help of your coworkers or designers to help you find the best graphics for the job, or use professionally designed graphics.

Rule 3: Defend Your Foundation!

At this stage in your BBP presentation, you've worked hard to create a strong foundation all the way from the words and structure of your story template through to your sketches. But if you're not careful to defend the foundation you've built, you might break the mechanisms that make BBP work so well and things can start to quickly unravel.

The main temptation is to add more to a slide than what you need to make your graphical point. But as Chapter 2 explains, research indicates that the more extraneous information you add, the more you increase the load on working memory and decrease learning. Every bullet point you add back to the slide, every additional color, and every extra visual detail can potentially clog the eye of the needle, the limited capacity of your audience's working memory to process new information. Keep subtracting from—not adding to—your slides. If you find yourself continuing to add more to a slide to make your point, most likely there's a problem with the structure and sequence of your ideas, and you should return to the story template to address the section of the presentation where the slide originates.

Although you might be able to control your own inclinations to add more visual detail to your slides, the biggest risk to your solid presentation foundation is from others who pressure you to keep adding information. For example, you might choose a simple illustration for a slide, as shown on the upper left in Figure 8-6—an image of a red toolkit to illustrate the headline "We study the market using our proprietary set of tools."

Perhaps you then invite your boss over to your desk to ask for his opinion. He thinks you should really emphasize the proprietary nature of the tools. He asks you to make the word *proprietary* bold and underlined. Then he says that he wants you to clarify the headline by adding the words *accurate quantitative-based*, which extends the headline from two lines to three (upper right). Not sure whether the slide is exactly right, he calls his boss over for her opinion. She says that you should emphasize the quantitative nature of the tools referenced in the headline by changing the word *quantitative* to uppercase and then adding a photo of a spreadsheet (lower left). Then the chief information officer happens to walk by and says that the slide looks unbalanced and that you should add a photograph of an IT team (lower right).

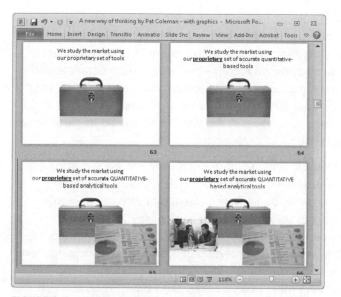

FIGURE 8-6 A BBP graphical foundation as it is eroded over time.

In spite of everyone's good intentions to make the slide better, the combined additions made it much worse. As the old saying goes, "If you emphasize everything, you emphasize nothing."

The headline on a BBP slide already sits in the most prominent position on the original slide (upper left), so there's no need to embellish it to make it stand out—there is an easy flow as the audience sees the headline, looks at the graphic, and listens to the speaker. The emphasis on individual words disrupts easy reading of the headline (lower right) and creates unnecessary visual competition about where to look first. The same happens when you add the other two photographs—they have transformed what was once a clear and easily viewable slide into a distracting hodgepodge. The audience can no longer easily see the meaning of the entire slide in seconds. The group process has broken the foundation of the BBP approach and rendered the slide ineffective.

Not only does breaking the BBP foundation impact an individual slide, it also disrupts the sequence of slides. It's easy to get lost in the individual slides instead of seeing the big picture of the story template. For example, for BBP to work, you should have the same font style and size of headlines on all your slides to ensure that each slide is easy to read and links together visually. Within the hierarchy levels of your storyboard, you should have consistent placement of headlines as each slide flows visually from one to the next.

You break the consistency in the BBP approach *only for specific reasons*—for example, when you disrupt the flow of ideas to indicate that the next idea is more important than the others, as determined by the story template. But in this example, other members of your organization broke the consistency *for no reason*—the unnecessary details added to the headlines do nothing to help the big picture of the presentation, and instead hurt it. The situation can get even worse if you start adding new slides to your storyboard and rearranging them without reflecting the changes in the story template. Soon, the internal pacing and flow of the presentation begin to unravel too.

The graphical way to fix the problems shown in Figure 8-6 is easy—remove everything except the minimum number of visuals needed to illustrate the headline, as in the original slide (upper left). But the organizational fix will take a bit more work. People's urges to add extraneous detail are most often related to habit or myths, such as thinking that the more you add, the more people will learn; or that you need to add pizzazz to catch someone's attention; or that you need to entertain people instead of helping them learn. To protect your hard-earned BBP foundation, stand firm on your research-based grounding from Chapter 2 as you help other people understand that "Less is more" is more than a slogan—it's a strategy and proven tactic for getting optimum results in your presentations.

THREE GROUND RULES FOR ADDING GRAPHICS

Adding graphics is the crucial last step in designing the storyboard. Follow these three ground rules to make sure you get the graphics right:

Ground Rule 1: See it in seconds.

Ground Rule 2: Align the aesthetics with the audience.

Ground Rule 3: Defend your foundation!

Starting the Production Flow

Aim for a first draft of your storyboard, not a finished product. Don't spend too much time on any single graphic—you could easily spend all day on one slide and get nothing else done. Instead, put something on the slide for the first draft, even if it's not exactly what you're looking for, and come back to work on the imperfect things later. Work in a sequence that will make most efficient use of your time, beginning with getting others to help you.

Note	This book assumes you know the basics of PowerPoint, such as using drawing tools and inserting, resizing, and cropping photographs. If you need a tutorial or a refresher on how to use the software, a number of basics books are available, such as Joyce Cox and Joan Lambert's, *Microsoft PowerPoint 2010 Step by Step* (Microsoft Press, 2010). To review the basics of working with photographs, see "Tip 2: The Photo Basics: Size, Crop, and Compress" later in this chapter.

Delegating the Graphics Tasks

If you have coworkers who can help you find or create graphics to add to your storyboard, get them started first so that task is underway while you do your work. A good way to provide these coworkers with the information they need is to save a new version of the PowerPoint file with another name, and delete all the slides that your coworkers won't need to see. When your coworkers open the file, they'll have the specific slides you assigned to them, and if you ask them to view the slides in Notes Page view, they'll see the headline that summarizes your point, the detailed off-screen narration, and the sketch you added to the slide in Chapter 7. They can replace the sketch with a graphic, and when they e-mail the file back to you, insert the new slides, copy and paste the entire slides, or copy and paste just the graphics from the slide area.

If you have the resources to have graphics custom-made, assign those tasks in the same way, providing the designer with the slides—see "Tip 4: Design for Your Designer" later in this chapter for additional advice about working with designers.

Getting the Graphics You Already Have

Next get the things done on the project that you can do quickly, to reduce the scope of the project. For example, if you already have on hand 10 preexisting graphics out of the 40 you need, adding them now to the storyboard means that you're 25 percent done, which will give you a better handle on the situation.

The first place to go to get graphics is your existing BBP presentations, if you have any. You'll be building a library of BBP presentations over time that will help your production process go faster each time. This library will save you effort as you build BBP presentations from scratch less and less. If you don't have previous BBP presentations, you might have some graphics in other presentations that are simple and illustrate the point of a headline—but if they are overly complex, or otherwise don't align with the BBP foundation of your storyboard, don't use them.

Getting Graphics at Stock Photography Web Sites

If you're a good photographer, take your own photographs using a digital camera to use on your slides; otherwise, visit a stock photography Web site. Search for graphics based on keywords you enter into a search box, such as "clipboard." You'll then see a search results screen similar to the one from the *www.iStockphoto.com* Web site shown in Figure 8-7.

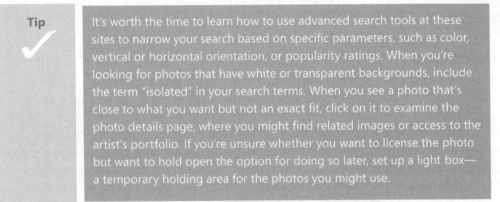

Tip ✓ It's worth the time to learn how to use advanced search tools at these sites to narrow your search based on specific parameters, such as color, vertical or horizontal orientation, or popularity ratings. When you're looking for photos that have white or transparent backgrounds, include the term "isolated" in your search terms. When you see a photo that's close to what you want but not an exact fit, click on it to examine the photo details page, where you might find related images or access to the artist's portfolio. If you're unsure whether you want to license the photo but want to hold open the option for doing so later, set up a light box— a temporary holding area for the photos you might use.

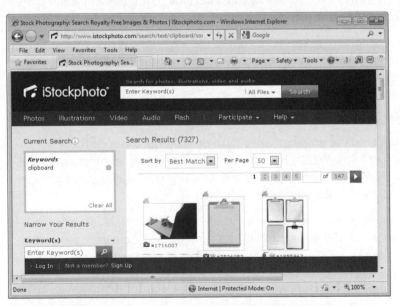

FIGURE 8-7 Search results for "clipboard" at *www.iStockphoto.com*.

As you consider where to get graphics, you probably have more readily available graphics than you think, especially if you work in an organization—for example, many marketing departments have libraries of photographs that are already licensed for use in presentations. In every case, make sure the photographs are optimized for presentation use at screen resolution—print resolution produces much larger file sizes that unnecessarily expand the file size of your presentations and can make them more difficult to use.

| **Tip** ✓ | The companion Web site to this book at *www.beyondbulletpoints.com* has a range of tools, training, techniques, and templates to make your graphics job easier and faster. |

Creating the Graphics You Can

PowerPoint includes a range of drawing tools that you might already know how to use, such as creating shapes, lines, arrows, callouts, charts, and graphs. Add any of these elements as a simple graphic on a slide, or use the drawing tools to add other graphical elements such as callouts to existing photographs.

Applying Final Slide Layouts to Your Storyboard

In Chapter 6, you applied preliminary sketch layouts to the Key Point, Explanation, and Detail slides so that you could see them clearly in Slide Sorter view and practice scaling your presentation to time. These visual cues indicate to your audience's working memory which slides are more important than others as you present them in sequence. In Chapter 7, you reviewed different ways to sketch these slide layouts to build on this foundation and keep the hierarchy of the presentation clear. You'll now apply a finalized version of these important layouts.

You have several options for your final layouts—use predesigned versions that are included in the BBP Storyboard Formatter you used in Chapter 6, have a graphic designer create layouts for you, or design layouts yourself manually by following the steps described in Appendix E. Whichever approach you choose, the layouts should adhere to the following guidelines to ensure you cue your audience to the type of Act II slide they are looking at, as show in Figure 8-8:

- When you apply the Key Point slide layout (left), it should call attention to these slides first out of all your slides. In this case, the Key Point layout features a full-screen, colorful pattern of blue and green.

- The Explanation slide layout (middle) should call attention to these slides second out of all your slides. In this case, the Explanation layout features a horizontal bar taken from the Key Point layout pattern, centered to hold the headline.

- The Detail slide layout (right) should provide a simple foundation for the bulk of your slides. This example of a Detail slide layout (right) includes a thin horizontal strip from the Key Point layout at the bottom of the slide, leaving the rest of the slide clear and open for a simple graphic.

Apply a layout that calls attention
first to the Key Point slides.

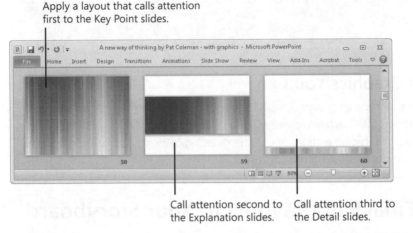

Call attention second to   Call attention third to
the Explanation slides.   the Detail slides.

FIGURE 8-8 Example custom layouts for the Key Point, Explanation, and Detail slides.

The completed Key Point, Explanation, and Detail slides from the example presentation shown in Figure 8-9 demonstrate how both layout and color work together to indicate the relative importance of these slides. As shown in this example, by applying these layouts to the corresponding slides in your presentation, you preserve the powerful hierarchy you created in Act II of the story template.

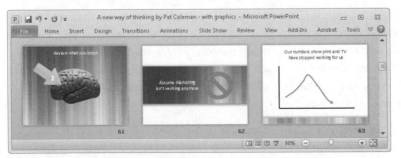

FIGURE 8-9 Custom layouts applied to sample Key Point, Explanation, and Detail slides.

Applying, Reviewing, and Refining the Layouts

Choose a layout set now, and apply it to the corresponding slides in your presentation. Be sure you use the BBP Storyboard Formatter described in Chapter 6 because conventional PowerPoint presentations don't include the BBP layout sets. To apply layouts, do the following:

1. In Slide Sorter view, press Ctrl+A to select all the slides in the presentation.

2. On the Home tab, in the Slides group, click the Layout button to display a drop-down menu of your custom layouts. Scroll through the built-in layout sets, and choose one that's the best fit for your slides.

3. Within your layout set, click the Detail slide layout to apply it to all your slides.

4. Hold down the Ctrl key again while you select each of the Key Point slides, click Layout, and then click the Key Point slide layout.

5. Hold down Ctrl while you select the Explanation slides, click Layout, and then click the Explanation slide layout.

6. Last, click the Title slide and apply the Title slide layout, and then hold down the Ctrl key while you click the Act I slides and apply the Act I slide layout (if you have one) or the Title Only slide layout (if you don't).

After you finish applying custom layouts, the slides of your storyboard should appear as shown in Figure 8-10. Now that you have custom layouts in place, you have a foundation for the graphics that you'll add to individual slides next.

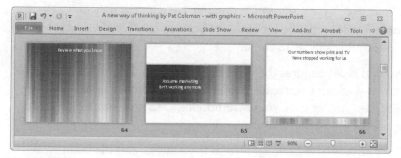

FIGURE 8-10 Examples of Key Point, Explanation, and Detail slides with the corresponding custom layouts applied.

CUSTOMIZING LAYOUTS

Customizing your slide layout sets as described in Appendix E will give you tremendous flexibility as you get to know them better and find ways to make your graphical work easier and faster. The great thing about custom layouts is that experimenting is easy—if you create a layout you don't like or that doesn't work, or if you make a mistake, it's easy to return to the layout in Slide Master view and make changes there that will be automatically updated on the corresponding slides built from the master. If a slide is not updated, select the slide, and on the Home tab, in the Slides group, click the Reset button. When you have a set of custom layouts you like, copy and paste them from the Overview pane in Slide Master view to other presentations, and save them to use again later.

Adding Graphics to the Call To Action and Key Point Slides

When you apply custom layouts to your storyboard, you now have a graphical foundation established for all of your slides. The next step is to add graphics to the Call To Action and Key Point slides you sketched in Chapter 7, as shown in Figure 8-11. The Call To Action slide sketch (upper left) features a simple illustration of a brain to illustrate "Change your way of thinking." As you learned in Chapter 7, if you had only one slide to show in a presentation, this one would be it because it both visually concludes Act I and visually summarizes the Key Point slides to come.

Each of the three Key Point slides features the same brain from the Call To Action slide, except an incoming arrow is added to indicate "Review what you know," upper right; an outgoing arrow to illustrate "Step outside your assumptions," and an incoming arrow to indicate "Step back inside a new way of thinking."

In Figure 8-12, Key Point layouts have been applied to these slides, and the brain photograph and arrows added. By using only a single photograph and arrow shapes, these Key Point slides manage to tell a simple story that captures and keeps the attention of the audience in a memorable way.

When your Key Point or Explanation slides feature the same underlying graphic—in this example, the brain—add the graphic to the underlying custom layout so you don't have to add the graphic to the individual slides.

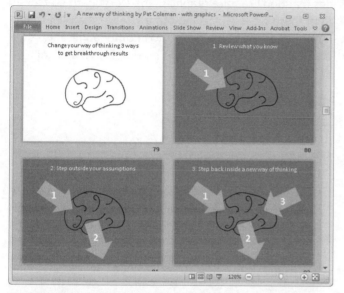

FIGURE 8-11 Original sketches of the Call To Action and Key Point slides.

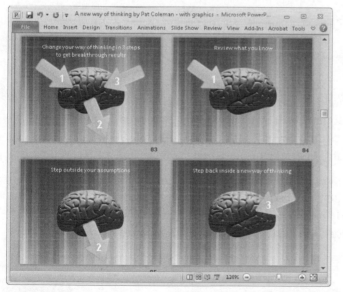

FIGURE 8-12 The Call To Action and Key Point slides with graphics added.

Preparing Slides That Don't Require Graphics

Now that you've taken care of the most important slides in the presentation, the next thing to do is take care of the slides that don't require graphics. The storyboard sketches in Figure 8-13 show four examples of these slides—blacking out a screen on an Act I slide (upper left), displaying a physical prop (upper right), switching to another application on an Explanation slide (lower left), and using only a headline and no graphic on an Explanation slide (lower right).

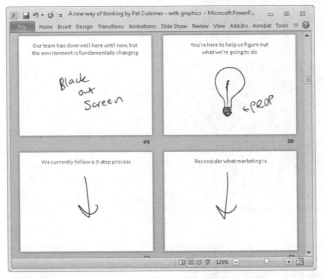

FIGURE 8-13 Example sketches of slides that use techniques other than graphics on PowerPoint slides.

As described in Chapter 7, black out the screen, as shown in Figure 8-14 (upper left), by right-clicking and formatting the background color as black or by inserting a black rectangle to fill the screen. Drag the headline outside of the slide area so it will not appear on screen. If you plan to use a physical prop, drag the headline down to the middle of the screen (upper right) or black out the screen.

To switch to a different application on the screen when you get to a slide, center the headline and add a simple graphic (lower left) to introduce your activity as you switch applications. If you are pressed for time and would like to include a headline-only on a slide, apply the Explanation slide layout and leave the slide as it appears (lower right).

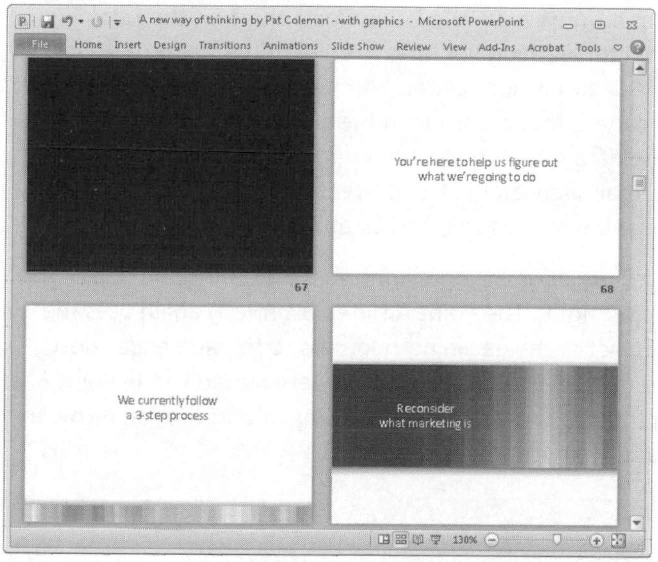

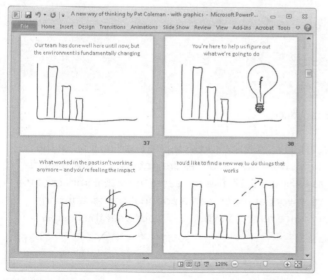

FIGURE 8-14 Completed slides, without graphics.

Adding Graphics to the Act I Slides

Now start at the beginning of the presentation and add the graphics to your Act I slides that you sketched in Chapter 7. Those sketches are shown in Figure 8-15.

FIGURE 8-15 Original sketches of the Act I slides.

In the completed example shown in Figure 8-16, the PowerPoint chart on the Setting slide (upper left) conveys a chart with declining volumes in an extremely simple way without detail. The usual detail in a chart is not needed here because in this specific context, the reason you chose this image is that everyone in the audience is already familiar with the chart and agrees that the data is true. Here the purpose is not to analyze the graph as you will likely do on a Detail slide later in the presentation, but rather to visually cue the audience as quickly as possible to the topic and establish the setting.

The Role slide uses the same chart, but adds a simple light bulb indicating the role of the audience is to generate ideas (upper right). The Point A slide (lower left) again uses the same chart, except adding the impact of the declining numbers to the audience—lost time and money. In the Point B slide (lower right), three bars were added to the Point A chart using PowerPoint drawing tools to show returns improving, along with an arrow to reinforce the upward direction the audience wants to achieve.

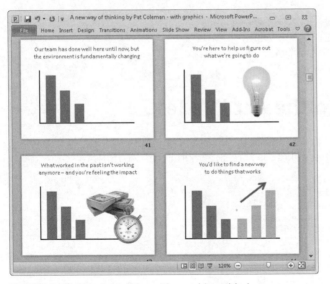

FIGURE 8-16 The Act I slides with graphics added.

An effective technique in your Act I slides is to click and drag the headlines off of the slide area when you work in Normal view, so the headlines are not visible to your audience when you display the slides as in Figure 8-17. This increases the visual impact of the Act I slides as they do their important work of making an emotional connection with your audience and making your audience reliant on you to explain what the images mean.

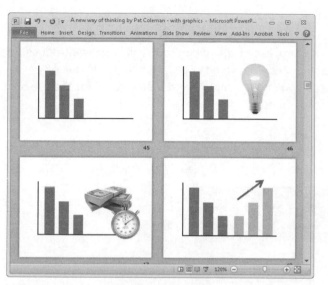

FIGURE 8-17 The Act I slides without headlines visible.

Adding Graphics to the Explanation Slides

As described in Chapter 7, the sketches of your Explanation slides might guide you toward adding a photograph, logo, diagram, chart, or other illustration on the individual slides. Figure 8-18 shows a Key Point slide with graphics you've already added (upper left), and the sketches of its three related Explanation slides.

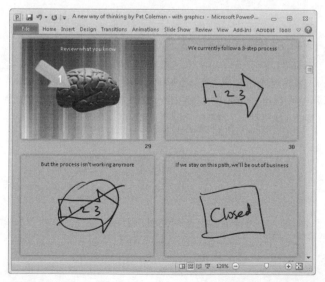

FIGURE 8-18 Key Point slide with graphics added and original sketches of the related Explanation slides.

Locate and add graphics that correspond to these sketches on each of these slides, as shown in Figure 8-19. Notice that these slides are telling a story, slide by slide, as they explain the initial Key Point slide—in turn, each Explanation slide will visually introduce and summarize its subsequent Detail slides. You would apply a similar technique of building a visual story step by step if your story template and sketches call for the use of a diagram or chart on the Explanation slides.

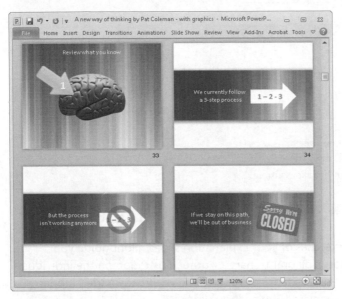

FIGURE 8-19 The Explanation slides with graphics added.

Adding Graphics to the Detail Slides

For a 45-minute presentation, the bulk of your work when adding graphics involves the Detail slides. As described in Chapter 7, you might have sketched photos, charts, or screen captures to add to these slides, as shown in Figure 8-20.

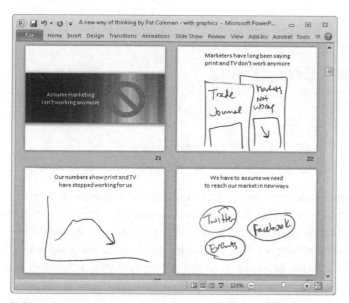

FIGURE 8-20 Explanation slide with graphic added (upper left), along with original sketches of the related Detail slides.

If you use images from *www.iStockphoto.com*, these slides might look like the slides on the upper and lower right in Figure 8-21 after you have added the graphics you found.

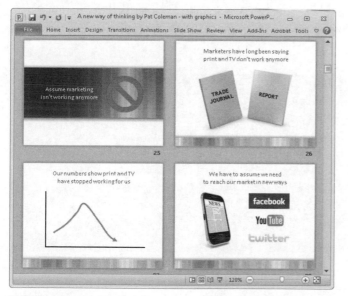

FIGURE 8-21 The Detail slides with photographs and a screen capture added.

Tip One of the simplest and most overlooked sources for graphics is your computer screen. To create a shot of your screen, press Print Screen (usually labeled PrtScn on your keyboard), and then on a slide in Normal view, right-click and choose Paste to place the image on the slide. Click on the image to access the Picture Tools and Format tabs, where you make adjustments to the screen capture. Commercial screen capture programs such as SnagIt (*www.techsmith.com*) allow you many more options for customizing your shots, such as adding a subtle drop shadow.

If you sketched a chart on a Detail slide, it might look like the slide on the lower left in Figure 8-21 in its final state. Although many of the guidelines and much of the writing and research related to charts deals with displaying them on paper, PowerPoint charts are usually projected on a wall with a live presenter explaining them. Because there is the added element of a synchronized verbal explanation in the live presentation environment, charts designed on a slide can generally be simpler than those displayed on paper without a live presenter.

With the BBP approach, you're certain that the main point of a chart is fully explained by the headline—that's because you always clarify your point in the form of a headline before you select the chart to explain it. If someone was not present to hear your narration, you provide them with a handout of a Notes Page version of the slide that includes the headline, chart, and off-screen notes area explanation. Displaying the chart over a series of slides that are mapped to a sequence of headlines, as described in Chapter 7, helps to introduce the new information in smaller pieces at an appropriate pace for the audience to understand.

Tip To keep a chart free of clutter and focused on the data at hand, simplify its formatting by removing excess lines, graphical treatments, colors, and grids. Avoid adding unnecessary ornamentation or special effects that inhibit the audience's ability to understand information, as described in Chapter 2. Strive for a minimalist style that allows the numbers to speak for themselves. When you need to show your numbers using a chart, consider consulting one of the books that can help you to display data effectively, including Stephen Few's *Show Me the Numbers: Designing Tables and Graphs to Enlighten* (Analytics Press, 2004).

Creating the Act III Slides

As you'll recall from writing your story template in Chapters 4 and 5, you never got around to writing Act III of your story—the resolution. You will quickly take care of the end of your story now with a couple of mouse clicks.

A classic way to end a story is to back out the way you came in. End your PowerPoint story the same way by holding down the Ctrl key while you select your Point A and Point B slides along with your Call To Action slide. With these slides selected, press Ctrl+D to duplicate the three slides. Now drag these duplicated slides to the end of the presentation, following the last Detail slide of Act II. If you haven't already done so, here you might differentiate these slides graphically from their Act I counterparts by dragging the headlines off of the slides so that they don't appear on the screen, as shown in Figure 8-22.

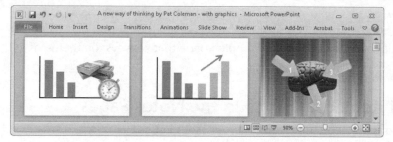

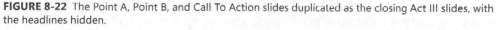

FIGURE 8-22 The Point A, Point B, and Call To Action slides duplicated as the closing Act III slides, with the headlines hidden.

When you reach the Point A slide in the closing Act III of the presentation, say something like, "You'll remember we started today by looking at the impact you feel because the old way is not working any more [advance to Point B slide] and the desire to find a new way that works. Well [advance to Call To Action slide], today we've shown that by changing your way of thinking in three ways, you'll get the results you want...."

These familiar images connect back to the core problem of the story you began and visually reinforce the messages you want your audience to remember. Just as you start strong visually and verbally, these same slides can help you end strong visually and verbally. Change the order of the slides, if appropriate, and otherwise adapt, innovate, and improvise verbally. Whatever you plan to say in your strong ending here in Act III, be sure to make the appropriate updates in the notes area of the corresponding slides that you duplicated.

Fine-Tuning and Finishing Up

Now that you have a first draft with a graphic on every slide, go back and review what you have with an eye toward refining your presentation.

Adding Graphics to the Title and Closing Credits Slides

In a film, the opening title sequence establishes the mood and tone of the story to come. Achieve a similar effect by adding graphics to the Title slide. Apply the same style to the Title slide that you did to the other slides in Act I. For example, if you use the photographic design technique for the Act I slides, use the same style for the Title slide. Then apply the same technique you use for the Title slide to a closing slide that will remain on screen when you finish your presentation.

To create a closing slide now, on the Home tab, click New Slide, and on the drop-down menu, click Blank. Now add a simple image or a line of text that you want the audience to remember after the presentation. This slide might include your organization's name, your contact information, a Web address, or a simple image that conveys the theme of the presentation.

Reviewing and Adding Graphics to the Notes Pages

The BBP Storyboard Formatter you used to create your slides in Chapter 6 includes formatting of the Notes Master that balances the notes pages equally between the amount of space you dedicate to the slide you show on screen and the amount of space you dedicate to the notes area, which holds the ideas you explain with your narration. In the example in Figure 8-23, the line around the slide placeholder was removed to open up the white space on the printed notes page. The Slide Master and Notes Master both have white backgrounds, and because neither the slide nor the notes areas will be bounded by lines, the headline of the slide summarizes the idea of the entire printed page.

To preview how the notes page version of any slide will look when printed, click File, Print. Under Settings, select Notes Pages. Add more graphics to the notes pages if you choose, such as the chart shown at the bottom of Figure 8-23.

When you finish making adjustments or adding graphics to all the slides, return once again to Notes Page view of each slide to review the notes areas and make sure your written words are clear and concise. Begin with the first notes page: read the headline, review the visual, and then read the notes area to make sure everything flows smoothly. When you've read the last line in the notes area, scroll down to the next notes page and make sure it reads smoothly as a continuation of the story from the previous notes page.

It's a good idea to print the entire document as notes pages at this point to check the wording and flow.

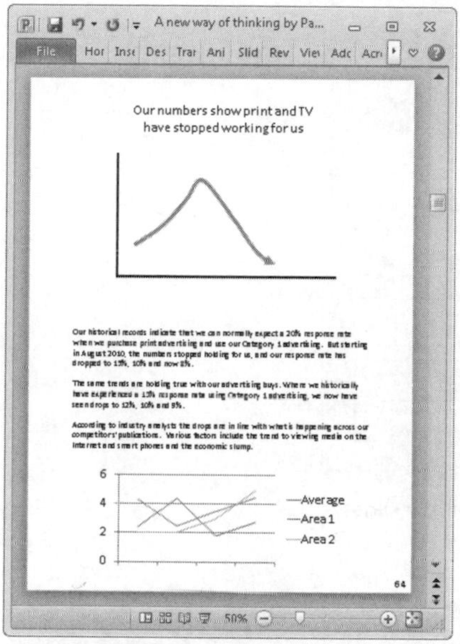

FIGURE 8-23 Notes Page view.

Reviewing and Finalizing the Storyboard

Congratulations on completing your PowerPoint storyboard! Your final presentation should look something like the one shown in Figure 8-24.

After you've reviewed the complete presentation, have someone with fresh eyes take a look at the presentation to verify that you didn't miss anything, make a typographical error, or misstate something. When you prepare the presentation for review, plan to send it as notes pages for review, not only of what appears on screen but also of the information covered in the notes area.

> **Tip**
> ✓
> Saving your PowerPoint file in PDF format allows you to send a version of the presentation electronically in a form that does not allow others to alter it. To save a presentation as a PDF file, click File, Save & Send. Select Create PDF/XPS Document, and click the Create PDF/XPS button.

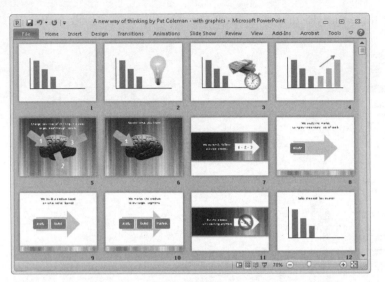

FIGURE 8-24 Completed storyboard with graphics added to all the slides.

BBP CHECKLIST: ADDING GRAPHICS TO THE STORYBOARD

Do your final graphics

- Clearly illustrate each headline in the simplest way possible?

- Show consistency within levels of the presentation hierarchy and variety across levels?

- Keep your slides free of any extraneous visual information?

- Align with the aesthetics of your audience?

You've come a long way since you started on the road to the BBP approach in Chapter 1, and the example presentation in this book should help you start applying the BBP approach to your next presentation. Next Chapter 9 will provide some ground rules and tips to consider when you deliver your presentation to an audience, and Chapter 10 will show you a range of presentations to review for additional inspiration.

As you get familiar with adding graphics, take a look at these 10 tips for improving on the basic techniques described in this chapter.

10 Tips for Enhancing Your Storyboard

Once you've prepared and planned both your spoken words and your projected visuals, try using these 10 tips to enhance the storyboard.

Tip 1: Clip Your Ideas

A great way to keep a fresh supply of creative visual ideas is by keeping a clipping file. Whenever you see an interesting layout, photograph, illustration, graph, or other visual idea in a newspaper, magazine, book, or other printed material, cut it out or copy it and place it in a folder in your file cabinet. Or for an electronic clip folder, create a folder in Microsoft OneNote and use the clipping tool to save an electronic image of the item. The next time you're stuck, refer to your paper or electronic file folders for creative inspiration.

Tip 2: The Photo Basics—Size, Crop, and Compress

You might find that a photo you choose to add to a slide doesn't fit or that it is too large a file for a PowerPoint presentation. To fix these problems, apply one of the three most important techniques you'll use to work with photographs: sizing, cropping, and compressing.

When a slide fills only a portion of the screen it communicates only a portion of its visual potential. To increase its communicative power, resize the photo to fill the entire screen. To do that, click the photo, and drag one of the round sizing handles that appear at each of the four corners to enlarge the photo to fill the entire slide area. Be careful not to drag a square sizing handle on one of the sides of the graphic, or you'll distort the photo as you resize it. You always want to preserve the image's original proportions so that your audience doesn't notice any distortion.

Review the picture to make sure that it's crisp and clear at its current size. If it isn't, find another image. Never use a photo that is unfocused, grainy, blurry, or otherwise unclear—you'll distract from your message and diminish your visual credibility. People are used to seeing sharply focused photographs in professional media, and if you don't deliver the same in your slides, they'll think less of the presentation, no matter how good the story is.

After you resize a photograph and verify that it's clear and focused, you might find that it extends over the edges of the slide. If so, crop the image to keep only the portion you want in the slide area. Click the picture, and on the Picture Tools And Format tab, in the Size group, click Crop, which will turn the sizing handles into cropping handles. To crop one side of the photograph, drag the cropping handle on that side toward the center of the photo to eliminate the part of the photo you don't want to keep.

The last tool to apply is Compress Pictures, available on the Format tab in the Adjust group when you click a picture. It's not uncommon for a single high-resolution photo-graph to be hundreds of megabytes in size, unnecessarily bloating the PowerPoint file. This huge image file can create problems when you try to e-mail the PowerPoint file or share it with other people. Solve this problem before it happens by making sure that the photographs are compressed to the smallest size needed for them to appear clearly on screen. Select the picture, click the Compress Pictures button, click Options, select the Target Output you prefer—the lower the ppi, the smaller the file size—and then click OK.

Tip 3: Try Three Treatments

You don't know what you have until you see it, and that's especially true with graphics. That's why you should create a range of options for yourself before you decide what to do with the design of your slides. When a professional design firm starts a job for a client, it's common practice to present the client with three design options. This gives designers a free hand to express their creativity by trying three completely different treatments. It gives clients a range of options from which they can select based on what works for them. For both parties, it provides a way of stepping back from the emotional attach-ment anyone has to the different designs and gives a point of reference and comparison that can be used in deciding which design direction to take.

This time-tested method will serve you well when you design your PowerPoint storyboard. Select the sketches for the Key Point slides from the presentation you've created, and try three completely different design treatments. Show the design treatments to your team, and test them on people unfamiliar with the presentation and ask for feedback. When you're satisfied with a design that will work for the audience, extend that design across all of the slides in the presentation.

Tip 4: Design for Your Designer

If you have the resources, invite a professional designer to help you design your slides and storyboard. Bring the designer in early—if possible, while you write the story tem-plate—so that the designer can absorb and learn from your thinking process. Working with the designer from the start avoids the frustration that graphic designers feel when someone hands them a PowerPoint presentation with the instructions to "make it pretty," and the designer has no ability to clarify the structure. In that scenario, no one is happy.

Instead, the story template places responsibility for the clear structure of the story squarely on the presenter. The resulting storyboard shows the designer the order in which you want the ideas to appear and how you'll reinforce the message through the presentation. Discuss how the Key Point, Explanation, and Detail slides form the hierarchy of a presentation, and explain that you want the backgrounds and layouts of these slides to cue the audience's working memory to the presentation organization. Always walk through the slides in Notes Page view to make sure the designer can see the relationship between the projected image on screen and your spoken words.

When everyone is in agreement, ask the designer to provide you with three completely different visual treatments of key slides in a test file that you select from Acts I and II. Then compare the treatments and choose the elements and styles that are the best fit with you and your audience. Ask questions to be sure you understand why the designer is proposing a particular treatment. Through your interaction, you're sure to spark new creativity and understanding that will set the stage for a well-designed presentation. Because the designer doesn't have to take on the unnecessary job of figuring out what you want to say and in what order, you'll accelerate the design process and avoid possible confusion. Instead, the designer is freed up to do what a designer does best—designing. Using this approach develops a smooth process that's sure to result in a PowerPoint presentation that gives everyone involved a rewarding communication experience.

Tip 5: Build a BBP Layout Library

If you have colleagues who are also using BBP, consider pooling your resources to create a BBP design library. If your organization uses Microsoft SharePoint Services, create a collaborative Web site for people who are willing to share their PowerPoint files. For example, create document library folders labeled Key Point Layouts And Slide Examples, Explanation Layouts And Slide Examples, and Detail Layouts And Slide Examples. Anyone who created a presentation using one of those design techniques would then post it in the corresponding folder. You and the members of your team would no longer have to begin presentations from scratch; instead, you'd have a library of ideas ready for you to check out.

Tip 6: Build a BBP Charts Library

Many individuals and organizations use a relatively limited range of diagrams and charts to explain the information that relates to their work. Instead of formatting diagrams and charts from scratch every time, design a single set of commonly used graphics that carry a clear and consistent design according to the best design principles. Whether you design the set of charts yourself or hire a professional information designer to help, standardizing the way you display quantitative information saves you time formatting and ensures that you maintain the integrity of the data you display.

Tip 7: Consider Color

Although this book is printed in black and white, color is also something you need to consider when designing the layouts for the levels of your presentation. According to widely accepted principles of color theory, some individual colors such as red or high-contrast combinations of colors such as black and white call attention to themselves before others.

Your choice of colors should always align with the hierarchy of your ideas. If you consider integrating your organization's colors into your custom layouts, be careful when you do that, because those colors might conflict with your goal of guiding the working memory of your audience. For example, you might use red in your company colors, but using a red element on your Explanation and Detail slide layouts will call attention to that element instead of the headline and the graphic, which will erode the way your slides are working to guide the attention of the audience.

You might run into resistance from others in your organization when choosing colors to indicate the hierarchy of importance of the ideas in your presentation. If that is the case, defend your BBP foundation by holding a meeting to convey the importance of verbal and visual hierarchy in communicating effectively to an audience, showing BBP and non-BBP versions of the same presentation to demonstrate how BBP uses color to guide the audience's attention.

Tip 8: Call Out Additional Information

To add a label to a graphic, on the Insert tab, in the Illustrations group, click Shapes, and then in the Callout group, select the style you want. After you add the label to the slide, modify it by adding text and adjusting the formatting as you would with any PowerPoint shape.

Tip 9: Sketch It All, Live!

If you are a good storyboard sketcher, consider something completely different and present your PowerPoint slides with only the headlines and no graphics added at all. When you present live, use a Tablet PC to sketch a graphic to illustrate each headline as you go along. It will be a deeply engaging and interesting experience for the audience, plus you can save the sketches you made with the PowerPoint file and send the illustrated file to everyone who attended.

Tip 10: Develop a Single Illustration, Slide by Slide

If you're feeling particularly ambitious, try developing a single illustration across the entire presentation. You'll have to plan this carefully in the story template, but the basic idea is that you introduce one piece of the graphic, one slide at a time, as you verbally explain each piece, until everything in the illustration comes together into a single graphic at the end of the presentation. This technique literally helps you explain the big picture to your audience.

CHAPTER 9

Delivering Your BBP Presentation

THE ROOT of the word *inspire*, spirare, means "to breathe," and that's one of the core objectives of the BBP approach—to inspire you with the confidence and tools you need to breathe deeply and relax more when you present. Most of the elements that contribute to your confidence are built into the BBP process every step of the way, but now, when you've finished creating your presentation, it doesn't hurt to revisit them before you make your live presentation.

Although BBP slides look dramatically different from conventional slides, the real fruit of your labor is your confident understanding of what you want to say and how you want to say it. You have expanded the capability of Microsoft PowerPoint beyond a tool for designing slides into a tool that helps your audience understand new information more effectively. When you open your BBP presentation, you actually have a sophisticated media toolkit that blends your clear ideas and story with the delivery technology.

Now it's time to use that toolkit to bring your story to life.

Delivering Your Presentation Using Three Ground Rules

The term *production* refers to the point when filmmakers capture live action on film. Film directors spend a great deal of time setting up scenes and filming the action many times so that they'll be able to use the best performances in the final cut. But you don't have that luxury in your PowerPoint production because you're presenting in a live environment, which means you typically get only a single shot at engaging the audience. Managing the complex mix of elements in a live presentation is challenging, but you already have firm control over the projected media, spoken words, and printed handouts in your BBP presentation. As you use the PowerPoint file to deliver your presentation, a set of ground rules can help keep the experience in balance.

Ground Rule 1: Step into the Screen

In conventional presentations, often a small screen sits to the side of a presenter, where it is a nonessential visual aid that could be turned off without much impact on the presentation. In contrast, BBP literally enlarges the visual aspect of your presentation. When you display your BBP presentation on a large screen, the audience should perceive you as inside the screen, as if it were a stage or a giant television set. Remember that you are a living, engaging presence in a presentation, and you provide the critical audio track that ties everything together. When you step in front of the large screen, you create a hybrid medium that did not exist before. The projected screen makes your abstract thoughts visible, your body keeps the presentation grounded, and your voice guides and informs the experience.

After investing so much time in creating your visual media, you absolutely need to ensure the screen and its placement are appropriate to your presentation. Many conference rooms are not designed well, often placing focus on a chandelier or other architectural element rather than on the media experience you need to produce. Make sure you communicate what you need to the meeting or event planner. Never allow a screen to be placed on the opposite side of the room from where you are speaking. This setup will cause a split-attention effect that places unneeded extra cognitive load on the audience by forcing them to continually look back and forth between you and the screen as they work to reconcile the two visual sources of information. Instead, make sure the screen is directly behind or just off to the side of you so that the light from the data projector does not shine in your eyes.

Ground Rule 2: Remove the Distractions

It's easy to lose your focus on the message when there are endless things you could do to fine-tune your slides, such as adding more graphical elements, animations, and special effects. One of the major advantages of keeping the slides simple, which you did in Chapters 6, 7, and 8, is that it keeps you from being distracted by unnecessary details and keeps the audience from being distracted because too much is happening on the screen. Removing distractions leaves you in control of the media instead of having the media controlling you.

You use PowerPoint well when people don't even notice you use PowerPoint at all. The last thing you want is for someone to compliment you on your slides—that would mean the medium called attention to itself instead of your ideas. The most important outcome of the presentation is that the audience understands the meaning you intend to communicate. When you finish the presentation, you want the audience to talk about your special ideas, not your special effects.

Ground Rule 3: Manage the Flow

It's important to align your PowerPoint presentation with your unique personality so that you make an authentic connection with the audience. For example, when you spend the time to carefully write the story template in your own words, you develop a deep confidence in your story that frees you to improvise your narration and tailor your words to your audience instead of being chained to reading bullet points in the conventional PowerPoint approach. All this leads to a more relaxed and comfortable approach that will make the audience feel more relaxed and comfortable too.

A presentation is not a free-for-all, however, so it's important to improvise within the constraints of a specified form. This fundamental principle is applied in many arts, including jazz, in which musicians improvise only after they've mastered the fundamental techniques of the musical form. In a similar way, improvise on the constraints defined in the ground rules presented throughout this book once you've mastered the basic presentation forms.

THREE GROUND RULES FOR DELIVERING YOUR PRESENTATION

Your single storyboard helps you manage your spoken words, projected visuals, and printed handouts. Follow these three ground rules to ensure that the rest of the live presentation experience is engaging:

Ground Rule 1: Step into the screen.

Ground Rule 2: Remove the distractions.

Ground Rule 3: Manage the flow.

Removing Distractions

Up to now, this book has concentrated on helping you to prepare a PowerPoint file that minimizes distractions that would otherwise overload the limited capacity of the working memory of your audience. You remove unnecessary information from the presentation by narrowing the focus of the story template. You keep extraneous information out of the slide area by following the storyboard and design ground rules. And you keep both graphics and narration focused on the headlines. After you've removed distractions from the slides, it's time to focus on removing distractions from the environment in which you'll present.

Preparing the Environment

The physical environment in which you present is just as important as the story you tell. The quality of your hard work is diminished if the room is physically uncomfortable, if there are distracting noises, if you don't have an electrical outlet within reach of the projector, or if the room looks just plain shabby. Just as you have a personal responsibility for the story template, you also have a responsibility for the physical experience of the environment in which you present. You need to use your leadership and diplomacy skills to work with facilities managers or meeting planners to ensure that everything is in order.

If you have access to the room where you'll present, visit it in advance of the presentation to plan for your needs. When you visit the room, review the options for configuring the physical space, and rehearse the presentation in the actual environment if that's possible. If you're not able to visit the physical location in advance, contact someone familiar with the room to find out about the room setup.

At a minimum, both you and your audience should be physically comfortable in the environment. You should have a base of operations when you present, such as a podium, and you should have the physical freedom to move around the room comfortably as you speak. If you use a Tablet PC to deliver your BBP presentation, place it on a podium or a low table out of the line of sight of your audience, and make sure that the projector cable and a power source are within reach.

When you're comfortable with the physical environment, turn to the technology you'll use to project the PowerPoint presentation.

> **Tip** ✓
>
> Lighting the room properly for a PowerPoint presentation can be a challenge. On one hand, you want people to see the screen clearly, but on the other hand, you don't want the room to be so dark that people start to doze off. The latest models of data projectors have brighter displays that allow the audience to see the images on the screen clearly without turning down the room lights.
>
> When you visit the room where you'll present, try out the projector and stand at the back of the room to review things from the perspective of audience members sitting there. Adjust the lighting so that everyone in the room can see the slides and see you clearly too. Ask a facilities manager to help if the lighting controls are not readily accessible or if you need additional lighting.

Checking the Technology

Stories rely on a strong beginning to set the tone and direction of the rest of the narrative. Although you have a strong beginning built into Act I of the story template, the presentation actually begins when the eyes of the audience turn to you and recognize you as the speaker. You're not off to a strong start if what they see is you connecting the projector cable to your computer, focusing the image on the screen, and searching for your PowerPoint file amid the clutter of your computer's desktop screen. Audiences are sometimes tolerant of these sorts of distractions, but don't count on that. That's why you need to prepare for your technical needs in advance.

When you survey the room where you'll present, take the time to perform all of the steps required to set up the technology for the presentation. Plug the projector into the computer, power up the equipment, and open the PowerPoint file. Make any technical adjustments you need, and then resize the image to fit the screen and focus it. If you use a remote control device to advance the slides, try it out to make sure it works properly. Test the Internet connection if you need one, and review any online materials you'll show on the projector during the presentation. If you plan to display Web pages, make a backup copy of them on your local computer if possible, in case you have problems with the Internet connection. If you will use the PowerPoint presenter tools in Slide Show view or on a Tablet PC, review the instructions in Appendix B to prepare the presentation.

If you're not able to set up the equipment and rehearse in the room in advance of the presentation, at a minimum you should set up the equipment before the presentation with enough time available to resolve any technology issues that might arise. You might also want to rehearse in a similar room beforehand.

Planning for Problems

Even if something goes wrong, you are still able to produce a solid presentation experience. For example, if your speaking time is unexpectedly cut from 45 minutes to 15 or even 5 minutes, quickly scale the presentation to the reduced time by hiding slides, as you did in Chapter 6. If your computer crashes and you have no way to recover it, cover all of the presentation points by using a printout of the story template, storyboard, outline, notes pages, or slides. If the projector bulb burns out and you have no spare, your simple slides might be clear enough to be seen on the computer screen by a small audience at a table. Your thorough preparation will enable you to carry out the presentation with confidence, no matter what problems come your way. If the presentation is particularly critical, such as the opening statement at a high-stakes legal trial or a keynote presentation to a large group at an important conference, arrange for your associates to run a second presentation in parallel as a backup, and connect both computers to a switch—that way, if something unexpected were to happen, you could switch to the second presentation without distraction.

Rehearsing Away Distractions

In the past, you might have waited until you had finished creating the slides before you rehearsed the presentation for the first time. But with BBP, you're really rehearsing through the entire process. You get comfortable with your story when you write the story template in Chapters 4 and 5. You become acquainted with the flow and sequence of the story when you prepare the storyboard and narration in Chapter 6. And you become familiar with the visuals on screen when you sketch the storyboard and add graphics in Chapters 7 and 8. Through each of these steps in the BBP process, you mentally rehearse the core of the presentation and address a number of possible distractions, such as becoming too reliant on the slides to remind you of every detail you want to present.

Now deliver an actual dress rehearsal of the presentation to remove distractions from the delivery of the presentation that come from being ill-prepared. When you check the room and technology setup, stand in the physical location where you'll present and give a complete delivery of the presentation.

During a presentation, all eyes are on you, and people will watch for cues that indicate your enthusiasm and interest in a topic. If you speak in a monotone and appear disinterested, you shouldn't be surprised if the audience mirrors your lack of enthusiasm. Instead, vary your voice to emphasize important points, and pause for effect when you want a particular point to sink in. You've been working hard on your story—let your enthusiasm come through your voice, as well as through your facial expressions. As you rehearse, you're sure to run into rough spots or things you want to change in the presentation, so keep a piece of paper handy for jotting down revision notes to yourself as you go. Then return to the presentation to make any final changes to the slides.

Ask someone on your team to attend your rehearsal and give you honest feedback about the presentation, because you're better able to improve with the help of an outsider's perspective. People are inclined to mention only good things, so ask your evaluators not only to confirm what you do well, but also to suggest specific ways to improve. It's a good idea to ask for a range of opinions, because each viewer will give you advice from a different perspective. Take account of whatever feedback you get, and make adjustments as needed.

Using Notes

Presenter view, described in detail in Appendix B, is a great asset to a presenter and provides helpful tools to remind you of what to say. Not only does the notes pane provide cues about what to say, but so do your headline and simple graphic, as well as the thumbnails of the slides below, which serve as visual summaries of the points to come.

> **Tip**
> ✓
> One of the most common verbal distractions is the use of filler words like *um, uh, I mean,* and *you know.* Most people aren't even aware that they use these words—even some of the most experienced speakers. To reduce distracting verbal fillers, record yourself when you speak and count the *um*s. Or ask someone you know to count the number of filler word occurrences while you speak. The surest cure for this distracting habit is becoming aware that you do it in the first place.

Although you should be intimately familiar with the presentation at this point, keep a set of speaker notes on the podium in the form of a printed story template or storyboard outline. Don't use the complete notes pages as speaker notes—the written text in the notes area might tempt you to read from the page, and you'd need to physically flip from one page to the next, which would be distracting. Instead, when you print your key presentation documents, consider using as speaker notes the story template, a text outline of the storyboard, or thumbnail images of the storyboard:

- To print the story template, open the Microsoft Word document that contains your story template. If you made any changes to the headlines in the storyboard, update the document to reflect those changes, and then print the document.

- To print a text outline of the storyboard, open the PowerPoint file, click File, click Print, and in the Settings area, click Print Layout and select Outline.

- To print thumbnail images of the storyboard in PowerPoint, click File, click Print, and in the Settings area, click the print layout drop-down arrow, and then click either 6 Slides Horizontal or 9 Slides Horizontal.

- To print handouts from notes pages in PowerPoint, click File, click Print, and in the Settings area, click the print layout drop-down arrow, and then click Notes Pages. Yet another option is to print the individual slides one per page, but you should have enough material with just the thumbnail images of the storyboard and the notes pages printouts.

- While you're at it, print any additional handouts you'll reference during the presentation, such as diagrams or flow charts, spreadsheets, and detailed charts and graphs.

Once you've printed all of the documents, assemble them in a folder so that you have them in a single place for reference.

> **Tip** ✓ To customize your speaker notes using thumbnail-size images of the storyboard, go to the View tab, and in the Presentation Views group, select Handout Master and make adjustments there.

Prompting a Dialog

When you make the audience the main character of your story in Act I of the story template, the story is *all about them* instead of *all about you*. So rather than the presentation being a performance in which you're the star who entertains an adoring crowd, you're part of the supporting cast in the service of the audience. This is a shift from seeing the primary function of PowerPoint as *speaker support* to a new view in which PowerPoint serves as *audience support*.

A presentation isn't a one-way street; it takes the interaction of presenters and audiences to create a dialog. You just happen to be the first one to speak, and because you're the presenter, you're the one who is in charge of getting the interaction started.

Being Authentic

The dialog you create with the presentation begins with you—after all, the audience is granting you their time to listen to what you have to say. An audience is more likely to give your presentation a fair hearing if they know you're being authentic. You communicate your authentic personal credibility in a number of ways, beginning with the introduction you planned in your storyboard in Chapter 7, continuing with the clarity of your ideas and the crispness of your message, and then carrying through with the visual credibility of your slides and the verbal credibility of your narration.

Adding your name to the byline of the story template when you begin writing the script establishes your personal responsibility for the presentation process from start to finish. The biggest benefit of being so closely involved is that the presentation eventually becomes an extension of who you are.

As you work on focusing the story in Act I and boiling down your ideas to three main points in Act II, you become increasingly confident in your message. And making creative choices for the design of the storyboard makes the PowerPoint presentation start to feel like an extension of your personality.

One of the biggest obstacles you can impose on yourself when you speak in public is the idea that you need to be someone you're not. This problem becomes magnified if you're handed a generic corporate PowerPoint file with the same overstylized but boring look everyone else uses. Although these presentations might look slick on the surface, they often lack the heart and soul that only the personality of a unique human being can bring.

Break out of this trap by using the new PowerPoint file you created, which should reflect your character and personality in the choices you make for the story and visuals. Then expand on that personal beginning by delivering a presentation that expresses your original voice. Audiences always prefer a presentation that's imperfect and a little rough around the edges—but still authentic—over a perfect and flawless presentation that has no soul.

When you present, never be afraid to be yourself, because that's what people really want you to be.

Working Confidently with Your Slides

For many people, the thought of public speaking inspires fear, not confidence. The fear often comes from speakers not being comfortable with their story, themselves, or their level of preparedness. You remove the elements that create fear by securing a strong story, extending your personality through the story, and rehearsing thoroughly along the way. Your confidence comes shining through most clearly in the way you use the projected slides you designed.

After working with the PowerPoint file in Notes Page, Normal, and Slide Sorter views, you should be very comfortable with the material. When you advance to a new slide in the presentation, that slide's headline will prompt you about what to say next. The headline also addresses the audience in a conversational tone, making them feel relaxed and helping them to easily understand what you want to convey at that point.

Next on the slide is the graphical element. One of the benefits of the BBP simplified design approach is that the slides are free of bullet points and excess clutter; instead, you show a meaningful headline illustrated by a simple graphic. The goal of simple slides like these is to inspire interdependence between you and the audience. By showing less on screen, you pique the audience's curiosity.

Next you answer the audience's questions about the slide with your spoken words, which you developed fully in the written explanation of each slide in the notes area. You explain the meaning of the headline and graphic to the audience in your own natural voice.

These three basic elements—headline, graphic, and your voice—work together to create an implicit dialog that engages the audience. When you finish the thought at hand, you advance to the next slide and repeat the process in a steady flow that naturally continues the dialog.

With the new PowerPoint presentation, you'll gain the focused attention of the audience through your relaxed approach, interesting story, and engaging visuals. Scan the room as you speak, making direct eye contact with audience members in every part of the room.

Handling Q & A

If you've done your work well in the story template, you anticipate questions by tailoring the presentation to the audience and addressing the questions they're wondering about as you complete each of the acts and scenes. However, having a Q & A session is impor-tant—even if you've covered everything, people who are making decisions will still want to ask questions so that they feel like they've participated in the experience. Depending on how you planned it into your storyboard, you might open up the floor to conversa-tion from the very start in Act I, or at the end of the first and second Key Point sections, or both. Or you might conclude your prepared remarks and then invite audience com-ments. In some instances, you might even want to purposely leave a few questions un-answered so that the audience will be sure to ask them and engage you in the Q & A. If you're speaking to a large audience and take a question, restate the question before you answer it to make sure everyone in the room hears it.

If someone asks a question about a particular slide, refer to the printed storyboard for the corresponding slide number (if you don't already know it), and then in Slide Show view type the number of the slide and press Enter to go directly to that slide. If you want to show a slide that relates to a general question from one of the Act II scenes, type the number of whichever Act II slide corresponds with the question and press Enter. If you have extra material that didn't fit into the Act II slides but you think you might still be asked about it, add the extra slides to the end of the presentation and refer to them if some questions relate to them.

> **Tip** ✓ As an advanced technique, use the PowerPoint storyboard on screen as a navigational aid. Before you start your presentation, go to Slide Sorter view and display the storyboard at a size that lets you see all of the slides at once—say, 33 percent. Leave the presentation in this view, and when you're ready to present, press F5 to begin. At the end of the presentation, press Esc to return to Slide Sorter view. This creates an interesting visual, and because you know the storyboard so well, when someone asks a question about a slide, click the slide to go directly to it.

Improvising Within Constraints

Because your new PowerPoint file is such a versatile platform, it lends itself to improvisation and adaptation to your personality and style.

Keeping Control of Your Story

Because of your relaxed approach, you might find that people ask you questions during the presentation or offer stories of their own experiences. This is a good sign that the audience is feeling comfortable with your speaking style, and it is perfectly fine if that's the way you planned the presentation in the storyboard. The danger is that these queries can also cause you to head off on a tangent that throws off your timing and story structure. Handle questions graciously by quickly answering them or by acknowledging them and, if necessary, deferring them to the Q & A session at the end of the presentation. If you don't know the answer to a question, admit that you don't know, and offer to follow up on the matter later.

It's essential to stay on course with your story; if you don't, you can easily lose control of the situation. The goal of the BBP approach is to create a compelling story that's tailored to the audience and anticipates their questions so that they're completely absorbed to the very end. If you missed the mark and your story wasn't a good fit for the audience, get as much feedback as possible and spend time later reviewing the story template to improve the next story you write. Pay particular attention to the Act I scenes to ensure that the story engages the audience fully.

At a minimum, present the 5-minute version of the presentation described in Chapter 6, which includes all of Act I, the first slide in each scene in Act II, and all of Act III, which together form the essential structure of your story.

Preparing for Different Contexts

The BBP approach is based on a time-tested classical story structure, so you should be able to use the same approach for audiences of different sizes.

For most audiences, a large screen is ample for projecting a presentation; for large audiences, the screen needs to be large enough for the people in the back row to see the slides clearly. A large audience size usually prevents you from getting feedback while you're presenting, but that doesn't prevent the experience from being an implicit dialog, as described earlier in this chapter.

For an audience of one or two people, give the presentation using a laptop with a large screen, printouts of the slides, or even a handheld computer. In each of these cases, you lose the power of a large projected image, but you gain in terms of a more casual and conversational approach and the immediacy of starting right away with little or no need to deal with technology setup.

Handing Out Handouts

Many presenters find it best to provide handouts after the presentation to prevent distractions. On the other hand, many audiences ask for handouts because they like to make notes on paper during a presentation. Try both approaches to see what works best for you and your audiences. One compromise is to print and hand out in advance a one-page version of the story template so that the audience has a basic road map of where you're going. Mention at the beginning of the presentation that you'll provide comprehensive handouts at the end, and at that point provide sets of handouts in the form of printed notes pages.

Presenting Without Being Present

If you can't present in person, you obviously miss out on the kind of communication that happens only in a live environment. But that doesn't have to stop you from presenting when you're not physically present—you just need to configure the PowerPoint presentation differently.

Sending Your Notes Pages (Not Your Slides)

When you add graphics to the presentation in Chapter 8, you know that the slides prepared using BBP don't make much sense unless you look at them in Notes Page view. The same holds true if you send the PowerPoint presentation to someone who couldn't attend the presentation in person, so never send just the slides—always send the notes pages.

Handouts in the form of notes pages offer quick reading as a printed document. Readers quickly understand the main idea of the document by skimming headlines and visuals from page to page, and they can also spend more time reading narrative detail in the notes area if they want.

An effective way to send notes pages is in PDF file format, as described in Chapter 8. When you e-mail the notes pages in this format, the audience has access to all of the information you want to present, but they do not have access to the original PowerPoint file where you keep the graphical materials and editable text you might not want to make available.

Producing an Online Presentation

BBP presentations work well in an online context because the same engaging story structure is there. The same simple visuals that support interdependence with your spoken words are there too, as well as the same evenly sized pieces of information, the same even pacing, and the same even flow.

BBP CHECKLIST: DELIVERING YOUR PRESENTATION

Before and during the presentation, do you

- Prepare the environment, check the technology, and properly rehearse in advance?

- Use your physical presence and voice to bring the experience to life?

- Engage your audience both implicitly and explicitly?

- Use the tools and techniques of BBP to manage the working memory of your audience?

The simplest way to put a presentation online is to post a PDF file of the notes pages on a Web site. Or convert the presentation to an online format using a conversion tool that allows you to record your narration as you display the slides. With most of these tools, the slides are displayed in a browser, and you use a microphone to record what you've written in the notes area. When the audience views the slides, they hear your spoken narration through their computers. Some online technology solutions also make the notes area viewable, in case people prefer to quickly scan what you're saying and skip ahead.

And Now, Presenting. . .

You should now be ready to present to your audience. With the thorough presentation you've prepared using BBP, you're sure to persuade the audience with your focused, clear, and engaging story.

As you apply this system to other presentations, keep this book handy, and visit the companion Web site for this book at *www.beyondbulletpoints.com* to get a steady supply of ideas and inspiration.

Now that you've seen why and how BBP works, it's time to get started on your own presentations. As you begin using BBP, use this book to guide you through the process step by step. Find others in your organization who are willing to help. As you apply the approach and get good results, you'll quickly create momentum that will propel clearer and more effective communications throughout your organization. As you start to live a life *beyond bullet points*, there's no turning back—you're on your way to a much more engaging way of presenting.

10 Tips for Enhancing Your Delivery

You now have a flexible and robust system for bringing your ideas to life using Power-Point. Before you give a presentation, review the following 10 tips to find ideas to spark your imagination or inspire you to try something new.

Tip 1: The Living Brand

In the conventional bullet points approach, it's common for presenters to place a logo on the Slide Master, which means that the logo will appear on every slide in the presentation. There's no problem with including a logo in the introductory and concluding slides, but a problem arises when the logo is on every single slide. Based on the research realities in Chapter 2, adding a logo to every slide amounts to extraneous information that does not further the focus of the specific point being made in the headline. Eliminating the logo from the Slide Master increases the amount of screen real estate available for presenting information and opens up the many creative options that an empty screen allows.

Beyond those reasons, in a live presentation context, the concept of a visual stamp on a slide diminishes in importance because all eyes are on you, and you are actually *living the brand*. The high quality of your ideas, the compelling story, the interesting visuals, and the high level of engagement all contribute to an experience the audience will not soon forget. And just in case the audience does forget some details of the experience, they'll always have the handout, which includes your logo on the notes pages.

Tip 2: Toastmasters

If you're not a member of a speaking club, you should be. Any speaker can benefit from attending a regular meeting with the sole purpose of learning and improving a full range of speaking skills. Toastmasters International, at *www.toastmasters.org*, is a good choice because it's inexpensive and all clubs are run by the volunteer efforts of their members. When you join, you'll participate in speaking exercises during meetings and give a series of prepared talks according to a sequence in a training manual.

The biggest benefits will likely come from simply attending regularly. As you're exposed to more speaking opportunities in a supportive environment, you'll develop skills to manage your nervousness, and your confidence will increase not just in public speaking but in all aspects of communication.

Many clubs haven't yet embraced the use of presentation technologies. If your local club doesn't yet use PowerPoint, bring a data projector and introduce some of the ideas you've picked up in this book to blend projected media and solid speaking skills.

Tip 3: Stretch Yourself

A live presentation draws on the full spectrum of communication skills, but almost no one is good at everything. You're probably better at one part of the BBP process—for example, writing your story, editing your headlines, distilling your ideas to their essence, checking your reasoning, creating visuals, or actually speaking and presenting. When you know your strength, pick a different area to work on improving because you'll still need to use all your skills when you create and deliver a presentation. For example, if you're good at writing, learn graphics, or if you're good at graphics, work on your public speaking.

Tip 4: Innovative Handouts

Create an unconventional note-taking handout by including only the three Key Point slides on a single piece of paper. As the audience members see each Key Point slide on the screen, it will cue them to the corresponding image on the handout and reinforce the top-level, visual-verbal message you want to communicate.

Tip 5: Got Gobo?

Many standard meeting rooms feature fluorescent lights and ordinary tables, but with inexpensive lighting tools, you have the ability to change the atmosphere of the room to remove the distractions of a shabby presentation environment. For example, a simple way to light up the presentation environment is with a *gobo*, which is a partial screen with the cutout of a pattern that's placed over a light. When you turn on the light, it projects the image of the pattern onto a surface.

Use a gobo to project a subtle pattern to cover up an uneven wall or to add a soft color to make glaring lights less obvious. As with all the visuals you've prepared for the presentation, any visual effects should be transparent and never distract from the message. If you've "got gobo," or any other special lighting, keep in mind that people should remember the message and not the lighting.

Tip 6: Visual Mnemonics

Having problems trying to remember what you want to say? Try using the graphics on your slides to trigger your memory. For example, if you display a particular image on a slide and you plan to make certain points when you narrate it, associate each point with an element on the photograph. When you use an image on a slide as a visual mnemonic, you make your ideas, as well as the presentation, memorable.

Tip 7: Make the Conversation High Voltage

In *Moving Mountains* (Crowell-Collier Press, 1989), Henry M. Boettinger wrote, "Presentation of ideas is conversation carried on at high voltage—at once more dangerous and more powerful." This is one of the best definitions of presentations because it packs so much meaning into a brief sentence, which becomes even more meaningful when it's broken up into pieces:

- You're presenting *ideas*. Not your ego.

- A presentation is a *conversation*. There are at least two people involved.

- A presentation is *high voltage*. It's not boring.

- A presentation is *dangerous*. It's risky.

- A presentation is *powerful*. It has strength.

The next time you speak, keep Boettinger's wise definition in mind to stay focused on the meaning you pack into your presentations.

Tip 8: Magnify Intimacy

One of the most powerful techniques in film is magnifying the face of an actor to give the audience a feeling of intimacy with that person. Although you won't see that technique in most presentations, new technologies continue to transform the presentation landscape.

For example, in some presentations, an IMAG image magnification camera will zoom in on a presenter's face while he or she is speaking at a live event. The image is often featured in a split-screen format next to the speaker's PowerPoint slides on a wide screen. If you have the chance to have your face magnified on a screen, embrace the opportunity—you're giving the audience a chance to see you up close. But before you do, rehearse using a live camera similar to the one in the presentation along with the event producers, who will arrange for lighting and makeup to make sure that you look good on the big screen.

Tip 9: Flip Through Flip Charts

If you use paper flip charts along with your screen presentation, when you walk over to the flip chart, write out a headline in a complete sentence that corresponds to the point you want to make on that slide in the storyboard. Writing out the headline on the flip chart keeps your point persistent because it stays visible to the audience, reminding them of the point and reinforcing it. The headline on the flip chart will stay visible after you return to the screen media, so make sure that it's a point you want to make visible through the rest of the presentation—otherwise, cover what you wrote with a blank sheet.

Tip 10: Predesign Your Media Tools

If you work with a Tablet PC or flip charts, consider predesigning parts of the slides or printed pieces before you use them. For example, you might have the background scene of a slide set up and then write over it using the Tablet PC. Do this with scanned documents, screen captures, and just about any other type of media so that when you start sketching, you already have a visual beginning point.

Note	Be sure to visit the Microsoft Press Web site for the *Beyond Bullet Points* book, where you'll find a bonus chapter and a copy of the BBP Story Template and Storyboard Formatter.

CHAPTER 10

Reviewing a Range of BBP Examples

SO FAR, THIS BOOK has demonstrated how to apply Beyond Bullet Points (BBP) in depth to a single presentation example. Chapter 4 showed you how Act I of the story template helps you choose the specific ideas you'll present to your audience's working memory in the first five slides of a presentation, and Chapter 5 showed you how Act II guides you through the process of setting the priority and sequence of the rest of the slides. Chapter 6 offered instructions on how to set up your storyboard and narration in Microsoft PowerPoint, and Chapter 7 illustrated some of the many ways to sketch your storyboard. All of this came together in Chapter 8 as you added the specific graphics that are a good fit for you, your headlines, and your audience. Finally, Chapter 9 demonstrated how to deliver your presentation using your powerful new BBP toolkit.

Although these chapters used a single presentation example, the same underlying BBP process will unlock a clear message from any topic and guide the working memory of your audience to clear and memorable understanding.

What Other Examples Can I See?

The types of presentations that are possible to create using BBP are literally endless. This chapter shows you more examples of BBP in action as it is applied to a wide range of topics and purposes, showing what a presentation might look if you were to

- Introduce a case to jurors in an opening statement with The Trial.

- Keep your team on track toward completing a project with The Plan.

- Summarize your market research findings to your clients with The Analysis.

- Update and gain the support of your boss for your activities with The Report.

- Teach your students about a new topic with The Class.

- Sell the services of your company to a client with The Pitch.

Because of space limitations, the examples in this chapter show selected portions of story templates, storyboards, and slides, focusing primarily on the critical Act I, Call to Action, and Key Point slides rather than on the Explanation and Detail slides that will contain your own specific photos, charts, graphs, screen captures, and diagrams. Every presentation was built using the same process in this book, but each looks and feels very different. Likewise, your own presentations will reflect your understanding of your specific audiences that determines the words you write in the story template, the graphics you add to the storyboard, and the way you deliver the experience.

As with the financial services example presentation in the earlier chapters of this book, the example presentations in this chapter adhere to the design constraint of a limited budget to show you what is possible with an inexpensive stock photography Web site and your own creativity—if you have a larger budget or work with a professional graphic designer, you probably can do even better. If adding graphics is not your strength, work with others who can help.

Introducing a Case with The Trial

This book began with the example of a headline-making BBP presentation used in a courtroom in Chapter 1, and it's worth taking a quick peek under the hood to see what made the first slides of that presentation work so well. Although you might not present the opening statement in a trial, when you explore the thought process behind this example, think of how you will write your own clear and concise words in Act I of your story template and apply equally effective yet simple visual techniques to your own storyboard.

Act I: The Classical Storytelling Foundation

Chapter 4 explained that at the beginning of your presentation, you are faced with the formidable challenges not only of setting up the framework that will help the working memory of your audience understand what is to come, but also of making an emotional connection. Mark Lanier, the plaintiff's attorney who presented the opening statement using BBP as described in Chapter 1, accomplished both goals by the way he structured his ideas in Act I of his story template, as shown in Figure 10-1, which established the story thread and pattern that would help the jurors sew up an understanding of the case.

The Trial by Mark Lanier		
Act I		
Setting	Bob Ernst is dead	
Role	You get to be like CSI detectives and follow the evidence	
Point A	**Call to Action**	**Point B**
The evidence will lead you to the pharmaceutical company	Follow the three parts of the case to bring justice for Mrs. Ernst	You'd like to bring justice to the situation
Act II		
Case Theme	**Explanation**	**Evidence**

FIGURE 10-1 Act I of The Trial presentation example.

Although the specific words in Act I are brief, they're a good example of how a sequence of concise statements works dynamically to create the underpinnings for a compelling visual story in PowerPoint. When you work on your own Act I statements, keep in mind the absolute importance of getting Act I right. If you know your audience well and you write the correct words, you'll hit your target, as the attorney did in this example; if you put too little effort into Act I and get the words wrong, you'll miss the mark.

> **Note** Notice that the Act II category headings have been changed in this example from "Key Point" to "Case Theme" and from "Detail" to "Evidence"—other examples in this chapter are also tailored to the presentation content, as described in the section "Tip 3: Tailor Your Act II Column Headings to Your Profession" in Chapter 5.

A Photographic Setting Slide

The Setting headline in the story template, "Bob Ernst is dead," quickly oriented the jurors to the context for the trial—Bob Ernst had died of a heart attack. As described in Chapter 1, this clear and direct statement is the foundation for the Setting slide, which in this example included three variations of a single photograph, here presented across three slides in Figure 10-2. The headlines of all the Act I slides are hidden in this example and the rest of the examples in this chapter. Although you should keep the headlines visible through most of Act II because they guide understanding of the in-depth new information on your Explanation and Detail slides, they are not essential in Act I because here you are primarily making an emotional impact. And, as always, your narration will supply the verbal information that synchronizes with your visual slides.

FIGURE 10-2 The Setting slide introduced to the jurors a gripping story.

As Mark told an anecdote about Carol and Bob while the first photograph was on the screen, his words packed the image on screen with meaning. Here the jurors could connect emotionally with Bob and Carol because anyone could relate to the details of their life together and be happy for them. But the emotion that had been attached to the first slide was suddenly stripped away visually with the removal of the background in the second slide, signaling that something unexpected was about to happen. The third slide becomes deeply poignant when visually Carol is suddenly left alone, with only an empty outline defining the space where her husband once was. Although the photo sequence is very simple, it had a deeply profound impact. When you think of writing and illustrating your Setting headline, consider how to use a simple anecdote and photograph to quickly orient your own audience in an equally savvy way.

Reviewing the Act I Slides for The Trial

Transitioning from the preceding photograph with a heavy black outline of Bob, shown on the upper left in Figure 10-3, Mark now "deputized" the jurors as crime scene detectives in the Role slide (upper right) with the simple phrase *CSI: Angleton* illustrating the hidden headline "You get to be like CSI detectives and follow the evidence." Mark knew that this technique would connect with his audience because many of the jurors had indicated in questionnaires that the popular *CSI* television show was one of their favorites. Even if all the jurors had not seen *CSI*, they would know its premise because of the show's broad market awareness. As you write and illustrate your own Role headline, consider what words and images will instantly place your audience at the center of the action in an effective way like this.

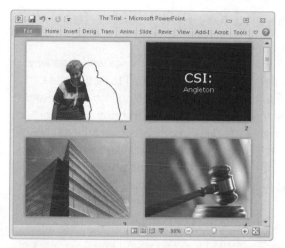

FIGURE 10-3 The Setting, Role, Point A, and Point B slides of The Trial.

In keeping with the classical storytelling form described in Chapter 4, Mark's next step was to present the main characters with a challenge they face on the Point A slide. In this case, Mark defined the jurors' challenge in the hidden headline, "The evidence will lead you to the pharmaceutical company," illustrated with an office building similar to the one shown on the lower left. In screenwriting terms, this introduced the challenge that is built into your Point A headline—an obstacle or an event that confronts the main character and begins the action that drives the story forward. Mark defined the obstacle as the evidence these "CSI detectives" would now need to follow. But for the problem to be fully defined, Mark needed to provide the jurors with a second crucial element— Point B, or where the jurors wanted to be, which is defined in the story template with the headline "You'd like to bring justice to the situation." The image of a gavel (lower right) along with Mark's narration reinforced the problem the jurors faced: they will follow the evidence that leads them to the company (Point A), and then they want to bring the situation to justice (Point B).

The underlying structure of conventional PowerPoint presentations rarely engages audiences at an emotional level, leaving them struggling to figure out why this information is relevant to them. But with Act I of the story template, Mark's presentation efficiently adapted a story technique to make the topic personally relevant to his audience. By creating a gap between Point A where the jurors stood and Point B where they wanted to be, Mark tapped into the core element of classical story structure— unresolved tension. People do not sit comfortably with tension, and it is the quest to resolve tension that compels a main character to action. By presenting the jurors with a problem, Mark engaged the jurors both emotionally and intellectually, and he answered the toughest audience question any presenter faces: "What's in this for me?"

Reviewing the Call to Action and Key Point Slides for The Trial

By using Act I of the story template, Mark would not leave his audience without a way to get from A to B. As described in more detail in Chapter 1, the Call to Action slide, shown on the upper left in Figure 10-4, distills the entire presentation into a single slide based on the hidden headline "Follow the three parts of the case to bring justice for Mrs. Ernst." With the three-part formula of *motive + means = death*, Mark introduced the vast amount of new information to the jurors as being as simple as 1-2-3. Just as the murder-mystery motif is a familiar structure, the jurors would also know the phrase "as easy as 1-2-3." If the upcoming story would be as easy to understand as that, the jurors could relax as they listened to the case.

Next Mark had written Act II of his story template to divide the story of the case into roughly equal Key Point (Case Theme) headlines that he would spend equal amounts of time explaining. Each corresponding Key Point slide carried forward the 1-2-3 numbering system along with an enlarged version of each icon from the Call to Action slide. Each image used on these slides was carefully chosen to convey the visual essence of each Key Point headline.

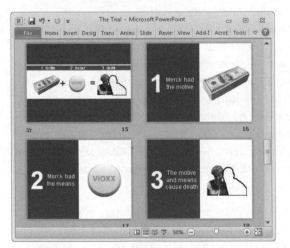

FIGURE 10-4 The Call to Action and Key Point slides of The Trial.

As illustrated simply yet powerfully here, the ideas and images and narration you use on your Key Point slides are the most important ideas you want your audience to integrate into long-term memory. In a similar fashion, you'll want to apply a blend of your best creative and intellectual thinking to design your Act I and Key Point slides because they represent the verbal and visual essence of the most important information you want to communicate.

With this familiar story structure in place on the Call to Action and Key Point slides, Mark solved the toughest communication challenge any presenter faces—how to make it easier for an audience to understand new information. As described in Chapter 2, as much as you might hope otherwise, the reality is that you cannot pour information directly into your audience's minds and have them simply "get it." The working memory of your audience can become quickly overloaded when the audience is unfamiliar with the information or if the material otherwise is not presented properly. To overcome this problem and increase his audience's ability to understand his case, Mark related the new information of the case using a story framework through Acts I and II that the audience already knew—the murder-mystery motif.

The graphics used on these slides are created using images from *www.iStockphoto.com*, family photographs, or PowerPoint graphical tools. This presentation is a good example of how the simple visual surfaces of BBP presentations offer few clues that there is a sophisticated verbal strategy beneath them, yet the powerful impact of the approach is very real and profound. As you apply simple visual surfaces to your own BBP verbal structures, you'll begin to tap into similar results in your own presentations.

Keeping on Track with The Plan

The Trial example showed a range of verbal and visual techniques to apply to your own presentations even if you never set foot in a courtroom. The next example, named The Plan, might come in handy if you find yourself leading a team toward accomplishing a project. In this scenario, your group has a deadline to accomplish a task, but you're running into problems that might delay the project. Most of the people on your team work in your local office, so you'll present this version live to them tomorrow morning; the rest of the team works in different cities, so you'll give the same presentation tomorrow afternoon using a Web conferencing tool.

Writing Act I of the Story Template

As you start your story template, you've done your research with your audience and know that there is a shared sense of frustration with the delays on the project, but as an experienced project manager, you also know what the basic problems are and how they can be resolved. The Setting statement, shown in Figure 10-5, affirms "We've been racing to finish the project and earn our bonuses." The reference to the bonuses establishes right away something the audience personally cares about.

The Plan by Pat Coleman		
Act I		
Setting	We've been racing to finish the project and earn our bonuses	
Role	But unsolved problems keep sending us back to the starting line	
Point A	**Call to Action**	**Point B**
A few key hurdles stand in our way	Overcome each hurdle as we face it, and we'll win the race	We will reach the finish line if we can overcome them

FIGURE 10-5 Act I of The Plan presentation example.

In the storyboard sketches shown in Figure 10-6, the reference to "racing" in the Setting statement plays out as a motif on the Setting slide as a group of people running a race (upper left). Remember, introducing a motif to a BBP presentation is not a "fluffy" nice-to-have addition in the story template and slides, but rather a strategy of introducing a familiar verbal and visual framework from the audience's long-term memory to introduce new information to their working memory.

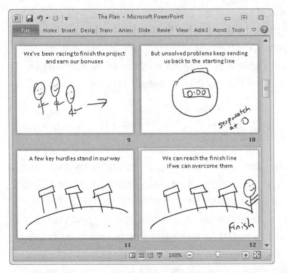

FIGURE 10-6 Sketches of the Setting, Role, Point A, and Point B slides of The Plan presentation.

The Role statement in the story template affirms, "But unsolved problems keep sending us back to the starting line," which plays out on the Role slide as the sketch of a stopwatch set to 0 minutes to indicate the beginning of the race (upper right). The Point A statement carries the motif further and engages the audience by visually describing "A few key hurdles stand in our way" with sketches of hurdles on the Point A slide (lower left). On the Point B slide (lower right), a runner is shown on the right in the slide, past the same hurdles and the finish line, to visually illustrate the headline "We can reach the finish line if we can overcome them."

Researching and Adding Available Graphics for The Plan

If you have a limited budget, as in this project, it's worth taking a few minutes to make a quick check of the graphical resources you have available before you commit to a motif you will use in your story template and sketches. You might have a great idea for a motif, but if you don't have the available graphics to pull it off, it won't become a visual reality. A *lightbox*, available at some stock photography Web sites, is a very useful tool in your research for available graphics. Use a lightbox to temporarily collect photos in a single place, without committing to purchasing licenses until you are ready to use specific photos. For example, create a lightbox named The Plan Presentation using your free account at *www.iStockphoto.com*. In keeping with the race motif of The Plan presentation example, search for terms such as "hurdles," "runners," and "finish line," and when you see a photo you like, click the Add To Lightbox button below the photo. In the pop-up window, select The Plan Presentation lightbox, and then click Add. When you have finished your search, visit The Plan Presentation lightbox, and you'll see thumbnails of all the images you selected in your search in a single area, as shown in Figure 10-7.

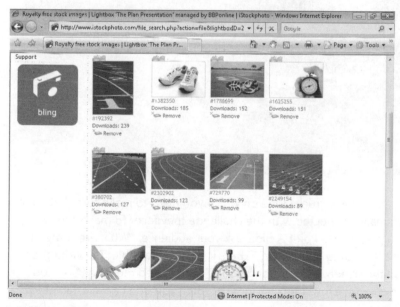

FIGURE 10-7 A lightbox at iStockphoto.

Reviewing the Act I Slides for The Plan

A search for the term "runners" on iStockphoto resulted in a number of good aesthetic matches with this audience, so add one to the Setting slide, as shown on the upper left in Figure 10-8, and then send the headline behind the photograph, as you'll do on the rest of the Act I slides. Then search for "stopwatch," and add the photo to the Role slide (upper right). A search for "hurdles" did not result in photos with three hurdles as the sketch described, but a single hurdle will work fine on the Point A slide (lower left). A search for "finish line" did not turn up a match for the sketch either, but a picture of a running track will work, along with a banner shape added using the PowerPoint 2007 drawing tools and showing the words *Finish Line*, as shown on the Point B slide (lower right). As these examples demonstrate, you won't always find the perfect match for your sketches, but you'll likely find something that will work.

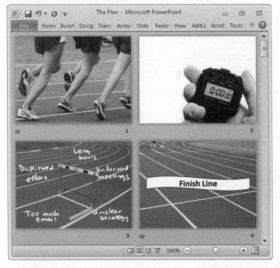

FIGURE 10-8 The Setting, Role, Point A, and Point B slides of The Plan presentation.

As described earlier, Point A is a crucial slide on which you need to make sure that your audience feels emotionally connected with the challenge they face. To make sure that is the case, when you present the Point A slide, ask your audience, "What are some of the problems you see that stand in our way?" Then, if you have a Tablet PC, write the responses directly on the screen, such as "long hours," "unfocused meetings," or "too much e-mail," as shown on the lower left in Figure 10-8. (If you don't have a Tablet PC, write the responses on a flip chart instead.) This shifts the dynamic of the presentation because you are not telling your team what their problems are; rather, they are telling you. Instead of risking that they will be alienated by feeling that you know it all, you give your audience a feeling of ownership. When you advance to the Point B slide (lower right), you affirm, "Yes, those are all valid problems, and we need to overcome them in order to reach the finish line."

Reviewing the Call to Action and Key Point Slides for The Plan

Although you opened the floor to the audience on the Point A slide, you also know from your research and your experience as a project manager that you need to cover the primary obstacles defined as the three Key Points in your story template, shown in Figure 10-9.

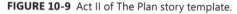

Act II		
Key Point	Explanation	Detail
Overcome the focus hurdle by reviewing the project plan each morning	The project plan changes periodically because of feedback from our client	Our client has been undergoing...
		Just last week, the board of...
		We have to be flexible in order...
	The project manager posts any changes each evening and sends out a reminder e-mail	The project manager keeps up...
		She makes sure to follow-up to...
		Each evening, she updates the...
	Without knowing about the changes, you may end up wasting effort	For example, the IT team started...
		Then they found out that the...
		They could have saved two days.
Overcome the communication hurdle by talking to someone directly instead of e-mailing	Many of the frustrations are coming from long e-mail messages	For example, the recent project...
		A total of 63 e-mails from 33...
		The final e-mail was 32 printed...
	It's easy to become detached from your coworkers if you only use e-mail	The situation could easily be...
		Ironically, the team worked...
		They finally solved it simply by...
	If there's a problem, it's more efficient to talk in person	When in doubt, talk to the...
		Project Team Alpha managed...
		Without a single e-mail, they...
Overcome the duplicated effort hurdle by checking off completed items on the intranet	The complexity of the project means there are overlapping tasks	Six project teams are handling...
		Eight off-site firms are coding...
		Together the teams manage...
	The intranet is designed to keep track of who is doing what	The central project site is now...
		Project managers are in charge...
		You can check the status at any...
	If you use the intranet to mark off what you do, you solve the problem	Every person is authorized to...
		By simply clicking the button...
		When everyone follows these...

FIGURE 10-9 Act II of The Plan story template.

Carry forward the race motif to your Call to Action sketch, shown on the upper left in Figure 10-10, and sketch the numbers *1*, *2*, and *3* on each hurdle. Carry through the numbering on each Key Point slide (upper right, lower left, and lower right) to indicate which hurdle in the sequence you are covering in that section of the presentation.

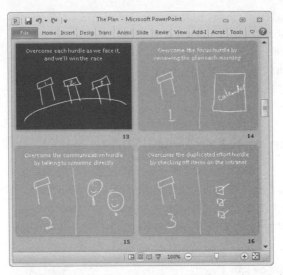

FIGURE 10-10 Sketches of the Call to Action and Key Point slides.

Since the three Key Point slides will all share the same photograph of a hurdle, create a Key Point slide custom layout that includes the photo. In this case, use the photo of the hurdle from the Point A slide, except tightly crop the photo and place it on the left side of the split-screen layout, as shown in Figure 10-11.

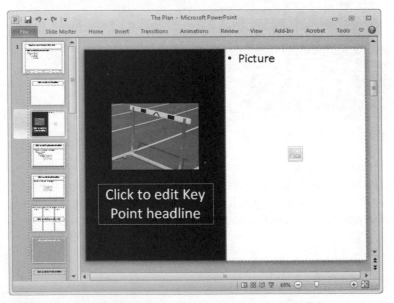

FIGURE 10-11 Creating a custom layout to apply to the Act I slides.

Return to Normal view of the Call to Action slide, and add three photos of the hurdle. Apply the new Key Point custom layouts to the Key Point slides, and add photographs to the Picture placeholders, as shown in Figure 10-12. If you have a Tablet PC, when you present the Call to Action slide (upper left), write on the screen with your stylus the numbers *1*, *2*, and *3* below each hurdle as you relate the headline, "Overcome each hurdle as we face it, and we'll win the race."

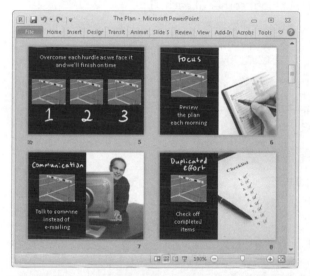

FIGURE 10-12 The Call to Action and Key Point slides with graphics added.

When you reach the first Key Point slide, write the word *Focus* in the blank space above the photo of the hurdle as you relate the topic to what your audience told you on the Point A slide and as you convey the message of the headline, here shortened on the slide from the original, "Overcome the focus hurdle by reviewing the plan each morning" (upper right). Then write *Communication* on the second Key Point slide (lower left) as you relate the headline, shortened on the slide from the original, "Overcome the communication hurdle by talking to someone directly." Last, write *Duplicated Effort* on the third Key Point slide (lower right) as you relate the headline shortened from the original, "Overcome the duplicated effort hurdle by checking off items on the intranet."

Note	The headlines were shortened on the Key Point slides to leave empty space on the screen where you could write with a Tablet PC stylus to increase engagement—if you don't have a Tablet PC, insert text boxes on the screen instead.

As you sketch the rest of the Explanation and Detail slides, use the range of graphical possibilities as described in Chapter 7 to sketch the slide headlines and then to add graphics, as shown in Figure 10-13. As you saw in earlier chapters, these graphics might include photos, screen captures, diagrams, charts, or other media elements. Add a navigation bar to your custom layouts for the Explanation and Detail slides to provide a cue to the presentation's organization and also to consistently carry through the visual motif in the form of a hurdle in the lower-right corner of each slide.

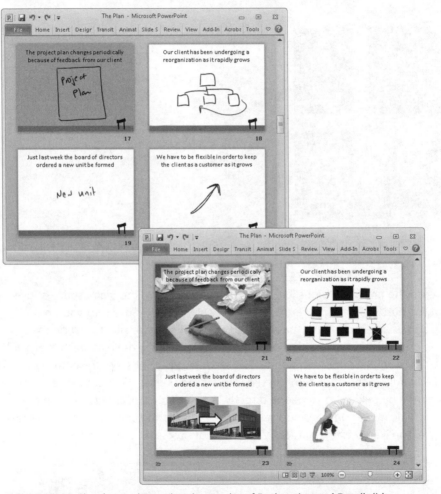

FIGURE 10-13 Sketches and completed examples of Explanation and Detail slides.

These completed slides use photographs from iStockphoto to communicate the message of the headlines. The photo used on the Explanation slide (upper left) fills the screen, and a fill color was added to the title area to make the headline text legible. The Detail slide with the organizational chart (upper right) has additional arrows to denote "reorganization" in the headline, and the Detail slide with the office buildings (lower left) shows the photograph of an office building duplicated and an arrow added to illustrate "a new unit." The Detail slide with the person doing a yoga pose to illustrate "we have to be flexible" might come across as too playful to some audiences, but for this presentation to a team within an organization, it is perfectly fine to have a visual sense of humor.

Tip

✔ Stock photography Web sites usually offer different sizes of graphics for licensing. For example, at iStockphoto, the small size of a photograph with a resolution of 72 dpi is generally fine for on-screen presentations, which will fill a standard PowerPoint slide measuring 7.5 inches by 10 inches. Carefully read all licensing agreements and size specifications for graphics before purchasing to make sure you are covered for the appropriate use.

Delivering The Plan Remotely

When you deliver the same presentation to the rest of your team the next day using a Web conferencing service, you'll present using a Web browser along with a telephone or a computer microphone and speakers. In a virtual environment such as this, you obviously cannot use flip charts and other off-screen media that the audience can't see. Instead, you'll use Web conferencing services. For example, when you present the earlier Point A slide using your online tools, ask your audience the same question, except now annotate the slide by using the tools to insert text boxes to record the audience comments, as shown in Figure 10-14. Alternatively, use your Web conferencing tools to create a poll that allows respondents to vote on your question, or use a text screen to write down the notes of your conversation for all to see.

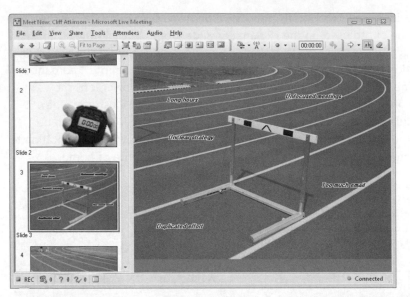

FIGURE 10-14 Using Microsoft Office Live Meeting to present the Point A slide with text boxes added.

BBP works particularly well in online meeting environments because it counters the lack of in-person dynamics with its visually engaging style. You will also make full use of the built-in tools to prompt engagement and involvement because you know exactly where you will use them—for example, on the Point A and Point B slides as well as the Key Point slides.

Presenting Results with The Analysis

Now that you've had a taste of using BBP as a way to present The Plan, the next example presents a new challenge—communicating the results of market research you conducted to your company's clients with The Analysis. Your client's sales have dropped, and the client has asked your market research firm to help.

This type of presentation featuring quantitative information is typically called a "data-driven" presentation. In spite of the research realities presented in Chapter 2, it's ironic that many conventional PowerPoint presentations that are considered to be data-driven do not use research as the foundation of the presentation approach itself. These presentations subscribe to the myth that you can simply drive data into your audiences' heads and they will "get it," and they don't take into account the importance of respecting the limits of working memory, synchronizing the visual and verbal channels, and guiding the attention of an audience in specific ways.

BBP, on the other hand, accepts these research realities and subscribes to the idea that there is no such thing as a data-driven presentation—there are only "cognitive-driven" presentations, because ultimately the audience's minds will determine whether understanding happened, not the data.

Act I of The Analysis presentation, shown in Figure 10-15, is a good example of how dramatically different a formerly data-driven presentation looks when you restructure it using BBP. In this example, the Setting statement summarizes that your client has hired your market research firm because "Your sales dried up last year in your most lucrative market segment." Next the Role statement puts your client in its proper place as the main character of this story as "You asked us to drill into the numbers and analyze the situation." The Point A statement explains the challenge you believe the client faces: "You have tapped out your existing revenue base." Point B then goes on to confirm to your client that "You need a strategy to get profits flowing again." Now what should your audience do to get from A to B? They should "Tap into three undiscovered wells of revenue by reaching new customers in new ways," according to your Call to Action slide.

The Analysis by Pat Coleman		
Act I		
Setting	Your sales dried up last year in your most lucrative market segment	
Role	You asked us to drill into the numbers and analyze the situation	
Point A	**Call to Action**	**Point B**
You have tapped out your existing revenue base	Tap into three undiscovered wells of revenue by reaching new customers in new ways	You need a strategy to get profits flowing again

FIGURE 10-15 Act I of The Analysis presentation example.

If it's helpful to you, rename the Act II column headings for this type of presentation from "Key Point" to "Recommendation" and from "Detail" to "Methodology/Data." As always, you end Act I of the story template with the Call to Action headline and expand on it with the Key Point (Recommendation) headlines in Act II. Then you flesh out each Key Point (Recommendation) headline, as shown in Figure 10-16, with further Explanation and Detail (Methodology/Data). With this approach, you know that you have logically organized your thoughts and built in scalability to present the same material in 5, 15, or 45 minutes (as described in Chapter 6) without losing the integrity or quality of your critical thinking.

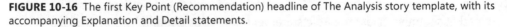

Act II		
Recommendation	**Explanation**	**Methodology/Data**
Reach suburban commuters and increase share 22%	More than 66% of your customers travel at least one hour per day	We conducted a random survey in your three target geographies
		More than 4,000 respondents completed the survey
		An analysis found that two-thirds travel at least one hour daily
	The right mix of radio ads will help you reach them	Your customers break out into three types of listeners
		You can reach them by allocating revenue based on their listening preferences
		Targeted buys like this produce consistent results
	A $5 million investment in advertising can produce a 10% increase in sales	Company X faced a similar situation in Q1
		They invested $5 million in a similar ad buy
		The result was a 10% increase in sales

FIGURE 10-16 The first Key Point (Recommendation) headline of The Analysis story template, with its accompanying Explanation and Detail statements.

Although the BBP structure might look straightforward and logical, it literally turns upside-down the most common structure of data-driven presentations. In the conventional structure, you normally jump right into the detailed data and the methodology and then finally make your recommendations on the very last slides. It's natural to think of structuring a presentation this way because you might think that if you start from the beginning of a project and go one at a time through the detailed steps you took to arrive at a recommendation, your ideas will have more credibility. However, the huge risk you take when you do that is that you overwhelm the limited capacity of working memory of your clients with so much new information, as shown in Figure 10-17, that they are disoriented and confused—which, ironically, diminishes your credibility.

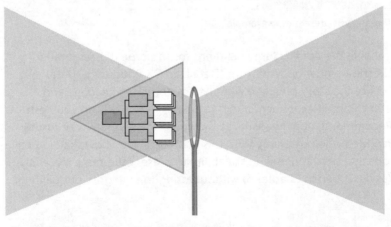

FIGURE 10-17 Presenting your methodology and data first, before your recommendations, quickly overwhelms working memory.

A symptom that overwhelm has happened in your presentation is if your client asks you to skip ahead to the end, starts looking at her phone or laptop, or asks you to get to the point—which indicates you didn't get to the point in the first place. Remember, journalists call this ineffective structural approach "burying the lead," because you put the most important information somewhere other than at the top level of attention of your audience. The good news is that you likely don't have to create new information for your presentation—you just have to restructure what you have using the story template to ensure that you present the most important information to the audience's working memory first.

None of this is to say that you will not present detailed data or complex charts when you show the Explanation and Detail (Methodology/Data) slides. If your clients have prior knowledge of complex data structures, the slides can include those elements without overwhelming their working memory because the understanding of the structure of this information is already held in the audience's long-term memory. If the source of the data is important to have available for detailed discussion, provide that on paper or in an electronic document to accompany the presentation.

Researching and Adding Available Graphics for The Analysis

Now that you have addressed the data you will cover in the Explanation and Detail (Methodology/Data) columns and you have determined the priority and sequence of all the slides in Act II, free yourself up creatively to make the critical top level of the presentation as interesting, engaging, meaningful, and memorable to your clients as possible. Being visually creative in what is supposed to be a data-driven presentation might initially be perceived as intellectual fluff, but with BBP, you know that your creative visual surfaces rest on a foundation built from a rigorous critical-thinking process. If your graphics are an aesthetic match with your audience, your clients will find the images refreshing, and the presentation itself will differentiate you from the boring, disorienting, and lifeless bullet-point presentations of your competitors.

As with the preceding examples, if your budget for your presentation is limited, you'll want to take a quick look to see what graphics are available to integrate as a motif into your story template and storyboard. In keeping with the "tapping into wells" verbal motif, a search for "oil well" in iStockphoto turns up the result shown in Figure 10-18—a series of icons including oil wells. This particular graphic is termed an "illustration" in iStockphoto, which means that it is not a photograph but instead a vector art image that can be opened and manipulated using a vector illustration software program. If you don't know how to use that type of software, most illustrations also come with a version of the illustration that you can insert on your slides and crop to use only the parts you want, as in the following examples.

FIGURE 10-18 Search result for "oil well" in iStockphoto.

CREATING YOUR OWN GRAPHICS

If you can't find the illustrations you need, create your own or hire someone to create them using a vector illustration software program. Aim for a simple, pared-down style for the illustrations. If you export these graphics in .emf or .wmf file formats, you might be able to group, regroup, and recolor the elements using the PowerPoint graphics tools.

Reviewing the Act I Slides for The Analysis

Following your story template and storyboard sketches as usual, set up your Act I layouts, apply them to your slides, and then add graphics. The example in Figure 10-19 features a split-screen layout, except this variation is horizontal, with a graphic at the top and a related photograph from iStockphoto below. The headlines from Act I of the story template are hidden in these slides to let the visual power of the graphics tell the story along with the narration. The Setting slide (upper left) uses a declining sales chart created from your client's data at the top and a photo of a cash register receipt below to illustrate the hidden headline "Your sales dried up last year in your most lucrative market segment." The Role slide (upper right) uses a photo of a spreadsheet below, but now it also shows an oil well above to illustrate "You asked us to drill into the numbers and analyze the situation." The Point A slide (lower left) uses the same oil well along with a "no sale" photograph to illustrate "You have tapped out your existing revenue base." And the Point B slide (lower right) uses the same oil well with an arrow pointing upward from a cash register drawer to illustrate "You need a strategy to get profits flowing again."

FIGURE 10-19 The Setting, Role, Point A, and Point B slides of The Analysis presentation.

The consistent horizontal split-screen layout across the slides creates an interesting dynamic as the changing photos carry through the meaning of the hidden headlines, which you will explain verbally. To set up the custom layout for these Act I slides, add a Picture placeholder to fill the bottom half of the screen, as shown in Figure 10-20, and then change the font color of the headlines to white to make them appear invisible against the white background.

After you create a custom layout using a Picture placeholder and apply the layout to your slides, right-click the placeholder and choose Paste on the shortcut menu to automatically crop and size the photo to fit; alternatively, click the picture icon to insert a graphic from somewhere on your computer. If you're good at creating custom layouts, share them with others to make their jobs easier—if you have used a Picture placeholder (not a Content placeholder) on the custom layout, all they do is click and add the photo without having to worry about designing layouts, cropping, and sizing.

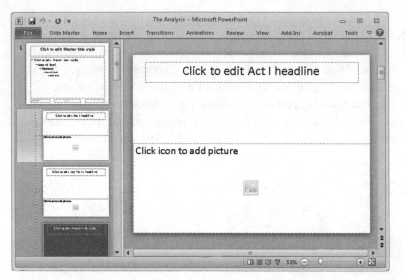

FIGURE 10-20 Horizontal split-screen custom layout for the Act I slides.

Reviewing the Call to Action and Key Point Slides for The Analysis

The horizontal photographic layout works so well in Act I that a similar layout will work on the Call to Action and Key Point slides as well, except this time divide the slide into thirds horizontally and leave the headlines visible in this version. The Call to Action slide shown on the upper left in Figure 10-21 features a photo of customers, except now there are three new oil well graphics to illustrate the headline "Tap into three undiscovered wells of revenue by reaching your customers in new ways." (The headline was shortened to fit the 2-line limit of the slides.) The first Key Point slide (upper right) features a single oil well with a photograph of cars on a highway to illustrate the first well of revenue explained in the headline as "Reach suburban commuters and increase share 22%." The second Key Point slide (lower left) features a second oil well with a photo of city traffic to illustrate the headline "Reach city travelers and increase share another 15%," and the third Key Point slide (lower right) features a third oil well with a photo of an airplane to illustrate "Reach frequent fliers and increase share another 7%."

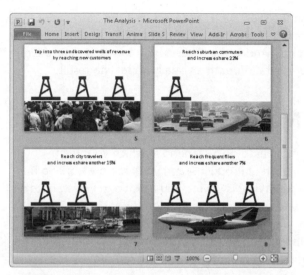

FIGURE 10-21 The Call to Action and Key Point slides of The Analysis presentation.

Together these Act I and Key Point slides create a compelling and interesting way to present the most important information your audience wants to know. The Explanation and Detail slides that follow, as shown in Figure 10-22, along with your backup printouts and spreadsheets, will go into the rigorous detail of quantitative-based reasoning that your client expects. A small oil well icon added to the Detail custom layouts carries the visual theme through the presentation on these slides.

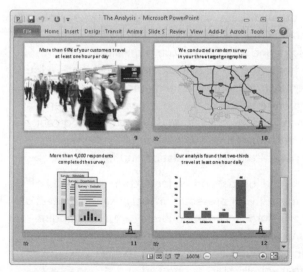

FIGURE 10-22 Examples of Explanation and Detail slides from The Analysis.

Much more than capturing the data on the slides, you have captured the imagination of your audience so that they can literally see what your abstract recommendations will mean to them in no uncertain visual terms. And in the process, you turned a data-driven presentation into a cognitive-driven presentation, with a visually appealing result.

Making Information Meaningful with The Report

The next example of a BBP presentation is based on a scenario in which your team recently contributed to the successful launch of Product A and you are now working on the launch of Product B. Your regional supervisor is paying you a visit and you want to let her know how things are going, so you prepare a presentation for her—The Report. You see this supervisor only occasionally, so this is one of your few chances to meet with her in person. Because this is just an update and not a set of recommendations, as in The Analysis, you initially plan to put together only an "informational" presentation to show her the facts.

Just as it's hard to let go of the myth of the data-driven presentation even in light of the research realities in Chapter 2, it's equally hard to let go of the idea of the informational presentation. You may hold on to the hope that you can present your supervisor with new "information" and she will automatically "get it," but the reality is that understanding happens only if she integrates the new information into her long-term memory. That means you must present the new information in particular ways that increase the chances that her working memory will handle it appropriately.

The phrase *informational presentation* often indicates that a presentation does not have a clear purpose. When you dig a little deeper into what people mean by this phrase, they usually say that they want to provide someone with lists of facts, typically in the form of bulleted lists of information. But without purpose or context, a list is just that—a list. If what you want to do is simply pass on facts for someone's reference, you don't need to go through the trouble of creating a presentation or having a meeting—just send the facts in an e-mail message, document, or spreadsheet and save yourself and your audience the time. But if you and your audience go through the trouble of gathering together, it should always be for a purpose—to make information and facts *useful*.

When you do have a reason to meet beyond just passing on facts, completing Act I of your story template is a reliable place to start your presentation, because the process of completing Act I always forces you to transform information into clear understanding that your audience finds meaningful and practical. Generic informational presentations normally lack a structure with a beginning, middle, and end, but with Act I as a structure for your introduction, you know that you will start strong and end strong every time. With Act II as a structure for the body of your presentation, you know that you will elevate the most important information to the top level of your audience's attention and cover the explanation and detail from there. Instead of listing every possible piece of information and showing *every* detail, you get right to the most important information and show only *the most important* details.

In this specific example, you might not be recommending or selling anything to your supervisor, but she does have something you need—her ongoing support. If your presentation fails to assure her you are handling your responsibilities, you likely won't carry those responsibilities for much longer because she wants to know you are on top of things so that she can focus on handling problems elsewhere. With this perspective in mind, Act I of your story template for The Report takes shape, as shown in Figure 10-23. In this example, the Setting statement explains, "Product Launch A went like clockwork," and the Role affirms, "You'd like to make sure Product Launch B goes just as smoothly."

The Report by Pat Coleman		
Act I		
Setting	Product Launch A went like clockwork	
Role	You'd like to make sure Product Launch B goes just as smoothly	
Point A	**Call to Action**	**Point B**
You haven't had a chance since last quarter to examine how things are working here	Be assured we will meet our goals	You'd like to be confident things are working smoothly

FIGURE 10-23 Act I of The Report presentation example.

The Point A statement summarizes the challenge your supervisor faces: "You haven't had a chance since last quarter to examine how things are working here." Where she wants to be at Point B is, "You'd like to be confident things are working smoothly." How does she get from a state of uncertainty at Point A to confidence at Point B? By following the simple Call to Action, "Be assured we will meet our goals." Instead of leaving your boss unclear about what she should do, you now have presented information in a way that ensures she can take action on it, even if that action is to believe something new or different—in this case, to be assured of your progress.

As shown in Figure 10-23, for this type of presentation change the Act II column headings from "Key Point" to "Summary," from "Explanation" to "Breakdown," and from "Detail" to "Backup." As you write your Key Point (Summary) headlines, you'll cover the three most important points that explain how your supervisor will be assured that you will meet your goals:

- **Key Point 1** We accomplished what we said we would.

- **Key Point 2** We are on track to accomplish our new goals.

- **Key Point 3** We will overcome our challenges.

As you complete the rest of the story template, you'll cover the Explanation and Detail slides that include the diagrams, charts, screen captures, photos, and anecdotes that back up your appeal for her support.

Researching and Adding Available Graphics for The Report

If your story template and storyboard sketches call for a verbal motif of clockwork (and that motif is a match with your supervisor), a search for "gears" in iStockphoto produces the photo in Figure 10-24, which will serve as the visual motif for several of the Act I and Key Point slides.

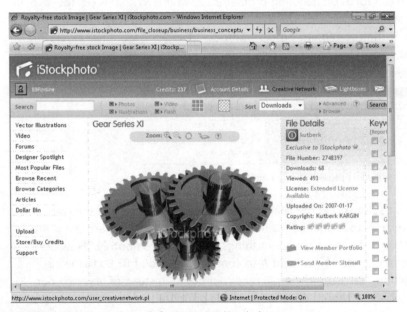

FIGURE 10-24 A search result for "gears" at iStockphoto.

Reviewing the Act I Slides for The Report

Although the headlines are hidden in the Figure 10-25 examples, the visual power of the images is clear. The Setting slide (upper left) features a photo of a clockwork from iStockphoto with a simple text box added that reads "Product Launch A" to illustrate the hidden headline "Product Launch A went like clockwork." The Role slide (upper right) features the same clockwork photo with a text box in the same position that reads "Product Launch B," referring to the headline "You'd like to make sure Product Launch B goes just as smoothly." Instead of the text boxes here, you could use the logos of the products.

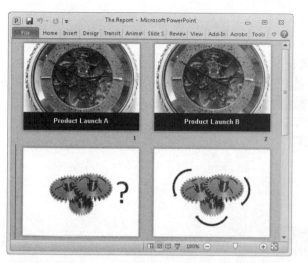

FIGURE 10-25 The Setting, Role, Point A, and Point B slides of The Report.

The Point A slide (lower left) features the iStockphoto graphic of three gears and a text box with a question mark to illustrate the headline "You haven't had a chance since last quarter to examine how things are working here." On the Point B slide (lower right), the same photo now includes three arrows created with the PowerPoint drawing tools to illustrate "You'd like to be confident things are working smoothly."

Reviewing the Call to Action and Key Point Slides for The Report

Next, insert three callouts with the numbers *1*, *2*, and *3* on the Call to Action slide next to each gear and arrow, as shown on the upper left in Figure 10-26—when the slide appears, you verbally explain that there are three reasons why your manager should "Be assured we will meet our goals," as described in the hidden headline. Then, on the first Key Point slide (upper right), use only the photo and add one arrow to illustrate the first Key Point headline, "We accomplished what we said we would." The Act II slides that will follow this slide in the presentation provide the breakdown and backup for these accomplishments. Then, on the second Key Point slide (lower left), add a second arrow and the second Key Point headline, "We are on track to accomplish our new goals." The following Act II slides will provide the breakdown and backup for your new goals. Then, on the third Key Point slide (lower right), add the third and final arrow and the third headline, "We will overcome our challenges." The following Act II slides will provide the breakdown and backup for how you will overcome those challenges. When you create your custom layouts for your Explanation (Breakdown) and Detail (Backup) slides, add a small version of the gears to the navigation bar to carry the visual theme through the presentation on those slides.

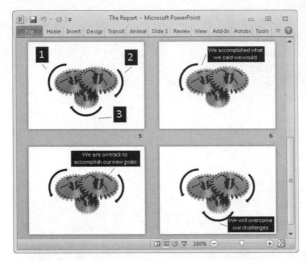

FIGURE 10-26 The Call to Action and Key Point slides of The Report.

Because you are giving this presentation to such a small audience, deliver it on a laptop screen or in a printed form using notes pages handouts. But whatever way you go, with the BBP foundation in place, you have transformed what normally might be an "informational" list of facts into a much more meaningful and useful story that you carry forward both visually and verbally.

Engaging Students with The Class

Beyond courtrooms and meeting rooms, BBP has tremendous potential to guide the structure of presentations used in classrooms and training rooms at every educational level. After all, the research realities described in Chapter 2 that inspire BBP are being extensively tested and applied by educational psychologists interested in improving learning using multimedia. If you use PowerPoint to teach, you'll find BBP a practical and effective method to help your students learn new information. And just as with The Analysis example, applying BBP to an educational presentation usually does not involve creating new material; rather, you restructure existing material in a new way to make the material easier for your students' working memory to handle.

As with the applications of BBP in other contexts, with an educational presentation, you always start with Act I of the story template. Here your aim in the first few slides of the presentation is to make the topic of your course emotionally relevant to your students and set the framework that will guide your students' understanding of the material to follow in the class. Instead of potentially losing students' interest and dampening their motivation to learn, you'll help them maintain interest from the first slide to the last.

In the example Act I shown in Figure 10-27, you are an instructor teaching a class on DNA. You introduce the Setting as "DNA is one of the great scientific discoveries of all time" and then engage the students by placing them in the Role as "In this class, you will get to play a role in discovering it for yourself." Next the challenge the students face in Point A is "Without knowing how to approach it, DNA seems like an unsolvable puzzle," and Point B is "You'd like to solve the puzzle to discover the big picture." So how do the students resolve the tension between not knowing how to approach the puzzle of DNA and solving it? By following your Call to Action, "Solve the DNA puzzle in three steps."

The Class by Pat Coleman		
Act I		
Setting	DNA is one of the great scientific discoveries of all time	
Role	In this class, you somehow get to play a role in discovering it for yourself	
Point A	**Call to Action**	**Point B**
Without knowing how to approach it, DNA seems like an unsolvable puzzle	Solve the DNA puzzle in three steps	You'd like to solve the puzzle to discover the big picture
Act II		
Key Learning Objective	**Explanation**	**Detail**

FIGURE 10-27 Act I of The Class presentation example.

With an engaging start to the presentation in writing in Act I, the next step is to complete the Act II columns of the story template. Begin by renaming the Key Point column heading to "Key Learning Objective." Often the biggest challenge for educators when completing Act II is not completing the Explanation and Detail slides, because those usually already exist in some form. Rather the difficulty comes in distilling the Explanation and Detail columns into an even simpler set of three Key Point (Key Learning Objective) headlines. It is essential that you provide students with only a few Key Point headlines that they will certainly remember, which then will serve as long-term memory reference points to access your Explanation and Detail headlines. In this example, as you write your Key Point (Key Learning Objective) headlines, you'll cover the three most important points you want your students to remember from the class:

- **Key Point 1** Assemble the theory.

- **Key Point 2** Assemble the research.

- **Key Point 3** Apply what you know.

Continue by completing the other two columns of the story template, and then create your Act II slides from these according to the process described in the other examples in this chapter.

Researching and Adding Available Graphics for The Class

To visually realize your puzzle motif from the story template and storyboard sketches, in Normal view of any slide, select the Insert tab, and in the Illustrations group, click Clip Art. In the Clip Art pane, type the search term **puzzle**, and then click Go. When you find the puzzle shape you want, position the mouse pointer on it, click the arrow to the right of the puzzle piece, and choose Insert, as shown in Figure 10-28.

FIGURE 10-28 Inserting a puzzle shape from the Clip Art pane in PowerPoint.

You might not want to use all of the elements included in this particular puzzle graphic, but you still can work with it because it is *vector art*, called "resizable" at the Microsoft Office Online Clip Art And Media site (*http://office.microsoft.com/en-gb/images/*). The value of this type of graphic is that you can break it into its components using the PowerPoint graphics tools and use only portions of it on a slide. Another advantage of this type of graphic is that you can resize it without ever losing its sharp, clear lines.

Right-click the puzzle graphic you inserted on the slide, and on the shortcut menu, click Group, Ungroup. (If the Ungroup option doesn't appear on this shortcut menu, the clip art is not resizable.) If a message box appears that reads, "This is an imported picture, not a group. Do you want to convert it to a Microsoft Office Drawing Object?", click Yes. Right-click the graphic again, and then click Group, Ungroup again on the shortcut menu, which breaks up the graphic into its parts.

Tip ✓	When you search for vector art graphics at the Microsoft Office Online Clip Art And Media site, you'll know that a graphic you find is vector art if the search results box includes the term "Resizable" under Dimensions.

Click and delete any pieces of the group you don't want, and click and change the fill color of any of the objects if you want. When you have deleted the elements you don't want to keep and have made any other changes to resizable clip art, right-click somewhere on the graphic and select Group, Regroup from the shortcut menu—this regroups the graphic into a single unit again instead of leaving it as many separate smaller pieces. To resize a piece of resizable clip art on a slide, select it to display the sizing handles. Hold down the Shift key, and drag one of the corner sizing handles to change the graphic to the size you want. Holding down the Shift key while you drag a corner sizing handle preserves the proportions of the graphic as you resize it; otherwise, the image will be distorted.

Reviewing the Act I Slides for The Class

When you create a custom layout for your Act I slides, change the background color to black and then apply the layout to all of your slides—this hides the headlines, as shown in Figure 10-29. Based on your story template and storyboard sketches, add a text box that reads "DNA" to the Setting slide (upper left). Animate the word so that when you click the slide, the word *DNA* slowly fades into the background as you relate the headline "DNA is one of the greatest scientific discoveries of all time." On the Role slide (upper right), add a text box with question marks that fade into the background to intrigue the students as you affirm, "In this class, you somehow get to play a role in discovering it for yourself."

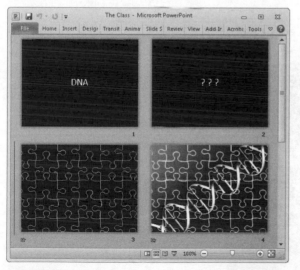

FIGURE 10-29 The Setting, Role, Point A, and Point B slides of The Class.

On the Point A slide (lower left), duplicate the puzzle pieces so that they fill the screen, change their fill color to black, and then animate the group to fade in when the slide appears and you relate the hidden headline, "Without knowing how to approach it, DNA seems like an unsolvable puzzle." On the Point B slide (lower right), add a photograph of a DNA strand from iStockphoto, copy the puzzle pieces from the Point A slide and paste them on top of the photo, and then remove the fill color of the puzzle pieces so that only the puzzle piece outlines remain. As the DNA puzzle appears, relate the Point B headline, "You'd like to solve the puzzle to discover the big picture." These Point A and Point B slides reinforce the puzzle motif and create a visually interesting framework for the topic the students will address through the class.

Reviewing the Call to Action and Key Point Slides for The Class

Next abbreviate your Call to Action headline to read "Solve the DNA puzzle," as shown on the upper left in Figure 10-30. Search for the term "custom puzzle" on the Web, and you'll find many companies that will create a custom jigsaw puzzle using your DNA photograph for as little as $11. If you have the budget, buy one, and then when you present the Call to Action slide as you relate the hidden headline "Solve the DNA puzzle in three steps," hand out the actual pieces of the custom DNA puzzle to the students so that they literally hold the motif in their hands. Tell your students that they now hold in their hands the puzzle they will solve, and ask them for their thoughts about how they think they can solve it.

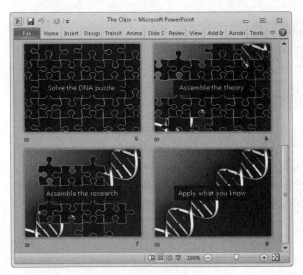

FIGURE 10-30 The Call to Action and Key Point slides of The Class presentation.

As you create your Key Point (Key Learning Objective) slides, leave your headlines visible, but delete some of the puzzle pieces from the first Key Point slide, "Assemble the theory" (upper right); delete more pieces from the second Key Point slide, "Assemble the research," (lower left); and last delete all of the pieces from the third slide, "Apply what you know" (lower right). Create the rest of the slides from the headlines of the story template, using these Key Point slides to guide you and your students through the engaging experience of solving the DNA puzzle.

THE THREE-YEAR TRAINING PLAN

Although this presentation example of The Class is designed for a 45-minute presentation, you can use the BBP story template to plan a much longer class or even a multiyear curriculum. Consider how much time you have—45 minutes, 2 hours, 3 days, or 3 years—and write in the Key Point column the three most important lessons you want someone to learn during that period of time. Then continue working in the story template from left to right—you'll add more columns to the right of the Detail column depending on how deep you want to go into the material.

Together with your engaging story template structure, these slides add a visual dynamism and interest that increase the likelihood your students will remember and apply the most important information you want to teach.

Putting Your Clients at the Center in The Pitch

The last BBP example in this chapter shows one more way BBP unlocks the verbal and visual power buried inside a presentation—this time with a sales pitch that your Internet services firm is making to a potential client. The typical outline in the old way of doing presentations would feature a structure with category headings like Our Company, Our Team, Our Services, Our Differentiation, and Our Clients—the message would be essentially "All About Us." Of course, each category heading would be followed by list after list of facts, without a story to be found anywhere to tie them together.

Often the origin of this type of presentation is the marketing department, where the goal of the marketers is to create a single, uniform, consistent message that they then distribute to the sales team to deliver exactly as it is. The only problem, though, is that the typical organizational process of making the presentation uniform also makes it canned, generic, one-size-fits-all—in other words, boring. Not surprisingly, even though some companies spend millions of dollars and countless hours and untold energy in creating these presentations, the sales team ignores them. And who can blame them? After all, the canned presentations in reality would likely cause them to *lose* sales rather than win them, because if they actually delivered these presentations, their prospective clients would send them out the door for wasting their time with a one-way, domineering recital of bullet points.

The problem is solved when the company gets the marketing and sales teams together in a room and then uses a projector to put the BBP Story Template on the screen so that everyone can work on it together, as shown in the example in Figure 10-31. Now, by viewing together the first five headlines they write of Act I, both marketing and sales can agree that the salespeople in the field need to start strong every time with a story structure that puts the company's prospective clients in the starring role of the presentation. With your Setting statement, you affirm to your client that "Your numbers have been off the mark" and in the Role that "You're under pressure to improve your game." With these two simple statements, suddenly the entire focus of the presentation has changed from "All About Us" to "All About You"—the salesperson's audience.

The Pitch by Pat Coleman		
Act I		
Setting	Your numbers have been off the mark	
Role	You're under pressure to improve your game	
Point A	**Call to Action**	**Point B**
Your current messages are not reaching your target	Aim for three goals, and you'll hit the marks you want	You'd like to hit the target more accurately and frequently
Act II		
Benefit	**Feature**	**Demonstration**

FIGURE 10-31 Act I of The Pitch presentation example.

Custom-tailoring this presentation to this specific audience continues in the Point A headline, which defines the client's challenge as "Your current messages are not reaching your target," and in the Point B headline, which defines the client's goal as "You'd like to hit the target more accurately and frequently." How does the client get from A to B? The Call to Action headline provides direction in the form of the statement, "Aim for three goals, and you'll hit the marks you want."

As your team moves to Act II to flesh out the rest of the presentation, change the Act II headings from "Key Point" to "Benefit," from "Explanation" to "Feature," and from "Detail" to "Demonstration" if you prefer. Now, in the Key Point (Benefit) column, write headlines that explain how aiming for three goals will help your audience hit the marks they want. By choosing to answer the question *How?*, you make this an explanatory presentation rather than a persuasive one, as explained in Chapter 5. This makes the presentation feel more like a consultative educational session than a stereotypical sales pitch. But even more importantly, this structure defines and elevates the three most important benefits as the client sees them from the context of Act I:

- **Key Point 1** Hit better sales numbers with Service X.
- **Key Point 2** Hit better margins with Service Y.
- **Key Point 3** Hit better customer ratings with Service Z.

Here the benefits for the audience have been tightly integrated into the wording of the headlines to bring these benefits to the top level of the audience's attention. You definitely will talk about your services throughout the rest of the Act II columns, but now each of three Key Point (Benefit) slides makes it clear how any and all of the information in the presentation is important to the audience. This ensures that from the start, your audience is perfectly clear about the answer to the continuing question, "What's in this for me?" If your service or product has more than three benefits, make the presentation modular by creating more Key Point sections and hiding the slides that do not apply or interest a particular client.

Researching and Adding Available Graphics for The Pitch

Following your story template motif and storyboard sketches as usual, search for the term "dartboard" at iStockphoto to find a result similar to the one shown in Figure 10-32.

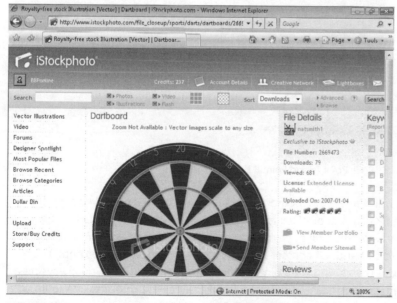

FIGURE 10-32 Search result for "dartboard" at iStockphoto.

Reviewing the Act I Slides for The Pitch

Next create and apply a custom layout for the Act I slides that leaves the headlines white so that they are hidden on the screen. On the Setting slide, include a chart tailored to your client's numbers, as shown on the upper left in Figure 10-33, showing the numbers dropping as you describe your hidden headline "Your numbers have been off the mark," and add the dartboard to introduce your motif. On the Role slide (upper right), continue the line upward so that it hits the bull's eye in the center of the dartboard as you verbally explain the hidden headline "You're under pressure to improve your game." On the Point A slide (lower left), add the photo of the dart and rotate it to point upward, off-target from a red bull's eye that you create using the PowerPoint drawing tools—here you'll relate the hidden headline "Your messages are not reaching your target." Next, on the Point B slide (lower right), rotate the dart so that it hits the middle of the bull's eye target as you explain your hidden headline "You'd like to hit the target more accurately and frequently."

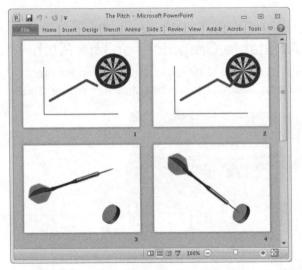

FIGURE 10-33 The Setting, Role, Point A, and Point B slides of The Pitch.

If you can pull it off, bring a real dartboard to the sales call that uses darts with plastic safety tips, and hang it on a wall or place it on a chair. When you click to the Point A slide, throw a dart and miss the bull's eye. When you advance to the Point B slide, place a dart in the bull's eye by hand. Of course, using a prop is a good way to prompt a conversation—for example, during the Point A slide, you might ask, "Do you always hit a bull's eye with your messaging?" and during the Point B slide, you might ask, "Would you like to find a way to hit the target more accurately?"

Reviewing the Call to Action and Key Point Slides for The Pitch

When you create the Call to Action slide shown on the upper left in Figure 10-34, place the dartboard graphic at the center, and duplicate the dart twice so that you have three darts to rotate and position at the bull's eye. Leave the headline hidden as you verbally relate the point, "Aim for three goals, and you'll hit the marks you want." For the Key Point (Benefit) slides (upper right, lower left, and lower right), apply a split-screen custom layout as described in Appendix E, using a Picture placeholder on the right half of the slides for the photographs. On the left half of the custom layout, include the dart and bull's eye to sustain that visual element through the presentation at these most important slides. The dartboard and dart are also elements that fit naturally into a navigational bar through the corresponding Explanation and Detail slides. It will be a nice touch to leave your audience with the plastic darts and dartboard, which will serve as persistent physical reminders of your motif and memorable message.

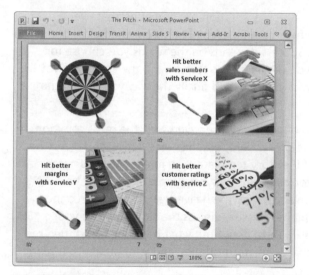

FIGURE 10-34 The Call to Action and Key Point slides of The Pitch presentation.

You'll continue to create your Act II slides as usual, and when you reach the Demonstration (Detail) slides, you'll switch over to another application on your desktop, as described in Chapters 7 and 8, to show sections of your live demonstration of Services X, Y, and Z at the appropriate places.

With the story template as a foundation, the BBP process produces a crisp package that is easy for any salesperson to tailor and customize, using custom layouts and placeholders that do not require the salesperson to have any graphical skill in creating layouts. But perhaps most importantly, because the sales force is involved in the creative conception and development of this story, they will feel they own it and this will be something they really use.

<table>
<tr><td>Note</td><td>As mentioned at the start of this chapter, the design constraints of the examples in this chapter include a limited budget, stock photography, and graphics that can be created within PowerPoint. With a larger budget, hire a professional designer to create custom layouts and graphics especially for your presentation. Within your budget and time constraints, only your imagination and creativity will limit the possibilities.</td></tr>
</table>

Handling Objections to BBP

As you begin the process of creating a BBP presentation, keep in mind that every decision you make along the way can mean the difference between whether or not you hit the mark with your audience. Your success depends on the words you choose for your story template, the illustrations you sketch on the storyboard, the aesthetics you create across the slides with the graphics you add, and finally the way you deliver the presentation and engage your audience.

If you try BBP and it doesn't work or is otherwise not received well, the most common reasons are because the story template, storyboard, graphics, aesthetics, or delivery need more work. Sometimes the content of the story template is an intellectual mismatch with the audience, or the wording is too simplistic—or not simple enough. At times the storyboard graphics are an aesthetic mismatch, or the delivery style does not connect with the audience. If any of these might be an issue, discuss the situation with your team—and with your audience, if possible—to figure out what happened, and then return to the story template, the storyboard, the ground rules, and your audience research.

However, you might present a perfectly good BBP presentation and still find that the audience is resistant to your approach. For example, if you give your first BBP presentation to a group where there is a strong bullet-point culture, their immediate response might be "Where are the bullet points that we expect?" or "This is too simplistic—where's the text?" If you expect you might get that reaction, prepare the audience in advance for what is about to come. Bring handouts of the notes pages, and pass them out while you verbally assure your audience that the detailed information is available here in printed format instead of on the slides. Assure them that you respect their time so much that you've done a great deal of advance work to identify only the most important information they need to know so that you don't waste their time.

BBP is a huge shift in thinking and action, and it can represent a threat to existing political structures within organizations. Some of the examples in this chapter demonstrate that there are deeply ingrained PowerPoint habits and cultures, and there can be a great deal of resistance to doing anything differently from what is normally done. Often the objections to BBP have nothing to do with the methodology or the content of a presentation, but instead are attempts to demonstrate an audience member's power by publicly raising doubts about the presenter's credibility. In other cases, using BBP well can make others feel uncomfortable that they don't know something that you do, and as a result, they might try to undermine you.

EASING BBP THROUGH THE EYE OF THE NEEDLE OF YOUR ORGANIZATION

It takes leadership to ensure that BBP works, especially when working with teams and within organizations. It's not a matter of simply having an effective approach, because even the best approach in the world can be stifled by an entrenched bullet-point culture. If your organization's culture cannot stray outside the narrow bounds of the conventional PowerPoint approach, it will take an organization-wide commitment from senior leadership that gives everyone permission and the resources to make a successful transition to a more effective approach. This has happened at the board of directors level of major organizations that have decided to move beyond a conventional approach that no longer works for them.

If you expect you might get these types of reactions, listen to the comments. If they are valid concerns, accept them and reply that you'll take them into account while you prepare your next presentation. But if the comments are more about politics than the presentation, defend your BBP foundation and explain how and why BBP works effectively to increase the audience's understanding of your material. Explain the research realities from Chapter 2, the classical story structure of Act I from Chapter 4, the logical critical-thinking structure of Act II from Chapter 5, and the way the storyboard balances verbal and visual channels from Chapters 6 through 8. If appropriate, set up a separate meeting at your organization where you use the Chapter 2 research realities to compare the old way and the BBP way side by side. When you are confident you have effectively prepared your presentation using BBP, you can be confident that you present a clear case for how and why your presentation works.

BBP Ground Rules and Checklists

BEYOND BULLET POINTS (BBP) includes sets of ground rules and checklists to guide you through the process described in this book—here they are compiled in one place for easy reference.

The BBP Ground Rules

The BBP Ground Rules cover the fundamentals you should follow through each of the key phases of developing a BBP presentation.

Three Ground Rules for Writing Headlines

Your BBP Story Template depends on a special writing style that boils down your story to its essence. Follow these three ground rules to keep your writing concise:

- Write concise, complete sentences with a subject and a verb in active tense.
- Be clear, direct, specific, and conversational.
- Link your ideas across cells.

Three Ground Rules for Storyboarding

Inspired by a filmmaker's storyboard, your Microsoft PowerPoint storyboard helps you manage both the words you speak and the images you show. Follow these three ground rules to keep your storyboard coherent:

- Be visually concise, clear, direct, and specific.
- In Act II, sketch consistency within columns and variety across columns.
- Sketch outside the screen too.

Three Ground Rules for Adding Graphics

Adding graphics is the crucial last step in designing the storyboard. Follow these three ground rules to make sure you get the graphics right:

- See it in seconds.
- Align the aesthetics with the audience.
- Defend your foundation!

Three Ground Rules for Delivering Your Presentation

Your single storyboard helps you manage your spoken words, projected visuals, and printed handouts. Follow these three ground rules to ensure that the rest of the live presentation experience is engaging:

- Step into the screen.
- Remove the distractions.
- Manage the flow.

The BBP Checklists

The BBP Checklists ensure that you cover the most important tasks through each phase of developing a BBP presentation.

Checklist: Planning Your First Five Slides

Do the first five slides of your presentation

- Orient your audience to the setting of the presentation?

- Interest them by acknowledging their role in the setting?

- Engage them emotionally by describing a challenge they face (Point A)?

- Motivate them by affirming what they want (Point B)?

- Focus them by offering a way to get from Point A to Point B (that is, deliver a call to action)?

Checklist: Planning the Rest of Your Slides

Do the rest of your slides in Act II

- Justify your Call to Action slide with your key points?

- Clarify your Key Point slides with further explanation?

- Back up your Explanation slides with the appropriate detail?

- Put your ideas in a logical sequence and priority?

- Integrate your motif verbally through your headlines?

Checklist: Preparing the Storyboard

Does your storyboard

- Include backgrounds that cue the Key Point, Explanation, and Detail slides?

- Provide you with the ability to quickly scale your presentation up and down to time?

- Contain notes in the notes area of what you'll say during each slide?

Checklist: Sketching the Storyboard

Do your storyboard sketches show clearly

- Where your Act I, Key Point, Explanation, and Detail slides are?

- How you tell your story across frames, at each level of the storyboard?

- Which graphics you'll use?

- Where you will use interaction, props, and other media?

Checklist: Adding Graphics to the Storyboard

Do your final graphics

- Clearly illustrate each headline in the simplest way possible?

- Show consistency within levels of the presentation hierarchy and variety across levels?

- Keep your slides free of any extraneous visual information?

- Align with the aesthetics of your audience?

Checklist: Delivering Your Presentation

Before and during the presentation, do you

- Prepare the environment, check the technology, and properly rehearse in advance?

- Use your physical presence and voice to bring the experience to life?

- Engage your audience both implicitly and explicitly?

- Use the tools and techniques of BBP to manage the working memory of your audience?

Presenting BBP with Two Views

MICROSOFT POWERPOINT offers you two views to present your Beyond Bullet Points (BBP) slides to your audiences: the usual Slide Show view and Presenter view.

Using Slide Show View and Tools

When you present BBP slides using Slide Show view, all the elements you designed into the slides to help the audience's working memory will also help you to present. The headlines will cue you about what to say, and the graphics will provide you with additional visual prompts. The changing layouts and optional navigational bar will keep you oriented to your place in the presentation and what comes next. These elements plus the thorough knowledge of your topic might be enough to keep you on track; if not, print speaker notes in the format that best works for you, as described in Chapter 9.

In Slide Show view, you see your slides on your own laptop computer screen in the same full-screen format that your audience sees on the projector screen in the room. As you prepare your presentations, always check how your slides will look to the audience by using Slide Show view. To do this, on the Ribbon, go to the View tab, and in the Presentation Views group, click Slide Show to begin the presentation from the first slide—you do this by pressing the F5 key.

Another way to start your presentation is to go to the View toolbar on the status bar on the lower right in the window and then click the Slide Show button to begin the presentation from the current slide selected on your screen—also do this by holding down the Shift key while you press F5. Yet another way to start your presentation is from the Slide Show tab—in the Start Slide Show group, click either From Beginning or From Current Slide.

When you present in Slide Show view using a projector, connect your laptop to the projector as usual, following the instructions that come with your laptop and the projector. Connect your remote control device to the laptop so that you are able to advance and reverse the slides without distracting your audience. When you are in the Slide Show view of your presentation, move the mouse pointer to the lower-left corner of your screen to display four icons that allow you to access additional presenter tools. Click the Pen icon to access a Ballpoint Pen, Felt Tip Pen, or Highlighter tool (as shown in Figure B-1) that allows you to draw or highlight information on the screen. Use these tools if you have planned for their use on specific slides in your storyboard. You'll be able to draw on the screen using a mouse.

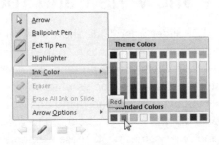

FIGURE B-1 Presenter tools available in Slide Show view when you move the mouse pointer to the icons in the lower-left corner of the screen—in this example, the Felt Tip Pen tool with a red color is selected.

Before you begin the presentation, while the screen is not visible to the audience, select the pen and color you prefer—the Felt Tip Pen in red is a good combination for visibility. You will see a small dot somewhere on the screen indicating where your pen tip is—move it to the corner of the screen so that it is not easily visible to the audience. After you draw or highlight on the screen in Slide Show view, press the E key to erase ink from your screen, or press Ctrl+M to show/hide the ink markup. If you do add ink or highlighting to a slide, when you press Esc twice to exit Slide Show view, you will see a window that asks whether you want to keep or discard the ink annotations. You'll normally want to keep the ink so that you have a record of what you wrote during the live presentation to send to audience members—you have the option to select and delete the ink from the slides later if you don't want it.

If you use a Tablet PC to deliver your BBP presentation, use the stylus with the Slide Show view drawing tools to produce smoother, more natural handwriting on the screen than otherwise is possible to create using a mouse.

Using Presenter View and Tools

Presenter view gives you a range of features to manage a live presentation.

To use Presenter view

- Connect your projector to the video port of your laptop.

- If you see a Display Settings dialog box, click the monitor where you want to display your speaker notes, and select This Is My Main Monitor. (For more information about selecting monitor settings, visit Microsoft Windows Help to locate your Windows Display Settings).

- Click the monitor icon for the second monitor where your audience will view the slides (the projector), select the Extend My Windows Desktop onto This Monitor check box, and click OK. Now the projector screen is an extension of your laptop screen—as you move the mouse pointer across your laptop screen, you should be able to continue to move it off the laptop screen and across the projector screen.

- On the Slide Show tab, in the Monitors group, click Use Presenter View. Under the Show On pull-down menu, select the second monitor where your slides will be displayed to your audience (the projector).

Delivering a Presentation Using Presenter View

Now start the presentation as you would using Slide Show view—you'll see the presentation in Presenter view on your laptop screen, as shown in Figure B-2.

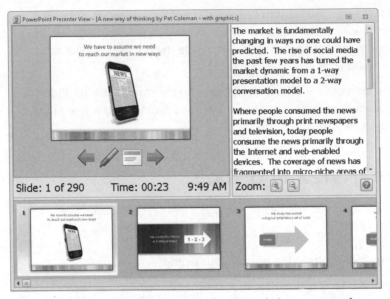

FIGURE B-2 Presenter view provides many features to help you present from your laptop screen.

Here you'll see many features that will help you as a presenter. The slide that your audience sees on the projector screen appears on the upper left, and below that is a bar that includes, from left to right, the current slide number out of the total slides, the time elapsed since you started the presentation, and the current time. On the upper right is a speaker notes pane that you zoom in or zoom out to resize, and at the bottom of the screen are slide thumbnails—the current slide is highlighted. Use the scroll bar to find another slide and click the slide to skip ahead to it.

Tip	To draw directly onto a slide in Presenter view using a mouse or the stylus of your Tablet PC, click the Pen icon and use the pens or highlighters to draw ink on the slide as you did in Slide Show view. When you add ink in Presenter view on your laptop screen, the ink image will not appear on the projector screen until you lift your pen.

APPENDIX C

Starting Your Point A and B Headlines

AS YOU WRITE your Point A and B headlines in Act I of your story template, as shown in Figure C-1, you might find it helpful to review a range of phrases that provide the words you can use to start each headline.

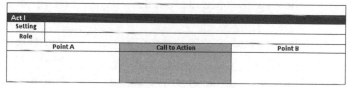

FIGURE C-1 The Point A cell, left, and the Point B cell, right, in Act I of the story template.

To use this table, look down the Point A column, and when you find a Point A phrase that matches the challenge faced by your audience, look across at the Point B column to see a corresponding Point B phrase. When you've found one of each, refer to Appendix D to fill in the space between Points A and B with a Call to Action statement.

POINT A (WHAT CHALLENGE DO I FACE?)	POINT B (WHERE DO I WANT TO BE?)
You're overwhelmed about x	You'd like to gain control
You're unclear about x	You'd like to be clear
You're uncertain about x	You'd like to be certain
You don't know what to do about x	You'd like to know what to do
People don't appreciate your value	You'd like people do appreciate what you do
You've got an unsolved problem with x	You'd like to solve the problem
Situation x is in disarray	You'd like to bring the situation into order
You don't suspect you have a problem with x	You'd like to know if there is a problem
Situation x is bad and getting worse	You'd like to turn things around before it's too late
Situation x is stagnating	You'd like to stir things up
There's a great new idea out there	You'd like to incorporate it into what you're doing now
There's a bad idea out there	You'd like to avoid it and stick with what you're doing
You're uncertain whether you should support x	You're certain you'd like to give your support
You don't know yet about x	You'd like to know about it
There is confusion about x	You'd like to clear up the confusion
There is ambiguity about x	You'd like clarity
You're feeling frustrated about x	You'd like to feel better about it
You feel like you're not earning enough	You'd like to improve your earnings
You're not sure if we're a good match	You'd like to know more so you can decide
You don't know us	You'd like to know us
You don't know how to begin x	You'd like to know how to begin
You don't know how you can help	You'd like to know how you can help

POINT A (WHAT CHALLENGE DO I FACE?)	POINT B (WHERE DO I WANT TO BE?)
You're unclear how all the pieces fit together	You'd like to be clear how the pieces fit together
You're not sure where you should go	You'd like to know where to go
You're unsure how we've been doing	You'd like to know how we've been doing
You're frustrated	You'd like to remove the frustration
The odds are against you	You'd like to find a way to beat the odds
You're dissatisfied with x	You'd like to be satisfied
You see a negative trend regarding x	You'd like to see a positive trend
Your numbers are down	You'd like to bring your numbers up
You face obstacles	You'd like to overcome the obstacles
You have several options	You'd like to choose the best option
You've been dealt a bad hand	You'd like to figure out how to win the game
You feel out of control	You'd like to gain control
You don't know how x happened	You'd like to know how x happened
You've heard one side of the story	You'd like to hear the other side of the story
You're concerned about x	You'd like to resolve your concern
You don't know what to do in a new situation	You'd like to know what to do
You don't know the topic	You'd like to know the topic
You're overwhelmed	You'd like to gain control
You see injustice	You'd like to find justice
The truth has been hidden	You'd like to reveal the truth
Something is irritating you	You'd like to remove the irritation

APPENDIX D

Starting Your Call to Action Headlines

ONCE YOU HAVE written your Point A and B headlines, you'll need a Call to Action headline to close the gap, as shown in Figure D-1, middle. As you consider what to write, review a range of phrases that provide the words you can use to start each headline.

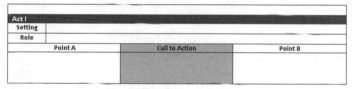

Act I			
Setting			
Role			
	Point A	Call to Action	Point B

FIGURE D-1 The Call to Action cell, middle, in Act I of the story template.

To use the table, which starts on the next page, look down the middle column to review words and phrases to begin your Call to Action headline, and then look at the range of phrases in the right column to complete the headline. You'll find a range of Call to Action headline possibilities, including motifs to integrate through the rest of the story template. This is only a partial list to get you started—feel free to keep building the table with your own headlines.

Explanation	Understand	how this works
	Observe	the way this is structured
	See	the three components
		the three sections
Recommendation	Partner with	us
	Work with	our people
	Hire	our team
	Join	our organization
	Ask	our network
	Make use of	
	Tell	
	Support	
	Approve	the idea
	Accept	the efforts
	Permit	the proposal
	Adopt	the budget
	Buy	the product
	Support	the service
	Facilitate	the initiative
	Be assured of	
	Disapprove	the idea
	Reject	the efforts
	Prevent	the proposal
	Don't adopt	the budget
	Don't buy	the product
	Don't support	the service
	Question	the initiative
	Doubt	
	Adjust	your strategy
	Change	your course
	Transform	your situation
	Share	your ideas
		responsibility
		the burden
		the risk
	Grow	more market share
		better relationships

The checklist motif	Check off	three items from the list three things you need to do
	Follow	three simple steps the formula (A+B=C; 1+2=3)
	Do Think	three things
The journey motif	Follow	the three road signs the roadmap
	Look for Avoid	the three pitfalls the three dangers the three missed signals
	Discover Find Uncover	the three elements the hidden treasure the three secrets a new route what has been hidden from you
The game motif	Put together the puzzle Solve the puzzle	in three steps to reveal the big picture to discover what happened
	Score	a touchdown a goal a run
	Win	a goal the game
	Watch	how the shell game was played how the house of cards was built how the hand is played how the cards were dealt
	Hit Aim for	the target the bull's eye

The project motif	Build	the structure in three steps
		the three parts of a strong foundation
	Tap into	three undiscovered wells
		three new opportunities
	Remove	the three barriers
	Avoid	the three obstacles
	Overcome	the three hurdles
	Build a bridge	to get to the other side
	Cross the chasm	to get what you want
	Turn it around	in three stages
		in three steps
The story motif	Watch	how the story unfolds
	Follow	motive + means = death
	Pay attention to	the three parts of the story
		Act I, Act II, Act III
	Find	the three clues
	Interpret	
	Follow	

Creating Custom BBP Layouts

TO CREATE custom layouts for your various levels of slides, on the View tab, in the Presentation Views group, click Slide Master. In the Overview pane on the left, you will see the built-in layouts to apply to your slides. Add any custom layouts here that you want, and as always, the best place to begin is with the most important slides in the presentation.

Creating the Key Point Slide Layout Manually

As you discovered with your sketches in Chapter 7, you use layouts in many different ways to make your set of Key Point slides stand out from the others. One quick and easy way to make these important slides stand out is to apply a split-screen layout to them. To create a custom split-screen layout to apply to your Key Point slides, follow these steps:

1. In the Overview pane, right-click the large Office Theme Slide Master slide. When you select any Slide Master in the Overview pane, all of its editable elements appear in the large view of the Slide Master in the slide pane. The Slide Master determines the formatting of any new Slide Masters and custom layouts you will create. Adjust the font type, size, and color if you want to apply those changes to all slides going forward, but do not delete anything from this particular Slide Master. When you finish, in the Overview pane, right-click the Slide Master and select Preserve Master.

2. In the Overview pane, position the cursor directly below the Slide Master slide, and then right-click and choose Insert Layout.

3. Right-click the custom layout you created, choose Rename Layout, and in the Rename Layout dialog box, type Key Point and then click Rename.

4. In the slide pane, right-click the large view of the Slide Master and select Grid And Guides, and in the Grid And Guides dialog box, under Guide Settings, select the Display Drawing Guides On Screen check box, and then click OK.

   This gives you temporary guides to help align objects on a slide; remove them by following the same steps and clearing the check box. See PowerPoint Help to learn more about how to use temporary guides.

5. On the Slide Master tab, in the Master Layout group, clear the Footers check box, and then click Insert Placeholder, click Picture, and drag a rectangle to fill the entire right half of the slide.

6. Next, on the Insert tab, in the Illustrations group, click Shapes. Click Rectangle, and drag a rectangle to fill the entire left half of the slide.

7. Right-click the rectangle, and specify a fill color—in this example, black.

8. Hold down the Shift key as you select both the rectangle and placeholder, right-click, and then click Send To Back.

9. Select the title area, and drag it down and to the center of the rectangle on the left, using the resizing handles as needed. Change the text in the title area to read Click to edit Key Point headline. If you need to change the contrast of the font color to make it readable against the color you chose for the rectangle, right-click the title area, and change the Font color—in this example, to white, as shown in Figure E-1.

10. On the Slide Master View tab, click Close Master View to return to Normal view.

Tip ✓ Instead of inserting and designing new custom layouts, rename and redesign the existing storyboard sketch layouts that you applied to your slides in Chapter 6. To do that, select and rename the Key Points Sketches custom layout to Key Point following the instructions in step 2 of the preceding procedure, and then make your design changes. When you have finished, return to Slide Sorter view, and you'll see that the layouts of the Key Point slides have been updated automatically according to the design changes you made.

Now that you have designed the Key Point custom layout, select a Key Point slide, and on the Home tab, in the Slides group, click Layout. The Office Theme window now includes the Key Point custom layout you created, as shown in Figure E-2.

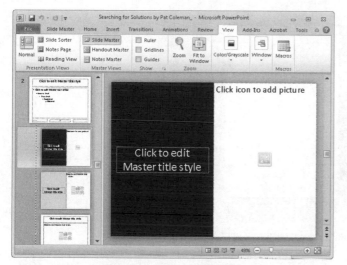

FIGURE E-1 Designing a custom layout for the Key Point slides.

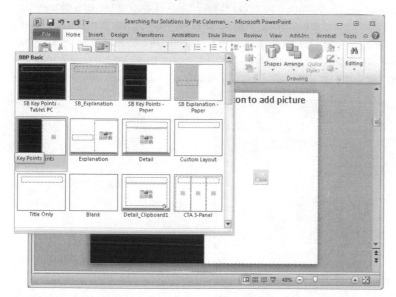

FIGURE E-2 Selecting the Key Point custom layout to apply to a slide.

Click the Key Point layout, and the formatting will be automatically applied, as shown in Figure E-3.

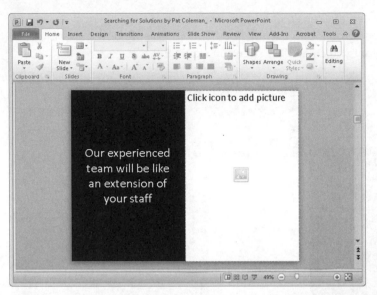

FIGURE E-3 A Key Point slide with the Key Point custom layout applied.

There are two ways to insert a photograph in the Picture placeholder on the right half of this slide. The first way is to find a picture and copy it and then click the Picture place-holder—not the Picture icon—and click Paste. The second way is to click the Picture icon in the center of the Picture placeholder to display the Insert Picture dialog box, as shown in Figure E-4. When you find a photo you plan to use, it is good practice to save it in a familiar folder on your computer or network to easily locate it.

FIGURE E-4 Selecting a photograph to insert.

Whichever method of inserting a photo you use, the photo automatically fills the Picture placeholder that you added to the custom layout, filling the right half of the screen. Although the original photo is horizontal, the Picture placeholder has automatically cropped the photo to fill the vertical space. If sizing photos is not your talent, this feature takes care of things for you. To resize or recrop the photo the way you want, select the picture, as shown in Figure E-5, and use the tools on the Picture Tools tab to make adjustments.

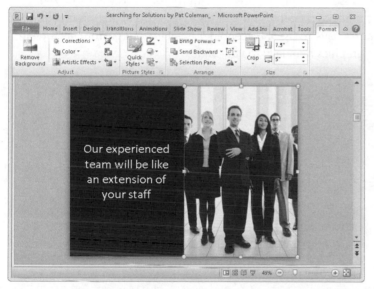

FIGURE E-5 A photograph automatically cropped and inserted into the Picture placeholder.

Creating the Explanation Slide Layout Manually

Next, follow similar steps to create a custom layout that you will apply to all the Explanation slides, based on what you sketched in Chapter 7. Again, using a split-screen layout for all the Explanation slides in this example presentation is only one way to go, but in this case, a similar layout will complement the Key Point slide layout. To create another custom split-screen layout to apply to all your Explanation slides, follow these steps:

1. On the View tab, click Slide Master.

2. In the Overview pane, position the cursor directly below the Key Point layout you created earlier, and then right-click it and choose Insert Layout.

3. Right-click the custom layout you created, choose Rename Layout, and in the Rename Layout dialog box, type Explanation and then click Rename.

4. On the Slide Master tab, in the Master Layout group, clear the Footers check box. When you click Insert Placeholder to add a placeholder on the right half of the slide, take a look at the range of other types of placeholders to use in the custom layout. On the Key Point custom layout shown earlier, the sketches indicated there would always be a photo on the Key Point slides, so selecting a Picture placeholder was a good fit and provided the added feature of automatically cropping photos to fit the space. But here on the Explanation slides, if you want flexibility beyond just photographs, choose Content, as shown in Figure E-6—this will allow you to insert a range of types of content on the slides where you apply this layout. Alternatively, you don't have to use a placeholder at all in your custom layout—in that case, later add graphics manually to your slides.

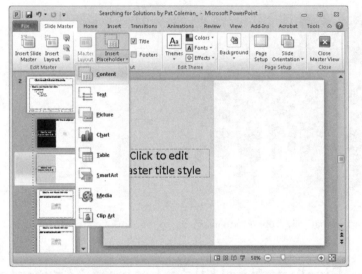

FIGURE E-6 Designing a custom layout for the Explanation slides—the Insert Placeholder drop-down menu shows a range of options.

5. As you did in the Key Point layout, add a rectangle to fill the left side of the slide. Fill this rectangle with a different color that in combination with the layout will call attention to these Explanation slides second, after the Key Point slides. As you did earlier with the Key Point custom layout, select the rectangle and placeholder and send them to the back, drag the headline over the box on the left side, and change the font color if you need to make it more legible. Change the text in the title area to read Click to edit Explanation headline.

Creating the Detail Slide Layout Manually

Now create a custom layout for the Detail slides. Because the Key Point and Explanation slide layouts are first and second, respectively, in visual prominence in Slide Sorter view, you don't need to create a split-screen layout here on the Detail slide layout to make these slides stand out. To create a custom layout to apply to all your Detail slides, follow these steps:

1. On the View tab, click Slide Master.

2. In the Overview pane, position the cursor directly below the Explanation layout you just created, and then right-click and choose Insert Layout.

3. Right-click the custom layout you created, choose Rename Layout, and in the Rename Layout dialog box, type Detail and then click Rename.

4. On the Slide Master tab, in the Master Layout group, clear the Footers check box. Leave the layout as it is, except insert a Content placeholder, and drag the placeholder to fill the slide below the headline; then delete the text from the Content placeholder. Change the text in the title area to read Click to edit Detail headline.

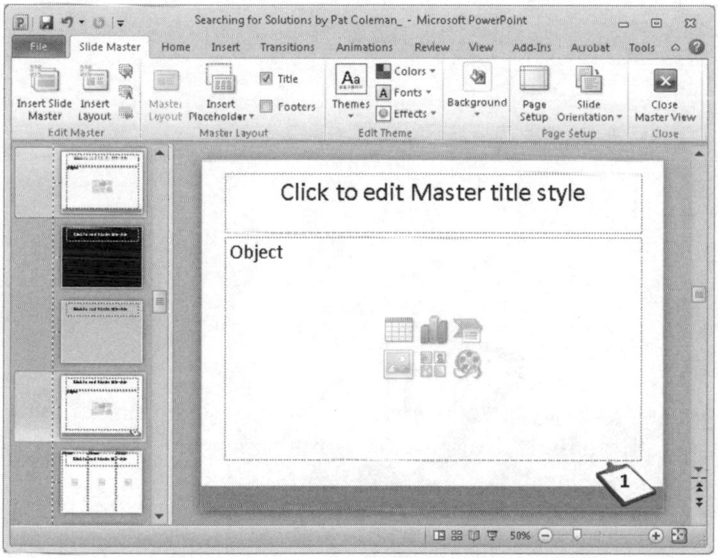

FIGURE E-7 Designing a custom layout for the Detail slides.

To create a navigation bar in the Detail slide layout, insert a rectangle shape, and drag and size it to fit across the bottom of the slide, as shown in Figure E-7. Placing the bar will not interfere with the simple visual reading of the slides, and its gray color will not call attention to it. Add the same bar to the Explanation slide layout you created earlier so that the bar visually links the Explanation and Detail slide layouts.

Adding an Optional Navigation Bar Manually

If you want to use an additional element to help viewers navigate the presentation, add a small icon in the lower-right corner. The magnification of the lower-right corner of the Detail slide layout, shown in Figure E-8, shows a simple clipboard that offers a subtle visual cue to guide your audience through this section of the presentation. Its small size ensures that it doesn't interfere with the overall composition of the slide. To add a bit more navigational assistance, add the number *1* to the clipboard to indicate the first section of this part of the presentation. If you do that, you will need to duplicate this Detail custom layout twice, rename the new layouts, and then add a *2* and a *3* to the duplicate layouts to apply to the other corresponding sections. If you're tempted to add your corporate logo here to the navigation bar, don't—it only adds extraneous information to the screen that neither illustrates the point of the slide headlines nor cues the audience about the presentation's organization.

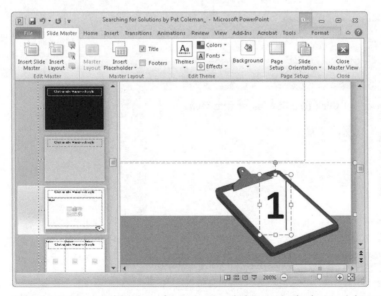

FIGURE E-8 A zoomed-in view of a navigational element in the lower-right corner of the Detail slide layout.

If you do create your own custom layouts and navigational elements manually, each time you do so, you will be building material to add to a BBP library to use in future presentations.

Adding Automated Animation

Remember to introduce information on the screen in the same order you want your audience's working memory to process it—first the headline you want the audience to quickly read, and second the graphical element you want the audience to see immediately afterward. Do this efficiently when you set up the custom layout with placeholders. For example, in the earlier Key Point slide layout, select the Title placeholder and the Picture placeholder, and then on the Animations tab, click Custom Animation. In the Custom Animation panel, select Add Effect, point to Entrance, and then click Fade. In the Start drop-down list, select After Previous, and in the Speed drop-down list, select Fast, as shown in Figure E-9. On the Slide Master tab, click Close Master View.

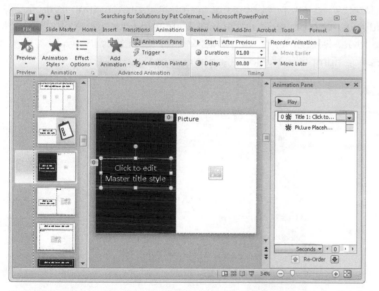

FIGURE E-9 Adding animation to the headline and placeholder in the Key Point slide layout.

Now every slide that uses the Key Point slide custom layout with a photo placeholder will automatically fade in the headline first and the picture immediately afterward—the sequence in which you want the audience's working memory to process the new information. Introducing the headline and graphic in this way adds a consistent and subtle movement to the screen without drawing attention away from your message. For the animation to work on your slides, insert graphics using placeholders as described earlier—if you add graphics to the slides manually, add animation to each one manually.

Tip ✓ Although they are not essential, create custom layouts for your Title and Act I slides. Alternatively, skip this step and later use the PowerPoint default Title Slide layout for your Title slide and the default Title Only layout for your Act I slides.

Adjusting the Notes Master Layout

When you finish making changes to your custom layouts, on the View tab, in the Presentation Views group, click Notes Master. Here add any more graphical elements that you want to appear later when you print notes pages of your presentation as a handout. For example, add the logo of your company to appear in your printed hand-outs by inserting it in the lower-left corner of the Notes Master layout, as shown in Figure E-10, or include a page number in the lower-right corner.

FIGURE E-10 Designing the Notes Master.

Including your company logo on the Notes Master so that it appears on printed handouts will not distract from the visual-verbal balance that you established with the slide area, selected in Figure E-10, and the notes area below.

When you finish making any changes here, on the Notes Master tab, click Close Master View.

Index

How To Download Your eBook

To download your eBook, go to
http://go.microsoft.com/FWLink/?Linkid=224345
and follow the instructions.

Please note: You will be asked to create a free online account and enter the access code below.

Your access code:

JRHXBDG

Beyond Bullet Points

Your PDF eBook allows you to:

- Search the full text
- Print
- Copy and paste

Best yet, you will be notified about free updates to your eBook.

If you ever lose your eBook file, you can download it again just by logging in to your account.

Need help? Please contact:
mspinput@microsoft.com

What do you think of this book?

We want to hear from you!

To participate in a brief online survey, please visit:

microsoft.com/learning/booksurvey

Tell us how well this book meets your needs—what works effectively, and what we can do better. Your feedback will help us continually improve our books and learning resources for you.

Thank you in advance for your input!

Microsoft®
Press

Stay in touch!

To subscribe to the *Microsoft Press® Book Connection Newsletter*—for news on upcoming books, events, and special offers—please visit:

microsoft.com/learning/books/newsletter